Face to
Face

Face to Face

VED MEHTA

Oxford University Press

OXFORD   LONDON   NEW YORK

OXFORD UNIVERSITY PRESS
Oxford   London   Glasgow
New York   Toronto   Melbourne   Wellington
Ibadan   Nairobi   Dar es Salaam   Lusaka   Cape Town
Kuala Lumpur   Singapore   Jakarta   Hong Kong   Tokyo
Delhi   Bombay   Calcutta   Madras   Karachi

The author wishes to thank the *Atlantic Monthly*
for permission to reprint material which first
appeared in their pages

LIBRARY OF CONGRESS CATALOGING IN PUBLICATION DATA

Mehta, Ved Parkash.
     Face to face.

     1. Mehta, Ved Parkash.   2. Blind—United States—
Biography.   3. Blind—India—Biography.   I. Title.
HV1792.M4A33 1978   362.4'1'0924 [B]   77-12984
ISBN 0-19-520014-4 pbk.
UK ISBN 0-19-285076-8

Printed in the United States of America

For

MOTHER & FATHER

without whom not

Publisher's Note

AFTER completing this book, in 1956, at the age of twenty-two, Mr. Mehta went up to Oxford, where he spent three years and took a degree in Modern History, and then, following a summer in India, he went on to Harvard, where he continued his studies for a year and a half longer; since 1961 he has been a staff writer on *The New Yorker*, and he has also held a Ford Foundation Travel and Study Grant for five years and two Guggenheim Fellowships. In addition to *Face to Face*, he has written *Walking the Indian Streets* (1960), a travel book about India and Nepal; *Fly and the Fly Bottle* (1963), a report on contemporary philosophers and historians; *The New Theologian* (1966), a report on contemporary Christian thinkers; *Delinquent Chacha* (1967), a comic novel about a middle-aged Indian; *Portrait of India* (1970), a study of a country trying to modernize itself; *John Is Easy to Please* (1971), a collection of essays on the written and spoken word; *Daddyji* (1972), a biography of his father; *Mahatma Gandhi and His Apostles* (1977), a biography of the Mahatma behind the myth; and *The New India* (1978), a history of Indira Gandhi's India. He is currently working on *Mamaji*, a biography of his mother. His books have appeared in numerous editions and translations.

A publisher's note that was included in the first English edition of *Walking the Indian Streets* read:

> As readers of *Face to Face* will know, Ved Mehta has been totally blind since the age of three; and they may be surprised to find no reference to his blindness in this book. This is entirely deliberate. By the diligent use of four senses Mr. Mehta is able to piece together the world of five; and when he describes what he "sees" he is in fact describing what he sees

through the eyes of other people. In re-creating the visual world for himself in this fashion, he finds that he is helped most by the chance and spontaneous remarks of friends and strangers.

By profession Mr. Mehta is an author and journalist, and he is anxious that no special allowance should be made for his work on the grounds of his disability. Indeed, he feels this so strongly that no note such as this will appear in any of his future books. It appears here only because some reviewers of the American edition seemed puzzled by this lack of any explanation.

To read this book, which is being reissued by Oxford, unaltered, twenty years after its original publication, is to have part of that explanation.

For now we see through a glass, darkly;
but then face to face: now I know in part;
but then shall I know even as also I am known.

I CORINTHIANS 13: 12

This entire book was dictated to my two fellow students, JoAn Johnstone (Pomona 1956) and Grace Kestenman (Radcliffe 1957); my labour was made easier by JoAn's patience and understanding – not to mention her well-cooked lunches – and Grace's cheerful and alert personality. The devoted and unsparing work of Nancy Reynolds (Atlantic Monthly Press) was invaluable in preparing and brushing up the manuscript for publication. Another good friend to whom I am deeply indebted is my sponsor, for it was her timely and generous help that made it possible for me to write at all.

Balliol College
Oxford

VED MEHTA

Contents

Publisher's Note
Foreword

Foreword

ABOUT three Christmases ago, I was invited by a group of students to speak on India. 'We want', the invitation read, 'something with flesh and blood, something which is more than just a talk on day-to-day happenings in your country.'

I rummaged through my file of previous talks, but none of them seemed to fill their order. The longer I sat by my Braille-writer, the harder it became to produce what was required. I was about to write and decline the invitation when one of my friends suggested that I use the form of a fairy story, but buttress it with 'real, live stuff'. I returned to my Braille-writer, and beginning with the sentence, 'Once upon a time there was a salt march led by a frail little man,' I constructed a success story of India's struggle for independence, complete with description, dialogue, action and pathos.

Full of trepidation I delivered my talk, but from the reaction it seemed that the teenagers had not lost their appetites for fairy stories. At the close of the discussion period a young lady on my right asked, 'Have you ever written anything?'

From the back of the room a boy piped up, 'It would be hard for him to write,' an allusion probably to my blindness.

This challenge, along with that speech, was the germ of the present narrative. The 'real, live stuff' I knew best was my own experience, yet I realized even before I began to write (I was then twenty) that no one man's experiences or reflections were sufficient to justify or inspire a book. But India, where I had been born and brought up, was. In that land there were colour, splendour and pageantry, juxtaposed with tragedy, division and change. I was all too conscious of my own limitations, but with the solace that everyone had to begin somewhere, I set that summer of 1954 aside to write, for my own diversion.

I began by trying to re-create a house of India, with all its colourful awnings, and portraits of family members, servants and *pandits,* and even the Kiplinglike curios which decorated the mantelpiece. In a way it was easier to build this house because its original had been drowned in the fast current of contemporary history. It seemed natural, then, to go on to describe the whirlpool of events which had divided my country.

After the intensive writing of that summer, I went back to the routine of a student until two years later, when with the kind encouragement of Edward Weeks and of Norman Cousins, the project was resumed. But before the book would be complete I would have to write a section on the United States, where I had been living for seven years.

This I undertook with mixed emotions. It would not be hard to write about a country to which I owed so much – my education and the use of the very language which made this book possible. And yet so many people had written about America, and with a much more eloquent pen and perceptive eye than I could ever command, that I wondered if I had much to offer that was fresh and worth being on a reader's bill of fare. Although the first two parts had to reflect larger issues, I decided that this final section should be wholly personal in tone.

And so I wrote about the experiences of a boy totally blind, set loose alone in the vast and bustling United States at the age of fifteen. The third part, then, is the story of the reception, problems and growth of this blind boy until he reached manhood, and of the pleasures and warm friendships he experienced in the West. Actually, the narrative is a succession of images, images collected from old and new India – one eclipsed, one rising – and from America, as these images appeared to that boy in the time of his growth.

I

INDIA & HOME

ONE

Surmas and School

In India as elsewhere every girl or boy has fond and warm memories of his childhood, from the day he begins to talk to his mother and father in broken syllables. Invariably a child learns and recognizes the faces of his mother and father, of sisters and brothers who play with him constantly, or the servants who prepare his meals or watch him play in a nursery strewn with knick-knacks and toys. He must also remember the rich colours of the butterflies and birds which children everywhere always love to watch with open eyes. I say must, because when I was three and a half, all these memories were expunged, and with the prolonged sickness (meningitis) I started living in a world of four senses – that is, a world in which colours and faces and light and darkness are unknown.

If my age and the length of the sickness deprived me of the treasured memories of sight, they also reduced things which are valued so much in the sighted world to nothing more than mere words, empty of meaning. I started living in a universe where it was not the flood of sunshine streaming through the nursery window or the colours of the rainbow, a sunset or a full moon that mattered, but the feel of the sun against the skin, the slow drizzling sound of the spattering rain, the feel of the air just before the coming of the quiet night, the smell of the stubble grass on a warm morning. It was a universe where at first – but only at first – I made my way fumbling and faltering.

It was good that I lost my sight when I did, because having no memories of seeing, there was nothing to look back to, nothing to miss. I went blind in November 1937. At that time we were living in Gujrat, in the province of Punjab in northern India. After my sickness we moved to Lahore, a few miles away, but the procession of relatives who came to sympathize made my father ask for another transfer, this time to Karnal, where we had neither friends nor relatives. There we got a cottage on the canal bank, built in very peaceful and quiet surroundings.

As might be expected, in the beginning it was tough for all of us – for my mother and my father, for my three sisters and my brother, and for me, too. The illness had left me weak. The servants shirked me as though I were an evil eye personified. My sisters treated me with care, as though I were a fragile doll, and my mother wept. My father, who was a doctor in the public health service, was grateful that my spine had been tapped in time, for a delay in the lumbar puncture would have affected my mind or endangered my life. But he, like the rest, despaired.

A state of complete inaction therefore followed my blindness. In part this was due to the immediate shock of the illness, but more important still, the impasse was caused by ignorance of the potentialities of a blind child, since the only blind persons my parents saw were beggars.

But now, by fate or by the will of God, blindness had struck not only a child of the well-to-do, but that of an excellently trained doctor, who found his training in this instance useless. Still, his wide medical experience had prepared him for an acceptance of this tragedy, and he understood that any course of action must begin with the realization that I would be blind for the rest of my life.

My mother, on the other hand, neither would nor could convince herself that my sight would never return; she did not have the medical experience of my father, and she blamed something in her past for the tragedy.

The family *pandit,* upon whose advice mother had relied almost from her childhood, was called in and consulted. 'He knows more about religion and science,' Mother said with pride, 'than any other *pandit* in our province.' I was taken before him, and for a long time I sat in my mother's lap while he was lost in reflection. After a while, he took my hand and thoroughly examined the lines. Then he looked at Mother's and he studied her forehead, mumbling steadily. He said he found himself inadequate, and more *pandits* would have to be consulted. At his request, they were called and questioned exhaustively as to what atonement could be made. Although their analyses and remedies differed considerably, they all agreed that by doing penance for her sins, my mother could improve my chance of regaining sight.

They prescribed methods ranging from intensive prayers to strenuous physical exertions, and for a fee they agreed to perform part of the necessary ritual. Each *pandit*'s advice was carefully heeded. Since my mother knew that my father would scorn such methods, she kept them secret, making it doubly hard for herself.

Along with this religious counsel was coupled a series of visits to *hakims* (physicians who followed the Greek or Unani system of medicine). These quacks prescribed all types of concocted drops to put in my eyes. The *surmas,* which were administered at all hours of the day and night, burned and stung my eyes; and the only soothing part of the otherwise miserable ordeal was the loving caress of Mother afterwards.

One night when my mother was administering these eye drops, and I was protesting with loud cries, my father unexpectedly returned. He asked and I told him why I was crying. He was outraged.

He questioned Mother as to how long this had been going on, but she would not answer him. She was prepared to bear any outburst silently and the longer she stayed silent, the more irritated my father grew. He said harshly that her superstitions far surpassed those of any village woman he had ever known. He went on to say that any person with the slightest consideration for her husband would have readjusted her ways in ten years of marriage. All his efforts to break her from her deplorable past had been in vain. He did not want his children brought up in such a tradition.

Even then she did not defend herself. Just as my mother had silently suffered the verdict of my blindness, the self-abasement imposed by the *pandits,* and the pleading which preceded the administration of my eye drops, so now she suffered my father's anger quietly. He forbade her to make any more visits to the *hakims,* and strictly prohibited the purchase of any more *surmas.* Then he gently lifted me from her arms, and took me away. With steady hands, he bathed my stinging eyes. After this incident, even though we stopped going to *hakims,* now and then applications of *surmas* continued until I was eleven. But they were very mild, and my mother always obtained my consent in advance.

I remember other little tests my mother put me through. One day she perceived that just before I arrived at a closed door I would stop and reach for the handle to open it. She began letting me go about the house by myself and she discovered that I seldom ran into things. She credited the *hakim* and the stinging drops, but every evening she would hold her hand up before my face and ask me to tell her where it was. She used to shake her hand before me so that myriads of pores next to, below and above my ears could feel her hand even when it was a foot away. The air currents helped me to spot it. But she wasn't satisfied with this. She wanted me to tell her whether the light was on or off. When I failed this test she was unhappy again, but I soon caught on and would listen for the click of the switch and then tell her. Sometimes she would flip the switch very rapidly time and again, and I would always count the clicks and give her the right answer.

The reason for the conflicting approaches of Mother and Father towards my blindness lay in each of their backgrounds. My mother had come from a large middle-class family, and had three sisters and three brothers. She was the eldest of the sisters, and at the time when she came to attend school it was still customary for even the best-educated women to go only as far as the eighth grade. Thus her education had ceased with simple arithmetic and Hindi grammar. From that time until her marriage five years later she had devoted herself to cooking, sewing, and caring for her younger brothers and sisters. While these skills trained her to be an excellent mother, they did not prepare her to cope rationally with an unfamiliar tragedy such as blindness. She found the weapons of love and affection useless. If she pampered me as her maternal instinct dictated, my father would scold her; and if she tried to use the medical cures which had been practised and handed down from mother to daughter for generations, my father would forbid their use.

My mother married my father when she was seventeen. They had little in common, for while my father had travelled extensively abroad, and had moved in a society completely foreign to our native culture, my mother had been brought up in the strict discipline of a very conventional Indian home. In fact, she had not even seen a white woman until she met one when in the company of my father. My father was a very restless person, quick-tempered and impatient. He often went to clubs and dinners where English-speaking people were present, and he would return home late at night from the club, where he had been playing a game of cards. I think my mother must have felt almost as apart from him as if he were an Englishman.

Then her first child had turned out to be a daughter, much to the disappointment of her relatives and friends, who blamed her for the miscarriage of their wishes. The second also was a daughter, and the third child was no more pleasing than the first two. Some hints were made to give up, since there seemed no hope of getting a son, although in all fairness to my father, he seemed to grow more and more attached to Mother and home, and he was very fond of all three daughters. In fact, he spoiled them.

At last a son came, and the event was celebrated with great joy and festivity. As an anti-climax to this addition I had arrived, and even more people with gifts had come to see me than had celebrated the birth of my brother, Om Parkash.

While my mother's parents had always lived in the congested city of Lahore, in a comparatively middle-class home, my father's childhood had been spent in the carefree atmosphere of village life. His grandfather had been the leader of a village on the bank of the Ravi River. In a small way, he had been a philanthropist, and had been loved and revered by all the villagers. At his death, he had given half his land to the Brahmans, and had left the care of the rest of his property to his eldest son.

According to the village tradition, the eldest son was charged with the care of the whole family. Thus my grandfather, Lalaji, was responsible for his two brothers' families as well as his own of seven children; the oldest of his boys was my father. These combined families formed one large household, typical of the village family system of India.

Recalling his experiences in this family, my father remarked, 'It was a village within a village.' He tells me that many relatives used to come to visit them, sometimes doubling the size of the household, and that 'visit' in those days was interpreted liberally. People would stay for months at a time, while my grandmother and the girls did all the cooking. Lalaji had inherited all the generosity of his father, and whenever any neighbours could not afford groceries, they came to him. He in turn would send them to my grandmother, Bhabiji, who had somehow to provide for them. One day my grandfather sent a neighbour to her in the middle of the month when supplies were nearly exhausted. Bhabiji knew that she had to make the provisions last until the end of the month, and it was impossible to do so unless every grain was conserved. She explained to the neighbour that there was nothing to spare, but when Lalaji heard of this he was enraged, and told Bhabiji that there was always plenty in his home. Whenever there was a shortage in the home it was the women of the immediate family who starved.

Of the seven children of the family, six were boys, and Lalaji was determined that every one of them should receive a college education, an exorbitant ambition for a person with limited means in a country where eighty-five per cent of the people are illiterate. When the children came of school age they started attending a government school located two miles from the village. They had to walk this distance after doing their chores each morning, and on the way home they rested under the trees to finish their homework.

Lalaji never treated them as children, but always as grown-ups, and from the time when he was nine years old my father was charged with looking after his younger brothers and setting them a good example. At the age of fifteen he entered Government College in Lahore for the premedical curriculum. Two years later, having passed the Intermediate examination, he joined the King Edward Medical College in Lahore, where he distinguished himself both in scholarship and sports – a rare combination indeed.

My father was very ambitious and independent. In April 1919, when Gandhiji was arrested trying to enter Punjab in spite of the ban on his entry, my father joined the college strike organized as a protest against this high-handedness of the British; therefore his merit scholarship was confiscated and he was dropped for a year. Although my father's punishment was rescinded a few months later by the committee appointed by the government to review these punishments, his scholarship was never restored.

In 1920, immediately on obtaining his degree in medicine and surgery, which entitled him to enrolment in the *British Medical Register,* he proceeded to England for post-graduate courses in tropical medicine and public health; this my father did in spite of the advice of the Government Advisory Committee, which doubted the possibility of admission of Indian students to the already crowded universities of Great Britain.

My father was the first in the family to venture across the high seas. All his relatives except Lalaji were opposed to his leaving for England. They believed he would lose his caste, and that such education was bound to change his way of life and destroy his native heritage. He would certainly be a misfit in Indian society if he returned. It was also argued that he might marry and settle down in England, which would prove disastrous to the education of his younger brothers; finally, it was considered most unwise to take the risk with the limited resources that the family had. However, he went.

In England my father attended the University of London, completing his education in public health in record time. He then returned to India, and as he disembarked in Bombay, his younger brother, who had finished his medical schooling in India, boarded a ship for England to receive the same training.

My father took a job in the newly created Public Health

Department as a Municipal Health Officer. Since he was the first to earn his living, he not only helped his younger brothers, but also contributed to the living expenses of the family. In 1922 he was selected as one of the first Rockefeller Fellows to tour Europe and the United States, and with this start he went on to a distinguished career in India. His success enabled him to assist his brothers and his older sister's sons in completing their education. From the very beginning, Lalaji had indoctrinated him with the value of education, and thereafter he never ceased to strive until all in his family who deserved an opportunity for education had received it.

Although in my case there was an obstacle which seemed insurmountable, he was determined to leave no avenue unexplored. He read all available literature on blindness. He learned that almost all India's blind people had turned to begging for their livelihood, or had become owners of *pan* and *biri* shops and spent their days rolling nuts and condiments in a betel leaf or tobacco in a cigarette paper. He was determined that this was not going to be the fate of his second son, and he started corresponding with many of the prominent educational authorities, asking their advice. The replies were not optimistic. For the blind, educational facilities and personnel were limited, and often the schools became semi-asylums with all ages grouped together in classes without any gradation system.

My father still persisted, for he knew that my staying at home would result in over indulgence. He realized, as well, that I would have difficulty playing with normal children, and that my mother would always be afraid to let me leave the immediate premises.

At last he heard of Dr R. M. Halder, principal of Dadar School for the Blind in Bombay. My father wrote to him asking advice. Dr Halder showed unusual interest in my case, and promised to take special care and personal responsibility for me if I were sent to his school.

When my mother learned of my father's decision to send me to the Dadar School, she was appalled. She had never been to Bombay, and to her it might have been a foreign country.

22

She could not understand the reason for sending me nine hundred miles away from home to attend school with orphans and children of the poorest classes. After all, another year at home could not but help my development. Yet she placed her faith in my father's superior judgement, and in her quiet way she acquiesced.

On 15 February 1939, when I was almost five, my mother and father took me to Karnal station. There I was to board a train for the first time, accompanied by one of my father's friends, who was going on to Bombay. When the whistle blew, my father said to me, 'Now you are a man.' Then he clasped my hands, and drawing the palms together within his own, he murmured the Hindu blessing, '*Namaste.*' I felt him lift me through the window as he handed me to his friend, and I leaned out just in time to kiss my mother before the train started moving.

It was an express train, and we covered the distance in a day and a half. My remembrance of the journey is that I cried and slept intermittently, overcome by all the strangeness which surrounded me.

My Cousin Prakash, who was posted in Bombay, met my train, and we took a *tonga* from the station to the school. I was overjoyed to ride in the familiar horse-drawn carriage, because it was something I could cling to from the past. After about an hour's ride, we slowed down and entered the congested, smoke-filled district of Dadar. The rhythmic beat of the tramway bells, the loud shouts of the conductors at each junction, the irregular rumble of the wheels on the narrow rails stood in sharp contrast to the quiet murmur of the canal water near our spacious bunga-low at home. I was frightened and I begged Cousin Prakash to take me home. We finally reached the gate of what Cousin Prakash described as a narrow three-storey building, sandwiched between a cotton mill and a congested shop district. Now I was at school.

It was about four-thirty in the afternoon, and the students had just finished their tiffin. Getting up from the floor, they greeted me in Marathi, the language of Bombay, which I did not understand. But we went on through the crowded dining-room to Dr Halder's office. In his high-pitched voice he said something to me in English, which I did not understand either. Without taking further notice of me, he turned to my cousin and started talking, and just then someone – I could tell it was an older boy – came and took me away.

He took me to the dormitory, which was on the second floor, and sat me down on his bed, which was four or five rough boards laid across a heavy steel frame. It might have been a wide bench had it not been covered with a single white cotton sheet. In his faltering Hindi he told me his name was Deoji, that he had come to the school eight years ago when he was almost as young as I and that he had been asked to look after me until I was settled. He said that this was the sleeping room, and that I did not have a bed yet, but they were going to bring one, and until then I could use his.

While we were sitting and Deoji was carrying on his mono-logue, I heard the rough laughter of other boys who started filing into the dormitory. Deoji said something to them in Marathi, and he lifted me up for exhibition to all who had some sight. Then he put me down on the floor to shake hands.

As each student took my hand and clasped it in his calloused grip I cringed. They laughed at my squeamishness, and one named Bhasker, who from his voice seemed about nine, said, 'Didn't your mother teach you how to laugh?' and some of them sniggered again.

Another named Abdul pulled both my hands into his, and feeling their texture, remarked they were smooth and asked if I had ever worked. I drew away from his rasping fingers, and stood there stupefied, to their jeering amusement.

Just then Dr Halder walked into the dormitory, and an uneasy silence fell over the boys. He took my hand and asked me to follow him, and to my great relief, we left the dormitory. We passed through a door which he unlocked and then closed behind us before we walked up the stairs to his apartment. He called his wife to say that I had arrived, and she took me in her arms and kissed me. She told me she was my aunt and Dr Halder my uncle, and she hoped that I would come to her just as I would to my mother. I was to eat in their private dining-room and not with the other children. Then Dr Halder took me back to the dormitory, where I waited the dreaded return of the students from the dining-room.

That evening a spring bed with a heavy mattress and a mos-quito net was moved in and placed beside Deoji's. From then on I was known as the boy with the good bed and soft hands. Later Deoji put me to bed and tucked the mosquito net under the edges of the mattress. I couldn't go to sleep, for the students were still in a fit of excitement over the arrival of a new student. They talked about how gently Dr Halder had asked me to follow him, and how neatly I was dressed. Abdul still contended that my hands were like a girl's and that I had never worked. Amidst this clamour was heard the loud coughing of Dr Halder and one of the older students shushed the others. Dr Halder, with quick, clicking steps, walked into the room, and turning off the light, reminded everyone in his shrill voice that it was time to go to sleep, and that severe punishment would follow if he heard any commotion.

The large, unfriendly room, the distant voice of Dr Halder, and the huge bed seemed far removed from my cosy bed in my parents' room, but soon sleep overcame me.

In the middle of the night I woke up sobbing and all the day's happenings came into focus. Pressing my face against the pillow, I cried silently. Then I felt someone gingerly pull back the mosquito net. It was Deoji. I clung to my pillow. I didn't want him to see me crying, but he gathered me up with the pillow.

I was frightened; suppose Abdul or Bhasker were to hear me? But Deoji carried me out of the dormitory and sat down on the steps. Clumsily he rested me on the steps, and asked me if he could do anything. He did not wait for an answer and started telling me about how he had felt when he first arrived there. He told me that I would soon forget about home, and would find school a very pleasant place. He described the games they played and said that before long I would be able to play also.

Listening to his gentle whisper, I felt a ray of kindness in that gloomy building. I even smiled at his faltering Hindi. He asked me to pronounce some words for him and then he tried to imitate them. When I was cheered, he told me he had broken a rule by leaving the dormitory and that we had better return, in case one of the other boys reported us. Then we went in on tiptoe, and so to bed.

In the morning Deoji helped me to dress and I was thrown into the general routine of the school. With the exception of learning how to cane chairs, which had been prohibited by my father, I was to follow the prescribed curriculum.

I went to the first class, where we spent our time looking over stuffed animals and birds to get their images in mind. With the help of an abacus we learned how to count. The first day I went up to eighteen in English, and the teacher complimented me on it in front of the class. I made rapid progress in my arithmetic class, as well as correctly associating the names and shapes of birds and animals.

When the boys found out about my progress their teasing subsided, and instead of letting me stand by myself while they played, they invited me to join them. Increasingly the teachers in class started referring questions to me when others could not answer; and what I lacked in physical activity at first, I made up for in the classroom.

For a while it remained a novelty in our school for everyone to ask me to teach them Punjabi, since I was the only one from that part of the country. They found the language extremely hard, and no sooner would I begin than they were ready to quit. Their perpetual question was how had I learned Marathi in only one week?

Abdul, however, never ceased in his contempt for my puny size. He would remark on my soft hands, my poor physical condition and my lack of facility in sports. One evening, when Abdul had just come from his dinner in the dining-room and I had just finished mine with the Halders, he asked me what

I had had to eat. When I related to him my dinner of freshly baked white bread and Dr Halder's favourite mutton dish, he sniffed sarcastically, and calling to his friends, repeated the menu as indicative of my pampered, effeminate ways.

In a tantrum, I cut his cane chair. Then I hid while he clumsily hunted for me. I was afraid Tarak Nath, who was Abdul's best friend and known for his meanness, would disclose me to him; but fortunately for me, and to his lasting credit, he stuck to the rules of fair conduct: namely, that no half-sighted person should interfere in the fight of two blind people.

Abdul strained to hear my breathing, or light movement, but I silently tiptoed, amid his characteristically vulgar profanity, to the dormitory and Deoji. Thereafter I earned respect and a particular following of my own.

Aside from these personal adjustments in my first few months there, I had to learn much about discipline. I had to make my own bed, and my first experience made me appreciate the value of having no mattress and no mosquito net. I had to sew on my buttons, polish my shoes, eat at regular times, and get up at the sound of the bell. As I grew more accustomed to the school life, the routine became easier.

After five months of school, when I had just about got settled, the summer came and it was time for me to return home. Cousin Prakash came to get me, and together we boarded the train for Lahore, where we were now living, since my father had been promoted and transferred in my absence. I expected that the noise and lively activity of the school would soon be replaced by a grieving silence, and I was filled with a longing to leave the train and return to school. Recalling my mother's pain and anguish after my blindness, I was ashamed of not wanting to go home, yet already I preferred the new taste of independence in school, and even the taunts of Abdul seemed more bearable than my sheltered, uneventful life at home.

TWO

Reality and the Dream

My parents met me at the station and I found my mother very cheerful. She was overjoyed at my return, and the same light-heartedness greeted me at our home. There was the infectious laugh of sister Umi to be relearned, the moist and warm hand of sister Nimi to rediscover. I had also to get used to taking orders from sister Pom, who was second in command to Mother. All these sisters pressed me about my doings at school and I repeatedly narrated to them and their friends my encounter with Abdul. They were amused that I had successfully defied an older boy and they were touched when I told them about Deoji.

In the morning it felt wonderful slipping my small hand into my mother's big one and running beside her almost at a trot for the family *halwaii*. As we neared the confectioner, there would be the smell of the steaming pots, the slow and deliberate noise of large spoons stirring the syrup, and an aromatic smell of freshly baked hot sweetmeats. At the shop, which jutted out on the street like a stand, Mother would lift me and place my hand on the *thalis* – the large platters which held a variety of roasted nuts and sweetmeats of different sizes and shapes. While my lungs breathed in the *halwaii* air and the old *halwaii* with rough and stubby hands gave me samples to taste and Mother held me loosely in her arms so that I could lean way over, I felt like a prince.

Sometimes Mother left me to go to the shop across the street, and the *halwaii* would let me sit with him on the platform crowded with *thalis* and say, 'Sahib, you have the nose, the mouth, and the ear, all cut out to be a *halwaii*. You just need a bigger stomach.' I would pick up one big piece after another with my sticky hands and put it into my mouth all at once. I

thought the *halwaii* was princely. We would return home with
enough sweetmeats for me to open a small shop in my nursery
room for my sisters and brother Om.

In the evening there were always the walks to Lawrence
Gardens, with its small mounds carpeted with lush grass and
the rich sounds of children running and playing hide-and-seek,
and the merry-go-round turning swiftly and the seesaw thumping against the ground. I ran and played too, but one of my
sisters always had to be at my side. The Carry-Home ice-cream
man seemed to be present everywhere, peddling his product in
small cups which my sisters would let me stuff in my pockets.
The open air of the huge gardens felt wonderful after Dadar.
So did the care of the servants, who made my bed and polished
my shoes, and the gentle hand of Mother, who bathed me. I
was glad Abdul was not there to see all this.

The summer ended, and once more my father clasped my
hands and said 'Namaste,' Mother kissed me, and I started for
Bombay with another of my father's friends.

In my second year at school I was old enough to have my own
little plot of land, where I planted vegetables, and I spent my
spare time, as did everyone else, caring for them. I had also
begun learning multiplication and division on an arithmetic
slate, and reading and writing Braille in English – at that time
there was no uniform Hindi alphabet for Braille. I learned that
each of the letters in Braille was formed by various combinations
of six dots. The Braille typewriter had only six keys.

Since I was slightly healthier now, I began to take part in
more games. Our games differed little from those of normal
children, with the exception of running. Behind the cotton mill
was an empty lot where half a dozen wires about a hundred
yards long were stretched between poles. We had our races
there, running with strings attached to rings on the wire. This
turned out to be quite a competitive sport, for the winner
received not only prizes but recognition from the other students.
Although we practised every day, the real contest was held
every two months between students of the same size. We would
all line up on one end of the stretched wires and Dr Halder

would give each one of us a biscuit. When he said 'Go!' we had to finish the biscuit before beginning to run. If at first I could not run as fast as Bhasker, I could outdo him in eating the biscuit and get a head start on him. I came in first in the fall contest. Organized tug-of-war and a ball which had bells inside provided us with other physical activity. Draughts, or chequers, chess and card games formed our indoor sports.

This routine, coupled with good friends, should have made anyone happy. But with the coming of war, prices had gone up, and the food at the Halders' had grown steadily worse. Hard pressed because of their low salary, they had to conserve their food, and, besides, items like butter and meat were already being rationed. This fact, plus the wet and oppressive climate of Bombay and my run-down physical condition, conspired to make me spend almost half my three years there in a hospital, with every disease of childhood, including malaria and typhoid.

Starting with this series of illnesses, I recollect little more than vague impressions of a hospital and severe fever, and all the fresh experiences of the early months at Dadar, which have left a lasting impression on my memory, begin from here on to be jumbled into a world half-dream, half-real. Each month my visits to the hospital increased not only in frequency but also in duration, until the hospital became home, while the school became a strange, illusory place. There is a sharp memory of someone feeding me, with a sticky spoon, soft boiled eggs, which went bad in my hot and dry mouth, and it turned my stomach to swallow them. I never wanted soft-boiled eggs, never again. I recall, too, my expectant waiting for my parents, and the repeated disappointment when they did not appear. When I asked whether they had been informed of my illness, the answer was always evasive.

Danger of death didn't seem too far away in that desolate hospital, where again doctors and nurses became my sole guardians, and an untrustworthy barrier at best against another tragedy. There was one comfort: a nurse whose name I cannot recollect. Neither do I recall her voice. Yet from the memory of her affection and kindness, I can readily reconstruct a clear, revealing image.

I remember she would come to visit me in her off hours, and even if I were asleep she would sit and watch over me. When I awoke, she would tell me stories of her childhood and amuse me. Then she would be talking about prayer, and of some figure in the distant past. She would ask questions about my mother and sisters, and would assure me they all loved me; that even if they were not present, their thoughts were with me. Each time I sneezed she told me that it was the surest indication that they had been talking about me just then, and that if I thought of them at once, they would sneeze too. She said she was a Christian, that she would pray to her God, and that I needn't worry. Her God, she said, had always looked after the sick and uncared-for, and no miracle lay beyond him. She would bring me fruit, and even sweets if I were well. I have often asked myself if I ever even thanked her. Probably not. After a while, I took her just as much for granted as a chair or a bed, and never once thought of her not being there. For me the hospital became her, and all my previous dread of that place left me.

When I returned to school I found that my energy had been sapped, and that I tired easily. I was ashamed of this and dreaded the play hour, knowing that I couldn't keep up with the others.

One day two boys were swinging on the single swing. Standing on the seat, they pumped until the chains squeaked shrilly with the motion, and I could tell they were swinging quite high. They had been in the swing long past their turn, and despite all my pleading for fair play they would not stop. I ran to grip the chain. When they heard me coming, they jerked the chain from my reach by throwing themselves to one side. Furious at my own lack of proficiency, I moved closer, only to collide head on with the seat. After that, I remember Dr Halder's arrival, the ambulance, and waking up to the familiar odour of the hospital disinfectant, which seemed less pure than the curling fog which hung over Dadar playground.

When I awoke, my nurse was not there. Disturbing thoughts rushed through my mind. Had she left the hospital, feeling certain I would not return? Humiliated at my own pride, I remembered she had other patients. Yet all of a sudden the same fear and despair I had experienced on my first night at Dadar School returned.

Weak from the blood I had lost, and exhausted by my dire thoughts, I lay there half-awake. Then I heard those soft, yet decisive, footsteps to which I had grown accustomed, and she was there. I clung to her and wept.

This accident was simply an interlude between one series of illnesses and another. During all these illnesses she talked to me about being good, and praying, but she never explained to my satisfaction what Christianity was. She always said that I was too young, and I would learn and understand some day. I do not know if it was she, but to something or someone must be attributed my lasting interest in this religion, and its continuous source of inspiration.

When I returned to Dadar School, I asked Deoji about it, and he told me he was a Christian, too; and added that the Halders were also. He told me that Dadar School was founded by American missionaries, and that I wouldn't be there if it hadn't been for them. I asked him if they were anything like the nurse I knew, and he told me, judging from my description, they were. He taught me an English prayer which I repeated every night before going to sleep.

Heavenly Father, thou wilt hear me;
Bless thy loving child tonight;
Through the darkness be thou near me,
Keep me safe till morning light.

All this day thy hand hath led me,
And I thank thee for thy care;
Thou hast clothed me, warmed me, fed me,
Listen to my evening prayer.

Let my sins be all forgiven;
Bless the friends I love so well;
Take us all at last to heaven,
Happy there with thee to dwell.

Since at my home no discussion had centred around religion, I only knew I was a Hindu, and no more. I prayed, of course, but they were only simple requests, and I had not learned to form an impressive prayer like the one Deoji taught me. Deoji also found for me some little stories about Christ which he translated for me, and before I left Bombay I was able to read them in Braille by myself.

While thus indirectly I was learning about the Western religion, so too I was being inspired to go across the sea into another land. Dr Halder, who had attended Harvard University, had visited the Perkins Institute near Boston (which today is still the foremost institution in the education of the blind) and was endeavouring to construct a small replica of it in Bombay. At the dinner table he often spoke of Perkins and of America, and one day even asked me if I would like to go there, and suggested that this was my father's wish. My father's enthusiasm for the West and Dr Halder's encouragement were enough to implant in me the desire to travel. A week after my seventh birthday, in March, Dr Halder took me to two of his friends, a Mr and Mrs Thomas, who were planning a voyage to America in the summer of 1942. Dr Halder told me it might well be that I could go with them to the States, and that he would ask their consent.

When Mr and Mrs Thomas decided to take the responsibility and when they told me of the two-month voyage on the ship, I was thrilled at the prospect. Dr Halder followed up this visit with a letter to Dr Farrell, director of Perkins Institute, on 19 April, 1941. Counting out the time for my illness and vacation at home, I had attended classes for only one year, and it was on this attendance that he based his recommendation. Since this letter was decisive in shaping my dream to come to America, I quote the important excerpts in full:

The boy has been in the school for about a year only. We do not have standardized mental tests to give the child, but basing on his responses and my observations during the period he has been with us, I have a feeling that probably he is a superior child. He is very much interested in physical activities as well. I should like to see that he gets an opportunity to be educated in the best institution in the world in his formative and most impressionable years. His father chose our school at Bombay though 900 miles away from home as he thought that the child would have the best opportunities of education, as they are available in India. We are teaching him through the mediums of English and an Indian vernacular. He understands English and can write on the Hall Braille Typewriter. When he joined the school, he did not know a word in English. Now he has a workable vocabulary of more than 200 words . . .

While I was too young to be acquainted with the full content of the letter, or understand its significance, I did, however, catch from Dr Halder that enthusiasm for an ocean voyage and a new country.

Dr Halder was still a very young man, and dedicated to improving the conditions of the blind; and if it happened that I should go to America, and return to India conversant with the more progressive Western attitude about this handicap, I might well help to change the course of Indian thinking about blindness, and indirectly help Dr Halder accomplish his aim.

At that time, Dr Halder was in the process of completing a book on analysing the dreams of the visually handicapped. It was to be an objective study as to how the dreams of the blind differed from those of the sighted; and he asked us students to help him by retelling our dreams to him each morning. For each dream correctly reconstructed for him, we would be given a piece of candy.

I used to, and still do, have numerous dreams. While I refrained from telling him all my dreams, I remember, however, going into his office and relating a dream that I was going to England with the Halders. There were details about the ship and sea on which he questioned me closely; for the theme of his whole book was to discover how blind people pictured their surroundings. Did they, for instance, see a tree with all its leaves and spreading branches; or would they only experience it in its tall, stark structure? Since my visual memory previous to blindness had been completely obliterated because of the long illness, my experiences in the dreams did not differ from those of waking hours.

A month later, Dr Farrell of the Perkins Institute replied, but he did not agree with Dr Halder that my most 'formative and impressionable years' should be spent in the United States. He strongly recommended that I should not leave my home environment. He said that his experiences with those coming from the East at an early age to study in the Western world indicated that there was a grave risk of becoming total misfits in Eastern as well as in Western cultures. Dr Farrell mirrored, as we were later to learn, the attitude of almost all the Western educators; and Dr Halder, realizing this, let the matter rest, and with this vanished my dreams about an immediate visit to America.

I continued my studies at the school for another year and a half, and within two and a half years I had absorbed all the school had to offer. To be sure, if I wished to make caning chairs my profession, I could have continued there and specialized in that work; but academically, Dr Halder considered my studies there completed. He wrote to my father to say that since no immediate provisions could be made for my trip abroad, the time could be more valuably spent at home rather than at another boarding school. What I needed most, he said, was family life.

In spite of climate, illness and food, Dadar School and Bombay had become home for me. As I boarded the train, bound for Lahore, I went with anguish and apprehension. I tried to remember Panjabi and couldn't. Indeed, I had a more workable vocabulary in English. I was no longer even a Hindu, for Deoji had convinced me that I was at heart a Christian. I thought and thought, trying to reconstruct the image of my family from their voices, but their voices were muffled and distorted, and echoed faintly in the corridors of time and distance.

I leaned forward, and tried to shut out the distracting and exasperating noises around me, but in vain. It seemed as though I were going to a place where nobody understood or even knew me. I had no friends in my family, for my friends were to be found in the nurse, in Deoji, the Halders, and my class mates.

35

Yet no one sympathized with me, and even the Halders were astonished by my apathy.

And then the compartment jarred, and I knew I would soon hear that definitive sound of departure as the train moved away from the station. It would overshadow even the loud pleas of the hawkers who clung to the train. Slowly the train pulled away as the wheels shrieked on the permanent way, and with their turning, completed a circle of my life.

THREE

Mehta Gullie

THE whole family met me at the Lahore station, and their happiness over my arrival was radiant and infectious. I soon forgot my apprehensions in that vivacious atmosphere.

Since our own house, which had been built a few years earlier, was being repaired, we moved in with my mother's family, where the whole lot of us were crowded into two rooms. But the cramped quarters were scarcely noticed by us children, since we spent all our waking hours in the Mehta *Gullie* and returned home only to sleep. The Mehta *Gullie,* or street, was separated from the main house by a five-foot wall.

Climbing this wall, we would find ourselves in a completely different world, for behind it and within a radius of two city blocks lay the houses of all the Mehta families, comprising a clan of some fifty persons. These houses opened on the *gullie,* which was off the Temple Road and formed a square. Our house was not included in the square, since it had been built before the planning of the Mehta *Gullie,* but it was only a block away.

There were many Mehta children, and all of us played together, but the family which was closest to us was that of my father's younger brother, who had received the same medical training as my father, and now worked in his department. He had five children, and they were about our age and had the same interests, although unfortunately there was no playmate for my baby sister Usha, who was born while I was away. The two older daughters, Shil and Lil, went to the same school as my sisters, Pom, Nimi and Umi. All of them played on the same ball team and often had the same assignments. Yog, their younger brother, who was three years older than Om, was the first boy in this generation of the Mehta families, and whenever we played any game, he was the leader. He chose the games and called the terms, and became the referee in any controversy.

Kite flying was the popular sport at this time, and while the girls knitted and sewed, we boys climbed the roofs to enter the competition. We had limited pocket money, and it was not enough to buy all the materials we needed to make our kites, but with *dor* (a strong thread) we could cut other kite strings and try, at least, to appropriate the fallen prize. During the day, someone was sure to fly a high kite, and as soon as it was spotted, other kites would go up to tangle in battle. Often three or four were hooked together, and with strong thread and the right pull a heavy kite could cut the snarl and bring them all plunging to the street. Yog posted us all at different stations, and as soon as a string was broken, a long cry of '*Bow-catta*' would resound to our posts. All eyes would focus skyward and we would try to follow the direction of the crashing kites. Everyone would rush to find the fallen booty, and sometimes a bitter struggle would follow. The rules of fair play were that no one was to snatch a kite once someone had placed both hands on it, but the rules were often broken. In the scramble which followed the kite's hitting the ground, more often than not a kite would be torn, but sometimes one party was able to take it undamaged. During the rush to follow the kite, we jumped from one roof level to the next, and each man looked out only for himself. My enthusiasm would never allow me to stand still while the others rushed to reach the prize, and I would follow the sound.

Sometimes one of the kite hunters would forbid me to follow him. 'Stay there,' he would shout. 'I'll be back in just a moment.' But other times boys tried to help me and took my hand while running. I scorned these gestures, because they annoyed me and interfered with the game. Soon, in the scramble of the play, my handicaps, indeed even my existence, were forgotten, and with very occasional exceptions, I was subject to the same rules and same fights. Though with this complete freedom came injuries, I did develop better co-ordination.

Once, though, I came close to a very disastrous fall. I remember my sisters, watching the rush and horrified to see me clambering from roof to roof, shouted that I must stop. Conscious of their attention, I thought of where I was, lost my nerve and sense of balance, and started sliding on the tin roof. Luckily, the sloping roof flattened to a three-inch ledge at the sides, giving me enough pause to regain my balance and miss the two-storey fall. When my mother learned of this incident, strict orders followed, forbidding me to take part in further activities. I was, she said, to stay with my sisters and let them watch over me, and all my entreaties were ignored 'in my own best interests'. I grew irritated and sullen, and my father, noticing this, finally resolved to let me learn my own lessons the hard way. He advised Mother not to be overly cautious. With this I gained my liberty and returned to my playmates.

I would often not see my mother from early morning, when we congregated for sports, until dusk. We were served food at whichever house we happened to be during the lunch hour, and my oldest sister, Pom, who was thirteen and who might as well have been Mother, saw that we were washed and clean. We all obeyed and respected her, for she was the only orderly influence in our disorderly group. Just as Yog was chief in the boys' games, she led the girls, but when we played together she was the undisputed head.

We returned home only in the evening, with healthy appetites for our eight-thirty dinner, but the dinner was not very leisurely, since there was yet another treat at the Mehta *Gullie* before bed. We assembled, tired and for the first time content to be still, in the room of Bhabiji, my father's mother. To drowsy but eager listeners, she told stories, stories which sparkled with her vivid narration. Sometimes they were about life on the farm when Lalaji was alive, and how the gathering of all the families made each dinner like a festival. More often, however, she told us tales with a simple moral, which had been handed down like Aesop's fables. She would vary these with tales about the dishonest shepherd who called 'Lion' too many times, or of the farmer who gave his life to save his family, and stories about Ram and Sita, the personifications of virtue – Ram and Sita were held up to us as models of manhood and womanhood. We were touched

39

and moved by their courage against the infamy of Rawan, and they high-lighted for us always the struggle between good and evil, and the triumphs of courage and sacrifice over greed and wickedness. After listening to these reminiscences and folk tales, we would return home refreshed and promise ourselves to live up to the ideals of Ram and of Sita. But the next day we were fighting again over the fallen kites.

When were still living in our grandparents' compound, my father went on an inspection trip and took Mother, leaving us in the charge of sister Pom. Once during our parents' absence, our grandfather returned from his evening walk, and when brother Om teased him for the promised sweets, he tapped him on the back with his cane. Brother Om thought this punishment unjust, since my grandfather had promised him a bag of hard orange candies. I was with sister Pom when brother Om came to her crying and told her, 'Grandfather beat me.'

Sister Pom was enraged, for our parents had never broken a promise. She gathered us together and said we were no longer to live with our grandparents and tolerate such insults. We were to pack our belongings and leave that very night. No one asked her where we were going, but we gathered our combs and wash cloths and soon we were on the road.

Holding each other's hands, we drew courage, and resisted our tears. Instinctively we turned towards Lawrence Gardens, which we had visited many times on evening walks. It was about a mile away, and as we got farther away from Grand-father's house, I wished that sister Pom had let me tell someone we were leaving. Then, at least, there would have been a hope of our grandparents' pleading, and maybe Grandfather's apologizing – and then we could have stayed there without having our dignity outraged.

We reached Lawrence Gardens around eight o'clock, and the clean, fresh air from the thick, tall grass which carpeted the hilly acres had a reviving influence. Sister Pom bought us all a cup of Carry-Home ice cream, which she said should take care of our dinner. Then we sat down in one corner under the tall, wide-spreading trees and prepared to spend the night. As it grew dark, all sounds subsided, and only the persistent chirp of the crickets remained to keep us company. In our intermittent drowsing, we heard the striking of nine, ten, ten-thirty.

Then, to my relief, I heard the faint, familiar calls of one of the servants who had often accompanied us to this favourite spot. We were all awake now. The party edged closer, and the shouts grew louder; still sister Pom didn't say anything. I wanted to shout back 'Here we are,' but dreading sister Pom's reproach, I didn't. Even when they spotted us with the help of their torches, sister Pom sat there immobile.

My uncle, who accompanied the party, scolded us for leaving and causing so much unnecessary concern. For all they knew, all six of us might have been kidnapped. But seeing his scolding was having no result, he paused and stood there silent, looking at us. Then he gently suggested, 'Let's go home.' But not until he assured sister Pom that Grandfather would make his apology to brother Om did she agree. We joined our hands, and with Uncle and servants trailing, headed towards our Grandfather's house in the Mehta *Gullie*.

FOUR

At the Foot of the Himalayas

IN September of 1942, my father was promoted and transferred to Rawalpindi, which was one hundred and eighty miles north of Lahore. At first there was talk of only my father going to 'Pindi and the rest of the family staying behind in Lahore, where my sisters were all enrolled in an excellent convent. But from the very outset we knew the fallacy of this arrangement. We had been a closely knit family, and from the very beginning, my father believed in home education just as much as in academic, and he himself played an important part in this. So, without any further argument, it was decided to leave Lahore. Within a week of his orders my father left, and in early 1943, when I was just nine, we started for 'Pindi, a city with excellent climate, bearing the exotic name of 'gateway to Kashmir', leaving behind our own home, the *gullie,* kites and Bhabiji.

In Punjab alone, where more Indians were to be found in the higher civil service than in any other province, recent developments had made possible the elevation of an Indian to the position of Assistant Director of Public Health. My father, because of his seniority and education, had received this job in 'Pindi, and with it the dividend of a house. Here, as in other big cities, the government had reserved areas for the homes of higher echelons in the civil service, who in the older days used to be Englishmen. We were delighted by the big government bungalow, with a built-in office for my father. While the house was in places a little dilapidated, the one-acre estate was excellent for raising chickens and buffaloes – our greatest source of milk – and we were able to build a pool for the accommodation of thirty goldfish. For a while we even kept a cocker spaniel. With our family, animal farm, and the six servants, plus the *dhobi,* our laundryman, and *chonkidar,* or caretaker, we had a holding comparable in dignity to that of any other official in the Indian Government.

By regulation of the government the road traffic of Civil Lines, the district where we lived, was limited, and for miles around it was quiet. The sticky heat of Lahore and the smoke-filled Dadar district seemed almost grotesque in comparison with this natural setting. The cold and pricking wind which grazed the icy peaks of the mountains swept down over Rawalpindi bringing the vitality and vigour of the Himalayas. I had never felt more exhilarated, or healthier. The vivacity I had experienced flying kites and jumping roofs returned afresh.

The rest of the family were happy, too. My sisters learned that there was a Presentation convent here as fine as Sacred Heart at Lahore. My brother was admitted to a good school also, and my mother was happy to have buffaloes of her own.

We continued to live at Civil Lines until October 1945, and those three happy years stand out in my mind as a buffer between my stay in Bombay and the break-up of India.

For the first time now, I noticed how smoothly the difference in my father's and mother's attitudes towards my blindness had been bridged. My mother encouraged me to play and run as I chose and to go on excursions wherever I pleased in the district. I was no longer pampered. One day when I had not eaten my meal, Mother gently scolded me, and then she gave me a banana to compensate for the small lunch. I told her I would eat it in a minute, and no sooner had she left the dining-room than I turned around to offer it to our little cocker spaniel puppy, Blackie. She swallowed part of it, but spat up the rest and there was no hiding what I had done. I was given a thrashing that day and made to clean up the mess. However much I valued my independence, I did like the pampering, too, but I was learning that my mother had decided to treat me according to my choice of independence.

My sisters treated me with no more deference than did my mother. In the past they used to buy me sweets with their own pocket money; and at the table, whenever there wasn't enough of some tasty dish, I had priority. But not any more. In fact I

43

have a slight suspicion that the sweets they bought with my own pocket money were not always all delivered to me. I was not even indulged as the youngest. Usha had replaced me in this advantageous position.

The Presentation convent was located about two miles away from our home, and at first this seemed to be at a prohibitive distance, because my father couldn't take time off from his work to drive my sisters there. After consultation it was decided to buy each of the girls a bicycle. For the past five years, the women in India had enjoyed increasing independence, thanks to the nature of Mahatma Gandhi's campaign; still not many women had taken to riding bicycles by themselves on the streets.

Since brother Om's bicycle was falling apart, he was given a new one also. I prevailed upon my father not to dispose of the one brother Om had outgrown, and it took me many days, learning by trial and error, to repair that bicycle. With an occasional direction from a servant, I kept on working at it until I had the wheels straightened out, put new spokes in them, and even replaced the seat. After this bicycle had been my toy for almost a month and a half, and I had well spotted my clothes with grease, it was fit to be put on the road once again.

Now I started learning how to ride it. This was very difficult, since I was afraid to ask anyone to teach me for fear the bicycle would be taken away from me as being too old and dangerous. Each morning, I would leave home and try to ride it in the compound. No sooner would I begin than I would fall, and would have to spend time not only hiding minor injuries, but fixing the bicycle. But gradually I learned to balance myself, and falls came less frequently.

One morning when my sisters were riding to school, I decided that I would try to follow them, keeping at a safe distance. I knew the streets would be empty at that early hour, and nothing would confuse the sound of my sisters talking to one another in the quiet of the morning. I was sure I could take my directions from their voices. At first everything went just as I had imagined. We didn't meet with much traffic, and in spite of occasional difficulties in hearing my sisters when they turned a corner, I followed them right up to the gate of their school.

Even if I had been concentrating on remembering the turns of the twisting road, it probably would have been impossible for me to find my way back. As it was, I was afraid to disclose myself to my sisters by shouting; I lost my nerve, and while I was still thinking about what to do, they were out of reach, inside the schoolyard.

Then I heard the bells and the retreating laughter of the girls as I walked around the wall outside the school. I thought about the Dadar School. Its wall had been high and impressive too, and no one inside the wall paid too much heed to what went on outside. Even the bells seemed to fit the atmosphere. They sounded much like the church bells I had heard on Sundays at Bombay.

I put my bicycle near the wall and sat down beside it on a patch of grass, leaning my back against the wall. When I was not dozing, I let my thoughts drift. After what seemed a long while the noon hour arrived. I heard the noise, the laughter, and the playing of games. I knew I was the only boy in that whole feminine vicinity, and I felt quite out of place. I wondered how it would be to find myself back in Bombay, competing in races, and swinging on swings. How noisy that place sometimes had been! Abdul? He seemed nicer now. I longed to be back there. Soon the girls' play hour was over, and they returned inside. But my thoughts lingered on.

I awoke with a jar; the bells were ringing three. It must be time for them to come out, I thought, and I picked my bicycle off the ground and stood up. When my sisters arrived, they were astonished, and I was overwhelmed with their questions — how I had got there, what I had been doing all day, why I hadn't told them. But I was saved the embarrassment of answering because their questions followed in such quick succession. Then we started on the journey home, and this time sister Nimi kept one of her hands on my handle-bar as we rode alongside each other. All the time I was thinking of what my mother would say, and I dreaded her reproaches.

But on my return Mother only made some comment about my not being there for lunch, and then asked how many new bruises I had added to my collection.

I grew more and more proficient on my bicycle and after a while I was even able to ride with my hands free of the handle-bars.

On Sundays, now and then, my father would take us all to Topi Park, where for a mile and a half there was a complete absence of obstacles and traffic. We would have races on bicycles, while father played golf. Usha had learned to ride a bicycle also, and with the exception of my mother, the world seemed to be on wheels.

One day when my father returned from a tour, he brought some squabs for me. Until then, I had had only chickens, which I diligently looked after. Ram Saran, a middle-aged peon who had accompanied my father, was supposed to help me prepare a place for these squabs, but having been delayed unloading the car, he did not come at my call, making me lose my temper. I called him a *pagal* – an idiot – and my father overheard me. He came out, and in front of Ram Saran, slapped me. Among other things, he told me. 'Ram Saran is your fellow man. See that you respect him as such!'

Humiliated and hurt, I cried. As soon as my father went in, Ram Saran, disobeying his instructions, tried to quiet me, and taking my handkerchief, he dried my eyes.

Starting with this incident, I came to know Ram Saran better than did any other member of the family, and whenever I accompanied my father on tours, Ram Saran was my constant companion and guide. Father would sometimes leave before I was up, and would not return until dinner-time and sometimes later. All this while I was left in the custody of Ram Saran, and it was he who took me on long walks through villages and farms. Until my father's transfer from 'Pindi in October 1945, it was through Ram Saran's explanations that I understood the significance of what I was witnessing on the farms, in the small shops, and in the village huts. Thus I came to know a point of view completely different from my own family's.

Even when we were not on tours. I would spend hours in Ram Saran's quarters, talking to him about the war. His quarters were a very small room located at the very farthest end of our estate. Stretching my arms, I could almost reach from wall to wall of his room, and the length was not much greater. Yet within that room, Ram Saran cooked, slept and kept all his belongings. On one side stood his small cot, which just fitted in the length of the quarters; and I remember wondering what Ram Saran would have done if he had been one of the Sikhs, six and a half feet tall. At the other side of the room was built a small *chula,* a charcoal burner over which he did all his cooking. I would often visit him in the evening during his off-duty hours, and while I sat on a small board, leaning against the cot, he would cook, and now and then I could persuade him to let me taste one of his pancake-like *rotis,* if I promised not to tell my mother.

Ram Saran hated Britishers, and he said the British officers whom my father had replaced used to return from their clubs at all hours of the night. In spite of being off duty, he would have to stay up waiting for their return, for frequently they would be quite unable even to unlock the door. Ram Saran, retiring after he had seen them to bed, would still be expected by the clerks to be on time next morning for his office duty, for he had to please the clerks as well as his officers.

Then Ram Saran had no use for war. The prices had gone up; his salary had not. He was having a hard time and he attributed all this to the British Government. He was a great admirer of Subash Chunder Bose, for he was sure Bose had acted rightly in starting the Indian National Army on the Japanese side and trying thus to undermine the British. Ram Saran had no doubt in his mind that the Axis powers would be victorious. He could read Urdu very well, and each evening he would run down to the home of one of his friends who subscribed to a morning Urdu paper and bring it to his quarters. While I sat, he would read me the pro-Nazi paper, and I was very much impressed. From his reading I would get fresh ammunition to fire at my father sometime after dinner or during the day, for he was for Allied victory through and through. My father was convinced that the coalition of the Allies would triumph; and the respect I acquired for the democratic nations, who were the constant topic of our meal-time conversations, convinced me that my father was right. After all, he had travelled, while Ram Saran had never ever left Punjab. So one day, Ram Saran and I made a bet of ten *rupees* – my one month's pocket money and one-fifth of his monthly pay – on who would win the war, and after that bet, we never wavered from our support of the opposing camps. Ram Saran had a good head, and argued very convincingly; but in all our heated discussions I never called him *pagal* again.

Ram Saran had yet another way of holding my attention. He used to read, sometimes even sing, the epic poem of *Ramayana*. Listening again to the struggle between the forces of good and evil, and the power of good to triumph against all odds, made a deep impression in my mind, and each time Ram Saran read it, I was enthralled anew.

Sometimes I reached Ram Saran's quarters before he returned from work, and I walked over to the *dhobi*'s dwelling only a few yards away. They were a family of seven, with two daughters around twelve or thirteen, and three younger boys, two of whom already went to the *ghat* with the *dhobi* to wash clothes. I would often find the girls feverishly ironing with their charcoal-heated irons, while their mother, when not helping, busily cooked and cleaned. Their house was just as spotless as Ram Saran's, and the same rule of leaving the shoes at the door was observed.

One day when I had entered their two-room house, which was little more than twice as large as Ram Saran's, I found one of the girls crying. They had never complained before, and always laughed and chattered whenever I came in. I asked her what was the matter, but she would not answer. Then her mother, who was breathing hard, began to talk.

For four years they had lived on the estate, washing the clothes of each new assistant director; they had always been careful with the clothes, and had never received any complaints. As the prices had risen, they had to take more and more customers, which forced them to work as fast as they could from early morning until late at night. Her daughter, while ironing an expensive *sari,* had scorched it badly; that very afternoon they had gone to the customer and reported the damage, but the customer had been furious, and had refused to accept the *sari.* Now the *dhobi*'s family was expected to make good the loss. 'A hundred and fifty *rupees,*' she said. Where can we get the money? We won't make that much in two months' time.' I was moved, and feeling helpless and awkward, without even saying a word of consolation I left.

I told Ram Saran about it and asked what I should have done, but he added to my discomfort by remaining silent. I couldn't approach my mother, for it seemed it was becoming a habit with me to tell her some new sad tale each day and then try to enlist her help for the *mali,* our gardener, or the boy who took care of the cows. So next day I asked sister Pom, who kept all our money, to give me all my savings, five *rupees* at the time. She wanted to know why, but according to the rules, she did not insist, and gave me my money. I put it in an envelope, and asked Ram Saran if he would take it to the *dhobi*'s family, but he did not want to take the responsibility. He said some day my mother would find out, and might think he had encouraged me; and all my assurance to the contrary had no effect. Finally I took the envelope and gave it to the youngest in the family, who was only five, and asked him to give it to his mother. Next day the envelope was returned to my mother, and at the dinner table she questioned me. I disclosed the whole matter, and to my great relief, all my family seemed to be as touched as I had been. All my sisters as well as my brother were willing to pool our savings and give them to the *dhobi*'s family, but my father said he would look into it himself, and that we need not worry.

When I saw the *dhobi*'s family again they were just as shy as I was, and the girls, who had greeted me before with lively talk, remained silent; but after their first awkward words of gratitude, we were again on the same terms. When Ram Saran heard about this incident, he was very happy, and gave me a piece of his *roti* without my even asking him, and that night he read a longer chapter than usual from *Ramayana*.

FIVE

The Juti

IT was fifteenth of June, and the cold winds of Rawalpindi had been replaced by the valley heat wave. It was hot and sultry outside, and the temperature was 106 degrees, although it was not yet eleven. The blazing sun heated the flat roof until we felt like pottery figures in a kiln; yet there was something singularly cold in the house.

Ashok, my younger brother, had been seriously ill for two days, and the lively activity which marks the home of a child was now suspended, and a depressing emptiness haunted the large house. Symptoms of his sickness were few, and made no sense. All that could be determined was that his temperature was above 102 degrees and did not change at all.

I had gone out to feed the chickens, and when I was through, hot and perspiring, I went straight to the drawing room. All my sisters sat on the couch. 'Gian Chand tells me Ashok has been taken to the hospital. What's the matter? Do they know what he has?'

After a painful silence, sister Pom answered in a firm and controlled voice, 'He has meningitis.'

I was stunned and suddenly felt chilly. All at once the house seemed cold and desolate. Only the ceaseless ticking of the clock on the mantelpiece disturbed the stillness.

I sat down behind the couch. I was not yet four when meningitis blinded me; Ashok was only a year old. What if he should die? I must do something, I thought; but the apathy was contagious. Lunch-time arrived, and no one ate anything. With the sound of every car on the street outside, the tension heightened, and my heart would throb violently. That might be Father, I would think, bringing us news, and I was sure that in every mind this hope was foremost.

My thoughts went back a year, to the day of Ashok's arrival in April 1944. It had been hot that day, too, yet the house had been full of happiness. There were no relatives in 'Pindi to celebrate his birth, and no festivity had marked his coming. It had been a quiet happiness which radiated and flowed through the big house, giving it new warmth. Everyone remarked on our resemblance, and someone called him my belated twin. Ashok had been like a toy to me, a diversion from chickens, fish and buffaloes.

As long as we had been in 'Pindi, I had never seen our house void of activity. But now it seemed so vacant, barren and spirit-less. Yet this condition had only existed for two days and already the nervousness in the house had reached an unbearable pitch.

I had often wondered what feeling must have possessed my family throughout my two months of sickness in Gujrat and Lahore. Now I knew: these two days multiplied thirtyfold. I remembered our house in Lahore, and the procession of relatives who had come to cheer the family with their expressions of sympathy until my father had been forced to seek a transfer. Even if Ashok survived, I saw graphically the whole scene of *pandits, hakims* and *surmas* repeated once more; and I felt sorry for Ashok, and agonized for my mother.

Thus my thoughts revolved in a vicious circle until my mind ached for action. Yet I listlessly leaned forward on the couch, and rested my head on its back, and once more I grew aware of the clock.

Suddenly the convulsive whines of a dog from somewhere in the heat of the empty compounds shattered the stillness of the house, and I jumped up. I heard the breathing of my sisters quicken. Then sister Pom said, 'We must be nervous to let a dog's bark startle us.' The howls increased in intensity until sister Pom got up and said she would see what was the matter. 'It must be sick,' sister Nimi said. We all got up and followed sister Pom.

As we stepped on to the veranda, the warm rays of the sun revived us. For a moment we stood there trying to determine the direction of the sounds, which were now short whines. Then

we moved forward to the back of the house and sister Pom
cried, 'It's Blackie!'

Panditji, who was head clerk of my father's office, was standing beside her. 'What's the matter, Panditji?' sister Pom asked.

'I don't know, Bahanji. I was working in the office when I
heard her.'

I could hear Blackie's short, rapid gasps and a sound like
scuffling gravel as she writhed between spasms. Nimi bent to
stroke her, but the yelps only grew louder.

'Leave her alone, Bahanji – she may bite,' Panditji continued.
'Do you know when she was born?'

'The same day as Ashok,' I murmured.

'I thought as much,' he said. Then he went into a long narration, but I was to depressed to listen.

I would catch fragments of his words, though, as he said,
'Their two souls were born on the same day, and since they
are both sick on the same day, only one of them must die.'
He sketched the details which led him to this conclusion, and
I was reminded of the *pandit* who had sat on the porch reading
my palm, pretending to keep me from following his intricate
reasoning, yet muttering loud enough to evoke my admiration.

No one had the strength or courage to contradict Panditji;
and he, taking our resigned attitude as respect and admiration,
was encouraged to go on further until he had calculated the exact
hours within which the dog must die if my brother were to be
saved. He fixed the time only an hour away. Stupefied at his
reasoning and by our misery, we all stood there, and before we
knew it, we were anxiously waiting, and I was even praying for
the death of the dog who only two days ago had been my constant companion, runinng behind the bicycle, fetching a ball,
and speaking for food. She was a member of the family, not
like the chickens, fish or buffaloes. Now I was feverishly longing for her death. Forever, I thought, we were to depend on
pandits' advice and follow their instructions. Whatever sinister
opinions I had formed about *pandits* and *hakims* now vanished,
and belief in Panditji's confident assertions seemed to be the
only escape from that gloom-ridden house.

He was saying, 'She's got to die a natural death. You can't kill her,' as if that had occurred to us. We were too confused, too weak to depend on our thinking, or even our ability to stand there longer. Yet determinedly we stayed with Panditji to watch the painful struggle. With each cry which was louder and more vigorous, or with each deep, gasping pant, I would become thoughtful. Maybe she will live and Ashok. . . . Blackie lingered on, and though I winced at each penetrating whine, I could have no pity for her.

When Panditji had repeated his argument several times, and could think of nothing more to say, even he stopped. Embarrassed probably that his stock of ideas was so soon depleted, he shouted for Qasim Ali, who immediately bustled from the office at his command.

'Bring an old shoe,' he said, 'and a long nail.' Qasim Ali obeyed at once, and rather than spend time hunting up an old shoe, he offered one of his own *jutis*. Then Panditji pounded a nail into the centre of the slipper-like shoe. Next Panditji and Qasim Ali sat down on the ground, each placing a finger lightly under the head of the nail, and balanced the *juti* loosely between them.

What followed left a deep imprint on my mind, for it was incredibly ridiculous. Panditji, a meek and pious man, destined by his birth to belong to the religious stratum of Hindu society, heaped such curses on the *juti,* accused it of such immorality, and shouted with such venom, and all this in front of my sisters, that we were aghast. Indeed, such was the strength of that masculine throat that the howls of poor Blackie became inaudible.

'You, *juti,*' he shouted, and began to curse it foully. 'By your mother's name you must tell the truth! Tell us the truth! Tell us the truth! Whose soul will be taken? Whose soul – do you hear?' He enunciated each syllable until even the *juti* could not possibly have missed them. Then he turned around to us. 'I am going to call names,' he said, 'and at the name of the soul which is going to be taken today, this *juti* will spin.'

Blackie's yelps seemed more anguished than ever, and she

whimpered as though exhausted. Her sides heaved with each breath of the heavy air, yet no one even thought of giving her water.

Panditji intoned monotonously, 'Is it Mohan Lal, Krishan Lal, Gani Chand, Tara Singh . . .' until at last he called, 'Is it Ashok Kumar?' A deadening silence followed. Had the *juti* spun? I wondered. Sick and dizzy with emotion, I was afraid to ask. Panditji resumed, 'Is it Taraknath . . . is it Blackie?'

Then I heard the shoe hit the ground and Panditji got up. 'You have nothing to worry about.' And without further ado he went back into the office. I took my handkerchief from my pocket and swabbed at the perspiration which ran down my forehead. We stood in apathy five minutes longer. Then Blackie gave one far-reaching cry and a last violent spasm.

With her life extinguished, there was not much left for us to do. Slowly we walked away as if from an uncovered grave, leaving Qasim Ali to dispose of Blackie's body. If anyone cried, it was silently, for I did not hear them.

We went into the drawing-room, and began our wait for Father's return. Half an hour later, around four o'clock, he arrived. As he came into the drawing-room, no one asked a question. He said only, 'Everything is all right. The lumbar puncture went off without a mishap.'

The news we had been waiting for ever since eleven o'clock had arrived, but the utter desolation of the house was unchanged. 'Are you all exhausted?' my father asked.

'Daddyji,' I broke in, 'why should this have happened to both of us?'

'I can't explain,' he said humbly.

In the silence that followed we heard the ticking clock on the mantelpiece.

SIX

From Mela to the Murree Hills

IN India, where hunger and poverty are the reigning monarchs and where all are at the mercy of any army of mosquitoes and flies, the sanitary conditions are at subhuman standards. The Health Department has a monumental job to perform. It not only must try to prevent outbreaks of epidemics by striking at the sources of poverty which cause them, but once they are in the open it must confine their spread. For this purpose, the British Government gave the Health Department top priority and a large number of personnel.

As an Assistant Director of Public Health in the divisions of Rawalpindi and Multan, my father toured the districts in the two divisions, and whenever an epidemic like cholera or plague overtook any vast area, he would immediately go there, sometimes on a half-hour's notice. He might be gone for as long as a week or a fortnight at a time. Since I was not attending school, I was permitted to accompany him now and then, provided his tour did not take him into an epidemic area.

One of these tours took me to a *mela,* a fair of provincial importance, which was held only seventy miles away from 'Pindi, and where my father was expected to go and make sure that good sanitary standards were observed. Sister Nimi and Cousin Yog, who was visiting us in 'Pindi, went too, and the peon we took with us was Qasim Ali, a pretentious, imposing man, conservative in outlook, and very conscious of his dignified position as the attendant of an Assistant Director of Public Health.

As we pulled away from 'Pindi, bound for the *mela,* Cousin Yog and my father's secretary sat in the front seat, while sister Nimi and I took the back with Qasim Ali. He immediately started telling us about the *mela.*

'It is too crowded, miss,' he said, 'and you have to be careful.' For ten years he had accompanied officers to the *mela,* and he said he had seen many, many terrible things happen. Farmers had no respect for his uniform, and refused to make way for him. He had seen children, just our age, separated from their parents, never to be found again. In his paternal, condescending way, he asked us to stay near him always. Sister Nimi, wishing to avoid argument with him, kept on nodding and agreeing. He warned us not to buy anything from the street hawkers, for it wasn't safe, and he did not want to be held responsible by my mother.

Incessantly, he talked, now demanding respect for his judgement, now planting fear, until sister Nimi switched places with Yog, who immediately started telling Qasim Ali about his experiences at the Karuk-Chheter *mela*; and whether Qasim Ali smiled or not, Yog laughed at each, only to relate one more daring. Even sister Nimi leaned back from her seat in front to hear Yog and thus encouraged him.

'A *mela*,' said Yog, 'is one place where you can let yourself go; do what you want when you want.' It was the freedom he loved, and once, he said, to frighten his sister Lil, he had persuaded a snake charmer to let him have a venomless cobra to wrap around his neck. Amid Qasim Ali's horror and sister Nimi's and my amusement, we finally reached the *mela,* and our car was immediately directed by a policeman to our pavilion.

After unloading there, we left our separate tent to join the press of the crowd. As we approached the main thoroughfare, and as the crowd grew thicker, pushing from all directions, our progress grew slower and slower. The hot sun beat down as if to establish its ascendancy and the smell which rose from the sweating bodies was equalled only by the aroma of steaming food.

Qasim Ali, dressed in the woollen gold-braid uniform and big red turban of an official, refused to mingle with the crowd. Playing on sister Nimi's 'good sense', he tried to restrain us, only to be out-talked by Yog, and drowned out by the crowd. Doggedly, Qasim Ali followed us as long as his dignified movements could compete with Yog's agile lead.

Then Yog suggested that we eat. Sister Nimi, looking over her shoulder for Qasim Ali and seeing that we had lost him, agreed. Now only the shrill notes of the bagpipe could be heard above the roar of the crowd, and once in a while, the voice of an over-energetic street hawker would beckon one and all to his *rehri*, a wheelbarrow, his shouts replacing the cautions of Qasim Ali. We finally made our way to one of these *rehris*, and each of us, folding banana leaves to make a cup, was served hot *alu-chhole, puris* and *halwa* (potato and chick peas in a pungent sauce; small wheat pancakes; and a sweetmeat made of flour, butter and sugar).

As we stood there licking our fingers, an incident occurred which to this day reminds me of the utter degradation imposed by poverty. The visual particulars I gathered later when the incident was related to my father. Among the crowd stood a mother with five children, one a boy about eight and four girls varying in age from five to ten. The healthy boy was heartily devouring his *alu-chhole* and asking for more. As his four sisters, whose thin, knobby legs were too weak to resist the push of the throngs, stood with their hands joined, their mouths half-open, and their hungry eyes turned to their brother, they made a piteous sight. Yet not one of them asked their brother or their mother for a morsel of food. Sister Nimi, noticing them, asked the little girls what was the matter. They looked at her uncomprehendingly. Then sister Nimi, turning to the little boy, said, 'Why don't you share with your sisters?' Bewildered, he turned to his mother, who appeared scarcely stronger than her daughters. Raising her tired eyes to Nimi's, she said in a weary voice, 'Some have to starve.' And pointing to the frail little girls, added, 'They will have to go first.'

Sister Nimi was stunned, but before she could do anything, the press of the crowd behind us swept us away from the family.

We continued to mingle with the crowd, making our way from shop to shop, from stand to stand, where we purchased token gifts for the family, and as darkness came on, tired and exhausted, we started picking our way back to the pavilion.

Beyond our pavilion, we saw the thick cluster of tall loquat trees, and wishing to avoid Qasim Ali, sister Nimi suggested that we go over to them. The trees were loaded with ripe loquats, and Yog, ignoring the sign NO TRESPASSING, RS 150 FINE, asked us to wait while he ran to the neighbouring inspector's cottage to borrow a flashlight and a basket. Before Nimi could protest, he was gone. Soon he returned. Then while he climbed the tree, he asked sister Nimi to stand lookout with the torch, and signal him if she found anyone approaching. He asked me to hold up the basket while he filled it with loquats. With his rapid movements from tree to tree, quickly the basket was full to the brim and he led us to a patch of grass, hidden by the trees. Abandoning all caution, we began eating the loquats. Yog was his cheery self, and the time passed all too quickly.

An hour or so later, his unrestrained laughter betrayed us to the *chonkidar*, who, pointing to the pile of seeds, told us it would do no good to deny our guilt, and choked off Yog's hastily con- trived defence. But just then Qasim Ali arrived, and drawing himself erect, demanded of the watchman, 'Don't you know they're children of the Assistant Director of Public Health?'

But if the *chonkidar*'s arrival was disconcerting, Qasim Ali's was no more pleasing. All the way back to the pavilion, he scold- ed us. 'I've been looking for you for hours,' he said. 'What if something had happened to Miss Nimi? Who would have been blamed for it? I, who else? What if something had happened to him?' he said, pointing to me. 'What would Dr Sahib say? Would I have my job left? Would I have anything left? Don't you have any thought for your servants?' And on and on he went, now sulking, now scolding.

'What have you been doing?' he said. 'Where did you eat?' Sister Nimi muttered without thinking. 'At one of the *halwaiis*.'

'Didn't I tell you that food was no good? What if you get sick by tomorrow? And where did you wash those loquats, Yog Sahib?' Yog tried to crack a joke by saying, 'Why, Qasim Ali, it rained only yesterday.' But Qasim Ali was not amused. As we reached the pavilion, however, he simmered down, for Father had returned. Yog later told us that when he went back the following day to pick up his torch, he saw Qasim Ali heartily feasting on loquats, and that his pile of seeds far surpassed ours.

The next day all of us went with Father on his inspection. It was still early in the morning, and as we neared the streets leading to the main thoroughfare, they were deserted. The restful silence bore witness to the frenzied activity of the night before, and only when we had almost reached the tents which housed the temporarily liberated peasants, their wives and children, was the lull interrupted by the children hustling to fetch water, washing, and getting prepared for the last day of the *mela*.

My father's staff of inspectors, who stood by the tents, greeted my father, and he inquired about unusual cases which might forewarn him of an epidemic. As each inspector replied in the negative, we felt a keen sense of joy. All morning was passed in visiting tent after tent, and then inspecting the midway.

The *halwaiis* had already reached their stands and were fanning their fires, while apprentices, scarcely in their teens, washed the pans, hoisted the canopies, and with cheap coloured papers and balloons, decorated their shops. Some *halwaiis* had already started preparing the batter, and I could hear the huge spoons slapping rhythmically in pots up and down the midway and the inspectors, walking to and fro, asking to see the cloths which were to protect the *thalis* and demanding to inspect milk and vegetables.

Watching these *halwaiis*, I was reminded of the family we had seen the day before, the incident which had been forgotten during our shopping and excursion for loquats. The same thought must have occurred to sister Nimi also, for she began to relate the incident to my father. She told him how shocked she had been, and how we had lost the family in the push of the crowd, before food could be bought for them.

My father told us that during his inspections he had encountered case after case where the girls were allowed to starve before a boy went hungry. 'Try,' he said, 'to see it from their point of view. A girl constitutes a heavy responsibility for a poor peasant. He is charged with finding her a husband, and often the success he meets in finding a suitable one depends on the size of dowry the poor man can offer. He is forced, therefore, to borrow money from usurers at exorbitant rates of interest, to insure his daughter's happiness. Sometimes,' he went on, 'the debt persists years after the marriage; yet according to the prevailing custom, the parents of the bride must never eat, or even take a drink of water in the village where a daughter is married.

'A son, on the other hand, can be relied upon to help on the farm from the time he is ten, and is also a security against sickness and old age. He takes care of his aged parents and assumes responsibility for the whole family on his father's death.'

My mind went back to the time when my parents in hushed voices first considered the chances of finding suitable matches for my sisters. We were comparatively rich people, and yet the responsibility of finding a husband, providing a dowry, and seeing that the girl was happily settled was evidently a problem for us, too.

Now the people were starting to fill the middle of the street, and the street hawkers had resumed their shouting, their voices somewhat hoarser than the day before. That afternoon we ate our lunch at the *halwaiis* and even Father joined us. We shopped some more, and tired but happy, we started for home.

As we eased our way through the crowds, my sister described to me the torn and shabby dresses, freshly dyed, which clothed the people.

Only the day before, Yog had made us laugh and chat, and events with Qasim Ali, though tedious at times, had continued to amuse us. But now, even though the bagpipes still played and the men and women responded to the gay music, simultaneously we all became thoughtful, and wondered about the the life each villager had left behind to attend this yearly festival.

Even Yog's lightheartedness was dampened. As we left the *mela* that night, my father did most of the talking, answering our inquiries about the people who did not live as we.

During the summer months when the direct rays of the hot sun would press down on the level plains, we would follow the cold, reviving wind of the winter to its mountain home. Hill stations, I believe, are a phenomenon peculiar to India, and more prominently so since the British *raj*. Unable to bear the heat of the plains when only a hundred or so miles away the towering and majestic Himalayas beckoned cool and green, Englishmen established small hill stations on suitable spurs in the lower and middle ranges, stretching along the fifteen-hundred mile range from east to west. For men with means, these hill stations became resorts where they could take their work in their briefcases and still enjoy all the life and scenery and freshness of the mountains. Indeed, during the British *raj*, there were two capitals for India: one in Delhi during the winter, and one in Simla for the summer.

For the British civil servants in Rawalpindi, Murree Hills was the Simla, and during the summer all the higher echelons would seek refuge in this small and compact town which lay only forty miles away from 'Pindi. We would start for Murree Hills every June, all nine of us and a servant packed into a car, with our bedrolls hoisted and strapped on the roof, our suitcases bulging from the half-open trunk, and the small British flag flying in front.

While my father often had to spend much of his time commuting from Murree Hills to 'Pindi and touring the villages in his district, we would all stay up in the hills, in a small secluded cottage buried in a steep canyon. In this summer vacation we lost all consciousness of time, and the early mornings would be spent taking long walks over twisted miles of winding trail, or riding horses for hours.

One grey, misty morning, before the sun was high enough to reach over the mountain-tops, we left our cottage for a walk. Sister Nimi and I were separated from the rest of the family, and as we wandered on a steeply sloping road which narrowed to a rugged trail when we passed the last house, I sensed for the first time why these stately mountains possess the thoughts of mountaineers the world over, why adventurous souls, hungry for the beauty and solitude of the lonely peaks, try to conquer the unconquerable, even though they perish in their attempts. As we tried to make our way up the rocky cliff, gripping the strong, sharp edges of the jagged rocks, and while sister Nimi nervously tried to make me feel the sweep of mountains and distant valley, I was seized with an insatiable urge to see these mountains for myself, to climb them by myself, and to aspire to the highest summits with the men who scale them.

I wanted sister Nimi to stop her description. It gave me the same feeling of being left alone that I was to experience at the hill station of Gulmarg, Simla and Mussoorie. 'Stop it, Nimi!' I said. 'Please stop it.' She broke off in the middle of her sentence, and I could tell she was hurt. No sooner had I said this than I felt ashamed at giving way to such rudeness. She was taking such pains, and trying so hard to make me feel with her. As I thought of this and of my ingratitude, my frustration grew and intensified, until I would have given anything to have retracted my words. Sister Nimi immediately regained her poise and changed the subject to how we would find our way back to the cottage.

Day after day was spent in the luxuriant surroundings of these cliffs and canyons. In the evening, however, we found diversion along the main street of Murree Hills; the Mall Road was about two miles long, with a quarter-mile stretch in the centre lined on both sides by small shops with Western-style show windows. The salesmen were well groomed prototypes of their fellow tradesmen in England, with jovial extravert mannerisms and hearty handshakes. All the summer inhabitants of Murree Hills flocked to the Mall Road after six o'clock, strolling up and down until they had sized up the bargains in the show windows, and greeted and chatted with their friends from the valley. Wearied by their walk, students might stop in at the coffee-house, where all the current political ideas clashed over *café au lait* and roasted nuts, until the growing heat of arguments rivalled the noise of the Mall.

A slender street sloped from the Mall Road like an outflung arm, and along this street was the Indian bazaar, with large baskets spread out from one end to the other, half-hiding vegetable vendors and the dilapidated shops of cobblers and blacksmiths. Economically minded housewives and domestic servants stood arguing with these vendors, trying to whittle down the price of a turnip or tomato a *pice* or two.

As I heard the vendors bargaining day in and day out, I never ceased to wonder at the incredible stamina of their vocal chords. Their whole success was based on one trade secret, how well they could out-argue their customers. This bazaar was the Mall Road of the poor, where the well-to-do only sent their servants, so that they might have fresh vegetables for their kitchens.

On the upper Mall Road, a segment of this bazaar could be felt; for at each end of the Mall stood coolies trying to enlist customers to rent horses or to take rickshaws. When I first arrived in Murree Hills, I had neither heard of nor seen a rickshaw. One of the first days when sister Pom and I were strolling the Mall, I heard the sharp, rhythmic slap of bare feet on the rough, hilly road, and a clipped voice saying, 'Faster – I must keep an appointment.'

'What is it?' I asked.

'A rickshaw,' she said. Then she explained that two men were sitting reading their papers while four coolies pulled the rickshaw up the steep street.

After that day, whenever we walked I would strain my ears to hear that sound, until I grew so proficient that I could even distinguish the racking gasps of the two men in front, who bore the brunt of the rickshaw's weight like buggy horses, from the coarse, heavy breathing of the two men who pushed from behind. Sometimes during our walks, we would stand by the railing at some high point and listen to arguments between submissive coolies, begging for an *anna* apiece more, and commanding customers, who would walk calmly into their homes, shutting the heavy doors behind them.

My father told us that these coolies lived in the mountains all the year round, and survived the bitterest cold, snows and storms in their shabby clothes, and with scant supplies. 'Often,' he said, 'they succumb to the rugged climate and strenuous life even before they reach forty, and they can survive at most only ten to fifteen years of steady rickshaw work.'

In the evenings we would return home tired and exhausted

from excursions on the mountains and walks on the Mall Road. We might linger by the fireplace, pressing close together, warming our hands and rubbing noses and ears to rid them of numbness. If the fire was burning low, we roasted chestnuts, and used them to drive the chilblains from our fingers.

Then one by one we would retire to bed, and if the cold, icy wind were not blowing too strongly, we would leave a crack of our window open, through which, faintly, we could hear the low, sad melodies played in the limited range of the flute, so typical of the mountaineers' music. Occasionally the powerful roar of the wind would obscure the low notes of the melody, and we would tax every sense to capture them, now barely succeeding, now failing altogether. Sometimes in the far distance, the fading sound of the flute would be replaced by some hillman's melancholy chant, swelling and sinking with the whims of the gusty wind.

With the passage of time, spectacular as well as simple happenings become mere items in the catalogue of memory; yet there is a power and strength in simple experiences which makes their impressions persist long after you have left the mountains and returned to the complex routine of the plains. I have spent almost every summer in the mountains, and after the break-up of India, even the icy winters, when the ground was covered knee-deep with snow. Each time I have returned, I have felt that same passionate longing revive, to hear again the mellifluous notes of the solitary tunes of the mountain dwellers, or walk undisturbed with only thoughts as companions.

SEVEN

The Dinner-Table School

BEGINNING with our stay in 'Pindi, several new institutions came into our lives and none more enduring than our dinner-table school. My three older sisters had entered college early at the age of fourteen and came home exhilarated by the new ideas of Western culture they encountered. Curious about Christianity and Western philosophy, they plied Father, who had travelled extensively in both Europe and America, with questions, and for the sake of convenience it was decided to hold all discussions at dinner-time.

We ate our dinner at half past eight, and where before, in Lahore, we had rushed off to Bhabiji, our grandmother, to hear her stories, now we lingered at the dinner-table while the servants cleared away.

At first these dinner-table discussions revolved around my sisters, who told of their college work under the supervision of the gentle Mother Superior and the Sisters. They would ask Father to tell them about Christianity and democratic ways in England; and sometimes their questions assumed the simplicity of asking only, for instance, if all Westerners were as quiet and gentle as the Sisters. It was soon clear that my sisters were subconsciously seeing the West as it was personified by the nuns; and their reading was making them believe that England comprised the whole Western Hemisphere. They said if you understood the struggle between the down-trodden workers and the industrialists in eighteenth- and nineteenth-century England, you could understand the identical conflict which spread to all the Western countries; and to them a look at the British Empire explained the whole imperial government of the Romans.

To correct such oversimplification Father told us of his experiences in Europe and America. He told us about the great democracy in America, the tyranny of Russia, the fascism of central Europe; and gradually we gained a whole new perspective of Christian society. We saw variety and diversity for the first time behind the white skin.

As my father described life in the Western world we were all moved with the desire to see it for ourselves. Gradually the conversations at night turned into an imaginary tour of the European countries and America with all of us packed into a big lorry. We would see the night clubs of France and hear the music festivals of Scandinavian countries and American jazz bands all at one time. Then we would imagine ourselves to be tasting Italian spaghetti, French wines and American hot dogs.

I do not recall when this casual narration of anecdotes and imaginary voyages became the actual planning of a tour of the hemisphere. Since we were so large a family, we decided we could not afford to go on a ship or a plane. We must have a lorry built in 'Pindi, and drive to England. To be sure, all roads did not lead to London, yet for a nominal fee our lorry could be ferried over any water we would have to cross. The next problem was where we would find such a lorry. We paid a visit to the Chevrolet dealer in 'Pindi, who promised to install an engine in the body which we would have built. Many nights were spent drawing designs for this vehicle; how the beds would fold in; where exactly we would place the water tank, and cook our food. 'Every attempt must be made to save space,' Father said, 'yet every provision must be made to meet emergencies in mountains and deserts.'

At last it was decided to call in the carpenters for consultation. They advised that the lorry would have to be two stories high; the body alone would cost about fifteen thousand *rupees,* then a little over four thousand dollars. These carpenters built a wooden model of the lorry, which we placed on view on the mantelpiece. There the matter rested, and our next question was what we were going to do once we got there.

My sisters, Father said, could dress in costumes from the peasant's simple *dhoti* and glass bangles to the luscious *sari* of Benares and gold necklaces. We would hire a stage and develop an act depicting a scene of typical Indian village life.

He told us how naïve Westerners were about the Indian way of life, or indeed about all Asian peoples. White men had curiosity, he said, but they were wanting in sources of information. To supplement my sisters' performances, therefore, he would lecture about Indian philosophy and history, and – if he could find an audience – tropical medicine. We were to take pictures exemplifying various facets of Indian life, from north to south and east to west, from simple villages to modern cities.

Even though British people had ruled India for two hundred years, my father said they had not been able to reach its soul or feel its heartbeat. While it was true that many factors entered into this lack of understanding, on the part of the British, the main reason was that even the simplest and poorest Indian peasant was a proud and reserved person, and his traditional ways, which the British thoughtlessly discarded as mere superstition, comprised his whole being, and gave him virtue and strength. In his person were reflected centuries of faith and suffering; and in part he summed up Indian history.

'One of these days,' my father went on in his enthusiasm, 'the present struggle for independence will culminate in freedom for India, and indeed for all subject nations. If all the nations around the globe are to live in a harmonious world, a better understanding among their peoples is imperative.' Our job, then, was to interpret for the Westerner the life of an average Indian and to capture his spirit. But to do this, we ourselves had to understand him. His mind was simple and straightforward, not confused by more than a few considerations. It worked on a white-or-black, this-or-that basis. It was this mind that we should try to clarify for Westerners. He pointed to the servants, and said when an Englishman entered the house, they would retreat into their shells, because they associated authority with white skin and a brusque voice. They felt inferior to the Englishman, and even after his long rule, they had not begun to assimilate this foreign element. While these servants would argue freely with my mother, and even with my uncles, they shied from speaking before my father. He attributed this to his holding a post previously held by Englishmen. Peasants in other districts, he said, were the same way, and whenever he went on tours, he had to make special efforts always to speak Panjabi, and thus win their confidence.

My mother hinted that this dream of travel was all very well if he had the money. But my father replied that industrious people with imaginative ideas were sure to be successful. We would surely be able to make enough money to finance the trip. Every day I looked forward to dinner, and to hearing that easy, confident, reassuring voice, interrupted by occasional questions. What had started out as a narration of interesting experiences and then transformed itself into daydreaming, now had assumed the character of serious study. My father bought some pamphlets and books on Europe and India, and after our meal he would real aloud in English, stopping only to explain various points in Hindi and colour them with his experiences.

I would understand very little of what he read, and hours would pass by without my comprehending any more than the verbs I had learned at Dadar School. Sometimes in passing he mentioned such names as da Vinci, Copernicus or Voltaire, and I often wondered what lay behind these names. Hearing them spoken at our house served to accentuate my curiosity and arouse my insatiable desire to go to America and to get on with my schooling. Sometimes I couldn't restrain myself, however, and would interrupt to ask him questions or to explain or translate, which he invariably did. For me these readings were like scriptures, reinforcing my belief that we would all one day pack into the lorry and leave India – my family to tour Europe, and I to attend Perkins.

Even though no definite date had been set for going abroad, my father had accumulated a leave of a year and a half to be used for just this purpose, and I never doubted for a moment the eventual reality of our trip.

Meanwhile my academic progress was still at a standstill while the other children were going happily to school. As I was to learn years later, immediately following my blindness my father had written in his diary, 'I will sell my soul to give him the highest education possible.' But his willingness to make sacrifices and his unwavering determination to treat me as a normal child and endow me with the same opportunities as his other children seemed now to be frustrated.

He had observed that in India the most self-sufficient blind people were musicians. Indeed, one of them, Master Kohli, had tutored my sisters in Lahore while I was in Bombay. So now in Rawalpindi, my father hired a tutor for me.

This teacher, Pandit Hukam Chand, called Panditji, belonged, like many Indian musicians, to the old school of Indian music, and had gained his training, not by attending a conservatory, but by living with his teacher, and attending to all his demands. In accordance with tradition, he became a disciple of his master, extracting concealed knowledge by massaging his feet, cooking his food, washing his clothes, and submitting to his will.

The *guru* imparted to his disciple his understanding of particular *ragas,* scale patterns for tunes, and music which he, the *guru,* had received from his *guru,* who in turn had received it from his. It was like the prescriptions of the *hakims,* never written, but entrusted to the safety of memory alone, and passed by word of mouth to the most devoted pupil through a long, impressive line of generations.

Panditji, regretting the changing society which was undermining his prerogatives, was forced to impart for a fee these secrets which were his legacy, acquired under unbearable conditions and through hardships which only he could relate. However much he might value the money, he could not quite reconcile himself to sharing the secrets of Indian music.

It was not surprising, then, that Panditji, in his bitterness, had also become an unscrupulous man. He came to teach me, not because he respected or had an affinity for me as a *guru* might for his disciple, but as a chore forced upon him which had to be performed, however detestable.

Panditji came three times a week in the afternoon to give his lessons. 'The primary thing in music,' he would say, 'is to get your voice trained, so that it can go from octave to octave without difficulty.' Thus the whole hour would be spent in exercising the vocal chords, and when he departed, I would be left hoarse and breathless.

While I sang, he sat playing the *tablas,* small drumlike instruments. With each thump on the tightly stretched hides, my heart throbbed. Panditji had a very short temper, and I knew that if I were to miss a beat, he would go into a tirade, wishing it were the old days so he could take a stick to me just as his *guru* had to him.

Since Indian music has no harmony, and centuries of change have left it untouched, understanding of rhythm and voice training are the major requisites for proficiency. And as Indian music is built on various scales, each scale definitely designated, because of the mood it creates, to the appropriate hour of day or night, the rest of our time was spent studying exactly which scales created what moods. In strict, classical Indian music, once a particular scale has been chosen, say *bhairon,* for instance, which creates a melancholy mood because of its minor quality and is thus appropriate to the early quiet hours of the dawn, no deviation from the accepted scale can be permitted. So the technique is to evolve various tunes constructed on particular *ragas.*

Thus our time was spent in learning rhythm, training the voice, and gaining appreciation of the various *ragas.* Panditji was very careful to drill me in a *raga* day after day, so that I would avoid the 'pitfall' of introducing a foreign note and thus corrupting the purity of the music.

He pointed out to me that the film industries, who were more interested in producing popular melodies, were determined to undermine the classical music, and it would be left to the younger generation to see that the classical form remained pure.

He imparted his knowledge more as favours than lessons. If I joined him in disparaging the pseudomusic of the film industry, he would feel well disposed towards me. Then he would condescend to teach me new variations on *ragas* which no one had as yet committed the sin of writing down on paper.

Panditji was not a conscientious man by any means, and unaware that even while I was singing, my ears still kept track of

71

his movements, he would get up, go to the mantelpiece, and set the clock ten minutes ahead so that he might shorten the time of his ordeal. Yet no one could summon enough courage to ever challenge, without proof, the integrity of the sage. For Panditji was a very learned man, and whatever faults he had, they were dictated by 'necessity'.

But one day, as chance would have it, just as he was tampering with the clock, my father walked in. Father was at first embarrassed at having caught Panditji red-handed. Then, unable to control his irritation, he asked, 'Panditji, what is it that makes you so uninterested in this pupil and moves you to set the clock ahead even though you admit he's a promising student? Were you prevaricating when you commented on my son's talent?'

Panditji retorted, 'I was not ... that time. But Doctorji, why would Almighty Providence have given lies to mankind if not to use? What chaos there would be if all men followed only the straight path of truth! Do you not admit it is so?'

'But, Panditji, God made snakes and poison as well. Would you by that reasoning drink poison?'

'Ah, Doctorji, you forget that I do take poison when I am sick. But however that may be, poison is not an innate quality like a lie, without which we could not see the truth. Even you, Doctorji, tell lies to a patient verging on death. You tell him he may get well, instead of the truth about the black and dismal fortune awaiting him. White lies or black lies, they are lies nevertheless. And besides, there would be no truth if there were no lies, just as there would not be good without evil. So, Doctorji, I tell lies just as often as truth, to give truth more value.'

Exasperated with this devious philosophical discourse, my father said only, 'Panditji, I hope under this roof the climate may be more conducive to truth than to lies.' Then he left the room, assuring Panditji, who was anything but insulted, that he had won his case, and that the long years of training under his *guru* had not been wasted.

But there was one thing Panditji did not teach, and I never dared ask him to teach it to me.

Only once a year could he be prevailed upon for his unique rendition of *ghunghrus*, the most treasured art which he had acquired from his *guru*.

In India, the dancers tie a tight band of small bells around their ankles, and as they dance, these bells ring out in rhythmical tunes, disclosing the precise movements of their feet. Panditji had learned from his *guru* to imitate the sound of these bells in his throat, and he did this with such precision and authenticity that one might have suspected him of hiding these *ghunghrus* somewhere in his chest. Once a year around Diwali, a great Hindu festival which celebrates the return of Ram from exile, by gradually preparing Panditji for three weeks by catering to his every wish in food, sweetmeats or services, he could be persuaded to give a rendition.

One of his conditions was that we would not invite any friends; and when Pushpa, a friend of sister Pom, and a great musician herself, wanted to come and hear him, we had to hide her behind the curtains during the performance.

A day before the Diwali, Panditji would stroll into the drawing-room, and instead of finding me there alone, he would discover the whole family.

'No lesson today, Vedji?' he would ask me. I would look somewhat puzzled, and then he would say, 'Well, it's holiday time – I'll come back after Diwali,' and start to leave. Then Mother would ask, 'Panditji, won't you stay for a glass of *lussi*?'

'No – no – no,' he would say, and my mother, in the typical manner of an Indian hostess, would refuse to take no for an answer, and would persist. While my mother and Panditji were still debating, I would run into the pantry and fetch a glass of *lussi*. 'Now you have to stay,' I would say; and he would finally answer, 'If you insist.'

Even though he took his seat on the floor by the harmonium, still there was no guarantee that the performance would be on. No one dared suggest it, for if once he said no, you could depend on his obstinacy never to relent. It was not like drinking a glass of buttermilk, which by custom Panditji could never accept at the first offering. His performance had to come from within, from an inner inspiration; no external forces would be permitted to interfere with it.

After he had taken his place on the floor, he would run his limber fingers lightly over the harmonium. First one could hear the soft tones forming, but as he would start pumping the bellows of the harmonium with more care, the tones would become complex scales. For half an hour or so he would just play scales. Then with the great ease of a *guru* he would shade into playing tunes, all the time trying to create a mood conducive to his rendition. We would all wait apprehensively, uncertain whether our weeks of catering would be rewarded.

Sometimes he would stop playing the harmonium and lift his hands completely off the keyboard. That's it, I would think, and a moment of suspense would follow, broken only when he rubbed his hands together; but then he would resume playing.

Now the early *ragas*, when he only skimmed the notes, would be transformed into melodious scales with the flat notes emphasized and prolonged until the tune took on the dignity worthy of his rendition. Our expectations would sharpen. Then I would hear a sound like blowing a noiseless whistle, and if I had not known what was to follow, I might have thought he was out of breath. Then this blowing sound would assume a more regular character. Finally, he would break into the bell-like notes. Slowly but surely the sound would grow more and more like the low jingling of the real bells. Then the tune on the harmonium and the resonant chiming would be co-ordinated until they blended into one sensuous melody.

In my mind, I could imagine Uday Shankar, the great dancer, dancing there himself. What skill, what perfect co-ordination of breathing, what control over his lungs, I thought. Sometimes for two or three minutes he could not breathe in any air, and the *ghunghrus* chimed from octave to octave without his interrupting the pattern for even the shallowest breath. For one precious hour, without stopping to take one long breath, he went on, never playing the same tune twice, as if he had an unlimited repertoire. His perfect rhythm and excellently timed cadence made the melody and the chimes rich and beautiful. We sat spellbound, and in ecstasy. At that moment, but only at that moment, I would gladly have become his disciple.

When he stopped, he was perspiring and gasping for air. He did not need any applause and compliments to assure him of his effect. He knew the full state of our rapture. After sitting immobile for fifteen minutes, until he had recaptured full control of his breath, he would quietly depart without any more ado, and for us, the celebration of Diwali, with its hundreds of candles and *diyas,* and appetizing aromas, was off to a good start a day before its arrival.

Whenever the family and I would despair over the nerve-racking idiosyncrasies of this man, we would always think of this occasion, and would be filled with admiration for his knowledge, which was not confined merely to a thorough understanding of *ragas,* but to a perfect control over his vocal chords. If his conceit and his eccentricities, ranging from tampering with the clock to flying into tirades at the slightest excuse, became sometimes unbearable, we continued to put up with him. We well knew that almost all good classical teachers in 'Pindi were no better than he, and though he taxed our endurance, and sometimes almost crushed the talent which I had for Indian music, nevertheless he was indispensable. It was a poor substitute for what I might have attained during those years, but it was at least a partial compensation. Had it been my fortune to have him longer than I did, I might have extracted more of that concealed knowledge which had ripened during its long contact with generations of sages, and perhaps even learned the art of imitating *ghunghrus,* so that this treasure would not have perished with his death. I might even have become a musician, entrenched in his school and versed in his techniques, for even he admitted I was a promising student; but this could be achieved by no less means than by becoming the most devoted of all his disciples, abandoning home and academic education to follow his solitary passion. Instead, my thoughts and aims were pledged elsewhere, in a different direction, and I cannot say I am sorry for it.

EIGHT

Inside Our Own House

In October 1945 Father brought home the papers which ordered us to return to Lahore. A couple of years earlier, we would have greeted this order with great joy, but by now we had grown accustomed to the tranquillity of spacious Civil Lines in 'Pindi and dreaded the change.

When we reached Lahore, our house, which had been rented during our long absences, seemed lonely and even gloomy – that is, until we plunged ourselves into making our home there, this time to stay for good. Within weeks, *mistrees*, skilled labourers, were called in to remodel the house and build new rooms for the needs of grown-up children. Now that we were to live in Lahore permanently, every *anna* the family could spare was to be invested in making this house a lifelong pleasure to us.

It took six months to furnish and decorate the house. The pictures which my father had collected in his travels were taken out of the storerooms, dusted and hung according to the unanimous consent of the family. Thick carpets absorbed the echoes of the *mistrees'* steady hammering. The hollow, unfurnished house was transformed into a home, and one had only to hear the incoherent exclamations of Ashok as he toddled across the carpet to feel that our house was restored to life.

It was in this house, where each of us had not just a single room, but a luxurious suite decorated with choicest paintings, adorned with moderately expensive furniture, stocked with relics handed down from generation to generation, that there took place a conversation which was made significant by the later turn of political events. The servants had just cleared the dinner-table, and the whole family was seated around it in a leisurely mood.

'Jio,' Mother began, 'I can tell you have something on your mind.'

Father had been unusually quiet. 'Shanti,' Father responded pensively, 'I don't like all that's been going on.'

'What's been going on?' brother Om asked.

While we listened, Father told us that a head-on clash between Hindus and Muslims seemed in the making. I could not help thinking of Ram Saran and Qasim Ali, one Hindu, the other Muslim. Both were my friends.

'In the history of India,' Father went on, 'the two most precious principles have been those of non-violence and renunciation. Leaders like Buddha, Asoka and Gandhi,' he said, 'have been the pathfinders in the long journey of our nation. These men have guided the course of history towards harmony and peace, but even as we sit in this dining-room, a storm is brewing which seems to be bent upon turning the work of the ages to ashes.

'While Gandhi's followers,' he said, 'were locked in the British jail during the war, so that Englishmen would not have to fight the war with their house divided, more militant forces seem to have taken over the country. I fear,' he pronounced solemnly, 'for the safety of our nation and our home.'

'Much of this, I am sure,' sister Umi said impulsively, 'is British rumour. If they can convince everyone, Daddyji, that as soon as they leave, the storm that you speak about will break out and our nation will go to pot, maybe they think we will change our tune and ask them to stay on in India.'

'Maybe,' Father said thoughtfully, 'but they are wrong. India will be free, but I fear what freedom will bring in its train.'

'I can hardly wait,' sister Nimi said, 'to see the lights glowing on Independence Day. It will be a real Diwali.'

'Like the one we had on V-J Day?' Usha asked.

'Much better than that,' sister Pom said.

'I think I will save the ten *rupees*,' I said, 'that I won from Ram Saran at the victory of the Allies, to buy *diyas* for our house.'

'Daddyji,' Usha asked, 'do you really think that Ram Saran and Qasim Ali are going to fight?'

There was a long pause.

'For the sake of Ram Saran and for the sake of Qasim Ali, let's hope not,' he said in a voice which was quiet and filled with emotion.

My three sisters, Pom, Nimi and Umi, were fast approaching their late teens, and thus their marriages were already a topic of indirect conversation. In India no direct allusions are ever made to this subject until a girl is engaged and well on her way to becoming a bride; so it is that they speak only of someone else's marriage, or a mother alludes to her own.

Once when my father was away on a long tour, and we were all sitting around the dining-table, this most sacred of all subjects was abruptly introduced by sister Umi. Umi was a charmingly easy-going person, less serious than Pom and Nimi, and often, when the conversation was too deep, she could be depended upon to lighten it with some witty remark.

When we were just finishing our dessert, Mother remarked what a relief it was to have everything finally settled between Dev and Nishchint. For months they had looked for a wife for Dev, who was my father's nephew, and finally they had decided on Nishchint, a close friend of sister Pom's.

Sister Umi, who had been silent throughout the dinner, which was very unusual for her, remarked how nice it would be to live in the West, where the girls were permitted to make their own choices, and no intermediate persons, like my mother, had to worry about the marriage of a distant nephew. Supposing Nishchint and Dev's marriage didn't turn out well? she asked. Some part of the blame would rest with Mother. It was no wonder, she said, that parents and in-laws greeted the birth of a daughter with solemnity that was more nearly gloom.

'How different it would be,' sister Umi exclaimed, 'if parents didn't have to feel responsible for finding husbands for their daughters and guaranteeing them happy marriages. I think myself capable of making my own choice, and if I did make a wrong one, I should take the blame, not my parents.' Then she went on to censure the custom of the dowry, which so often exceeds the means of the parents, simply because a large dowry may fetch a better suitor.

'When I married your father,' Mother began, 'I had nothing in common with him. I could not speak English, and had too little education even to talk with him intelligently. I had no hand in our marriage, and neither did he. It was all arranged by our parents. I went as his bride without having even a fragmentary picture of this man with whom I was to spend the rest of my life, and whose happiness was to be mine. And finding him so unlike myself, I was very disheartened, and my confidence in my parents' judgement was shaken.

'Had there been a way open to me to get out of that marriage, I gladly would have, but, thank God, there wasn't. Had I left him then, I would never have had all the happiness I have known since.

'So heeding my mother's advice, I continued to suffer in silence. "The only way," she would say to me, "is to win him by sacrifice." And had I not been brought up to love and adore my husband, we might have –'

Could my father have been heartless, I thought? He was so gentle and understanding.

'Yet when you children were born, he would rather play with you than go to the club, of which he was so fond. Urmil, when you arrived, I was not at all grieved, for he was by my side. Thus the sacrifice bore fruit.'

Sister Nimi interrupted Mother. 'But would you not have been just as happy – even happier – with someone else, someone who was perhaps less educated and Westernized?'

'Well, that's hard to say, for I'm very happy now, and in a sense I was happy even when I suffered most. I had been brought up that way, and now that I look back on it, the first years would have been much worse if I hadn't been prepared for them.'

'I agree with Mother,' said sister Pom. 'It's a different kind of education that makes a good mother.'

Sister Umi broke in again. 'I don't see what happiness there is in suffering.'

'I do,' said Pom. 'It is the same as pleasure in giving without expecting anything in return.'

'But how about the responsibility parents feel?' Umi continued.

'But our whole life is built around responsibility,' said my mother. 'When I was young, I used to take care of all my brothers and sisters, just as Promila looked after you when I'm away. You think this responsibility is too much? How about your father, feeling that he had to educate his brothers? When you have a large family, you must expect this responsibility. I don't know what I would do if I didn't have all of you to think about.'

'Wouldn't it be better, though,' sister Umi said, still unsatisfied, 'if I made my own choice?'

Pom said, 'I don't see how you could make a better choice than your parents. Their experience is so much greater than yours. I wouldn't even know where to begin if I had to find my own husband.'

Umi persisted. 'If the customs were different, I would know where to begin.'

Sister Nimi, who had sat quietly so far, said, 'I saw three girls standing in front of a *halwaii*'s, starving. Is this happiness, Pom? I almost cry when I think of them. If their parents didn't have to worry about their dowries, perhaps they would have been eating *alu-chhole* with their brother.'

'But some would starve anyway,' said Pom. 'You can't blame all that on the dowry. There still wouldn't be enough food to go around, and there would be just as many children dying from poverty. I think the dowry is detestable just as you do, Nimi.'

'Whatever the faults with our customs, you will have to admit,' Mother broke in, 'that ultimately our marriages work out very well. Of course, they wouldn't if we didn't accept the idea that we will try to make our husbands happy at whatever cost to ourselves. You can't imagine the happiness I felt when your father started taking more interest in you girls, and became so mild-tempered. Even in the arguments I had with him about Ved, he was right.'

'If I were to make a free choice, I still could think about my children,' sister Umi insisted, 'and still keep some of the old customs.'

'You can't just discard a few customs in the kind of society we live in,' sister Pom said. 'Perhaps we are subject to more suffering, but then we can endure more than we might otherwise.'

'But at what cost, Pom?' asked Nimi. 'The deplorable poverty – we have never gone hungry to know really what physical suffering is. Our mother has never been beaten by her husband, either.'

I thought about our grandmother Bhabiji and how she had sometimes suffered at the temper of Lalaji; yet she talked about Lalaji always in a very tender and respectful manner.

'But as I say, Nimi, you can't blame all this on how we marry,' said Pom. 'That is the way of life in this crowded country.'

'I think our whole family system would degenerate, Umi,' said Pom. 'We are taught from childhood to respect Father and to acknowledge that his word is final in all things. Perhaps there isn't as much freedom, but there is more than enough unity in love and affection to compensate for it. We don't have broken homes where the children belong neither here nor there.'

Sister Umi, half-laughing, went on: 'Pom, you have to admit this is a man's world, and in this country especially. I don't see why it should be. I'm just as good as any of them.'

'I hope you realize the consequences in our society if the women started leading independent lives, working like men.'

'But perhaps there wouldn't be so much poverty,' said Umi.

Then Nimi spoke slowly. 'I see with you, Pom. There is good in suffering. But not when it's carried so far.'

'Society will change,' said Umi, 'as we get our freedom and there is less subservience and useless misery in Indian homes. No theorizing is going to change matters. People will change of their own accord. I'm looking forward to that day.'

Soon the conversation turned to the anticipated freedom of India, and the subject of marriage was dropped. I wished Father had been there to say something about how the free system actually worked in the Western world.

NINE

Roar of Mr Baqir

In Lahore, once again I experienced that helpless feeling of not being able to attend school. As in Rawalpindi, a classical music teacher was engaged; yet that awareness of being isolated from the rest of the family for lack of education still persisted. My health had improved greatly during my three years in Rawalpindi, but my father was hindered in his efforts on my behalf by the fact that so few channels were open to me.

There are in India about two million people who suffer from visual deficiencies, as compared with one hundred thousand in the United States. The sight of three-fourths of this number could either be completely cured or greatly improved with proper medical attention, yet lack of eye specialists and, more than that, lack of understanding about the causes and prevention of blindness among the masses make the problem almost insuperable. The blind in India have no future, for in a country ridden with starvation and poverty, little attention can be paid to those with special problems. So it is that this blind population, whose number could be appreciably reduced if only they were taught the most elementary principles of eye care, has become parasitic.

My father tried to arouse a greater awareness of this problem. As he was now posted as the senior Assistant Director of Public Health in Lahore, he was in a better position to call the government's attention to the growing problem of blindness. In taking stock of the opportunities and facilities open to the blind, he learned of Emerson Institute.

Like Dadar School, Emerson Institute at Lahore was primarily concerned with teaching students vocations which might help to rehabilitate them. Their education followed no system of gradation by classes, and even if it had, the education would have ceased by the fifth grade because of the lack of funds to engage qualified teachers, who are so scarce everywhere. Apart from the principal, who was not blind, the teaching staff at Emerson consisted of six members whose education at best had terminated with high school graduation, a feat considered spectacular for the visually handicapped.

My father, upon visiting this institute, was very much struck by the financial needs of the school and was very disheartened by the inefficiency and substandards of education. So he approached the Finance Minister, Sir Manohar Lal, whom he knew personally, and requested him to increase the annual allotment to the school. Sir Manohar Lal knew of the special interest of my father and made a single grant of Rs. 45,000 (about £3,000).

While this allocation enabled the institute to add a new wing and admit students whose petitions had been pending for years, it did not improve the academic situation; and although later on another grant made possible the engaging of Mr Khanna, an excellent administrator, even his devoted efforts on behalf of better education for the blind were frustrated.

I tried to prevail upon my father to send me to this school, a request which at first he did not consider with much favour, for although the school was located only three miles away from our home, a maze of narrow streets and dirt roads made a prohibitive path from my home in Temple Road to Emerson School inside Sheranwala Gate. If no mills were present to mar the sky with suffocating smoke, as in Dadar, one had only to walk within Sheranwala Gate to find its substitute in the stench of rotten vegetables and human filth. Then, too, there was a question of how much I would gain from this trade school even if the hurdle of distance were overcome. But my father, seeing my unyielding determination to get away from the confines of the four walls at home, decided to give the project a try.

One of our servants, Gian Chand, was asked to cruise all the streets leading to Sheranwala Gate on his bicycle and map out a route which minimized the danger from accidents. If this route were satisfactory, then Gian Chand might carry me on his bicycle to school. He came home to tell my father that a way could be worked out, even though occasionally he would have to push the bicycle.

The first day my father took me to school in his car, and even though we took a roundabout route, the going was tedious and exasperating. That day I was simply introduced to Mr Khanna and shown around the building. The second morning, Gian Chand and I set out at about seven-twenty, while already the blazing June sun turned streets to dust and encouraged swarms of flies. As we passed the Mall Road, the streets grew stifling, congested with *tongas,* bicycles and streams of pedestrians. Gian Chand would often have to dismount and walk the bicycle while I hung on to the improvised seat, clutching my sandwiches. It took us forty minutes to cover the distance, and when we got there, Gian Chand was sweating from the exertion and I from the frightfully hot sun and nervousness.

I proceeded to my first class, which was with Mr Baqir. I learned that his was a small room, perhaps double the size of Ram Saran's quarters. A large thin-strip bamboo fan, draped with a cotton cloth, dangled from the ceiling and extended the width of the room; a rope led from it over a pulley, and a boy who stood by the door pulled and relaxed the rope to give some motion to the sluggish atmosphere. Mr Baqir greeted me and introduced me to the six other students, saying, 'A new lad — and a day scholar, no less.'

Every now and then he would shout, 'A little harder, my boy,' and the irritating noise of the swinging fan would become fast and ragged. It was no longer the deliberate motion of a tired boy, but the frantic one of a worried disciple. Mr Baqir sat there puffing his *biri* and loudly smacking his lips as he chewed *pan.* One hand nervously tapped a cane on the desk top. 'Be on the look out, boys!' How often I was to hear this phrase repeated! It was a sign for everyone to prick up his ears and listen for the clicking heels of Mr Khanna. Students divided their attention between this nerve-racking job and Mr Baqir, who, well versed in the art of circumlocution, now and again remarked about the Braille contraction and abbreviation system. He might ask a student to read from an old book with his calloused fingers, and when the student made a mistake, he would curse him violently.

I soon realized that it was political indoctrination, not teaching, that Mr Baqir considered his job. 'Boys,' he would say in his harsh and confident voice which challenged dispute, 'tell me, what is the Hindu religion? Do they have a prophet like Mohammed? Are they the chosen people? No, they are meek and servile, ridden with tradition and superstition. We Moslems conquered them with the greatest ease. Wasn't it the strength of our religion that converted so many heroes?'

I was too naïve, not initiated yet in the ways of Mr Baqir, and these perversions of the truth added to my confusion. I was terrified at being in a classroom with this teacher who could better educate us in the use of vile language, profane yet picturesque, than make us efficient in reading Braille. In the confusion of tapping cane, creaking fan, and the roar of Mr Baqir, it was indeed difficult to listen for Mr Khanna's footsteps and warn Mr Baqir in time to control his language and confine his remarks to Braille; for in the event that we let Mr Khanna slip up on Mr Baqir, we were assured of the stinging blows of a wet cane across our knuckles, which often missed its mark to strike another part more tender.

For two hours, Mr Baqir bellowed at his students without ever showing signs of vocal fatigue. I was frightened and shocked at the crudity of this man. I thought of the refined nuns about whom my sisters had talked so enthusiastically in 'Pindi, and felt depressed. My desire for education wavered as never before. I felt the four walls drawing in, closer and closer, and the low roof crushing my ambition, and I felt too dizzy to hold my head up. I longed for four o'clock when I might see Gian Chand.

The next two hours were spent in a better atmosphere, for they were devoted to my music lessons, which were held in the new wing of the building. Besides, my singing, the continuous rhythm of the *tabla,* and the shrieking notes of the harmonium checked forever any urge Mr Chander, my music teacher, might have felt to copy the mannerisms of Mr Baqir. They were two hours of calm, soothing to my tired body and discouraged spirit.

The lunch hour finally arrived, and I was happy to have an hour free to get outside the building. I was not hungry any more, and I gave away my lunch.

As I was to follow the prescribed curriculum, if indeed it could be called that, part of my afternoon was to be spent in caning chairs. This profession, deplorable as it is, saved many students from the cruelties of toiling from one street corner to another, begging. (Later when it was found that my fingers were growing calloused through continuous contact with the sharp edge of the split cane and impairing my ability to read Braille, and since I was still hoping for a career quite different, Mr Khanna was approached, and this part of my curriculum was dropped.) I returned home that night too ashamed to relate my crude experiences alongside those of my sisters at the convent. I had always prided myself on my ambition, and often, lying in bed at night, I had vowed to give all for education. I was humiliated to find how quickly my determination was crumbling. Only a few days before, this very resolution had persuaded my father to give the school a try. To let him know now that only one day in school had so disillusioned me was to admit that my perseverance was no more than childish enthusiasm. So I took refuge in complete silence, rather than risk an embarrassing narration of my school experiences.

Mr Baqir, the frightened boy swinging the fan and the anxieties I had felt as we made our way through the crowded streets seemed too out of place in the calm, pleasant atmosphere of our dining-room.

Although I had seen almost nothing of Mr Khanna, one day he summoned me to his office. I went in some trepidation, wondering what I had done wrong, but it developed that he only wanted a friendly talk.

'How do you like school by now?'

'I like it, sir.'

'I told your father I wasn't sure it would be helpful for you to come here. But he said you were determined. It's a long time since you attended school, isn't it?'

'Yes, sir, four years.'

'You were at Dadar School, weren't you? And how did you like that?'

'I was happy there, sir. But the climate didn't suit me, and so I was sick a good part of the time.'

'You were exposed, then, quite young, to what schools for the blind are like, and still you wanted to come back?'

'Well, sir, my brother and all my sisters went to school, and I admire my father, who is so learned and has travelled so much. He wanted me to have as good an education as his other children. He even tried to send me to Perkins a few years ago.'

'Why didn't they take you?'

'They said, sir, I was too young, and should know more about my country before I went there.'

'That's true enough. What have you been learning these last few years, my boy? If you want to go to America you must have much more preparation than this.'

'But, sir, there were no schools for me to go to here.'

'You could have been tutored at home.'

'I was, in music.'

'But why not arithmetic, or English?'

'No one knew how to teach blind children.'

'It's not too different from teaching other children. I admit, some understanding is necessary. Your sisters could have taught you.'

This was the first time that such a question had been put to me, and ever since then, it has been a recurring thought. Even if each one of them had helped me an hour a day, I would have learned just as much as though I were going to school.

'I don't know, sir. Perhaps they have always been too busy.'

'Too busy to teach you? That's not my impression of your family.'

'I can't think of any other reason.'

'Maybe they treated you too normally, and never considered your special problems.'

'My father always said that I would one day go to America and learn there.'

'But they took this too much for granted. Remember that you must know very much about your own country if you ever plan to come back here. What would you do, supposing you did go to America? Would you be interested in coming back to India and helping the blind people?'

'I don't think so. If I could see, I would be a doctor, just like my father.'

'But you can't see. What else but teaching would there be for you to do?'

'I could teach in a university. Maybe take up law.'

'Well, I don't mind telling you, you are too ambitious; and so is your father. I know you both and can make allowances, but I don't think that authorities in America will. Maybe I can help you. Say you come in here an hour a day – you spend two hours with Baqir, don't you? Well, you can spend one of them with me. I could help you some with history and we could talk this over. Would you like that, boy?'

'Yes, sir. . . .' Then summoning my presence of mind, 'I'd like it very much, sir.'

'Well, you just do that.' For the first time he fumbled for words. 'Well, we'll see. You can go now.'

Thus, gradually, time and again, Mr Khanna asked probing questions. He made me realize that my desire to go to America had overshadowed all other considerations. I knew what I didn't want to be – a beggar, shopkeeper or street hawker – but I did not know what my future should be. Whenever I put this question to my father he evaded it, and gave only vague answers. 'Education,' he would say, 'is a lifelong asset, and once you have it you can always find something to do with it.'

I was soon to learn how inadequate an answer this was. No educational authorities anywhere could reconcile themselves to this. Education, they maintained, was a liability if it made you a misfit for your own society. While Mr Khanna had refrained from disillusioning me completely about my ambition, he had frequently hinted at its vagueness. Once he told me, 'I admire you and your father for your ambition, but those who don't know you will consider it foolhardy. You will receive much discouragement, and you will have to learn to insulate yourself against it. You are too sensitive, and that's bad. Especially so since you are blind. Whatever you may do, you'll never convince the world that you are normal. And if you go abroad, you will be even more isolated, for you'll miss your home and country.'

These were the thoughts which added to the turmoil of my mind, and whereas in Rawalpindi I had considered education to be a panacea, now I was not sure. Mr Khanna was forcing me to be introspective, and at the same time making me aware of some of the problems which would come with education. Yet my ambition had taken too great hold of me. It had been a sustaining force throughout my four years of idleness, and no disillusionment could entirely checkmate it.

I spent one hour a day with Mr Khanna, which proved to be most valuable. We talked about history and he would give me some lessons in English vocabulary. Even Mr Baqir's classes grew more tolerable than my first day's impression.

Though the time might have been spent more advantageously in a better school, I did not regret my attendance at Emerson. I found the students very friendly, and the feeling of being independent, of having my own friends in students and Mr Khanna, was exhilarating and dispelled all my first day's misgivings.

I was very happy during the seven months at Emerson, for starting at seven-twenty in the morning until five o'clock in the evening, when I reached home, I was busy. Then in the evening, I would go to Rastriya Swayam Sewak Sangh, the R.S.S.S., a Hindu organization, determined to bring about political freedom for India. Sohan Lal, a student at Sir Gunga Ram Medical Hospital, would come by for me each evening at seven o'clock and together we would walk to the meeting grounds about a mile from my home.

We would stay there until nine o'clock, playing games, doing calisthenics, but, more than that, praying and singing hymns. Almost all the people present were college students, and certainly I, at twelve, was the youngest person. Since the day of independence was fast approaching, the topic of conversation with everyone, particularly students, was politics, and long after the last hymn had been sung, we would sit around on the ground talking over the current political situation. There were hopeful people; there were frightened people. Some said that when the day of independence came, India would start on a path of greatness equal to the Western world. Then there were others who saw nothing but gloom. They pointed to the increasing nationalistic sentiments among the Muslims as a sure sign of destruction of the very independence for which we had struggled so long. They felt that the Indians, divided among themselves, would soon prove their inability to govern, and if not the British, then some other great power would come to take over.

As the time passed, and we approached the months of December and January, 1946 and 1947, the tone of their talk changed. They pictured themselves as brave men who would rescue India from the bloody path towards which some fanatics were steering her.

'Give us time,' they would say, 'we'll stop bloodshed.' As the pressure mounted for the partitioning of India, all differences were resolved into one common purpose, to try to keep India united. There was no venom, no threat, nor, much less, any preparation for effecting these plans. But there was a sense of responsibility, of duty, of courage. Thus, if I were not learning much Braille or arithmetic, I was being exposed to a variety of views, from Mr Baqir's fanaticism, to Mr Khanna's historical approach, to the keen sense of the students who analysed the currents of the time. There was an awareness of movement, of living in a momentous hour, only darkened by the inward fear of the unknown.

TEN

Marriage in the Making

In the month of February, when we had been in Lahore almost four months, we heard through one of my father's friends about an eligible young dentist in Dehra Dun named Kakaji Mehrotra. As always in such cases, a thorough investigation followed, in which the young man and his family background were scrutinized. Even his friends were reviewed. Did they drink? With the precision of a lawyer, the liabilities and assets were carefully evaluated.

Even though her whole future happiness was at stake, sister Pom, who, as the eldest daughter, by tradition must be the first to marry, was given no hint of what was going on. For this there were several reasons: first, because when a girl reaches the age of marriage, many inquiries are made, and almost all the network of relations keeps on the look-out. Since the families are so large, and remain in such close contact, there may be hundreds of people who, without being told, bear the eligible members of other families in mind. So there are many leads, all of which have to be carefully tracked down, and it is thought best not to worry the children with these steps. Then, too, since the parents ultimately make the decision, they deem it unnecessary to consult the child prior to the settlement of final arrangements.

As Kakaji was a more attractive prospect than any other leads, his parents were finally approached – for the initiative always rests with the girl's parents. Then his family follows the same intricate process of thorough investigation, often with the help of relatives on the spot. If they are favourably impressed, then the parents, sometimes with their son, come to view the girl in question. But since Dehra Dun was so far from Lahore, Kakaji came by himself.

In the early part of March, he arrived in Lahore and casually dropped in for tea. I say casually because his manner was that; but with the network of elaborate planning behind the event it was actually anything but casual. Sister Pom – she was now nineteen – was sent for, and came with Mother into the drawing-room. Dressed in a soft silver-bordered *sari*, she shyly served Kakaji tea, while he continued to talk to other members of the family. During the tea, he addressed some remarks to sister Pom about her studies in college and the painting over the mantelpiece, and told her about his summer practice at a hill station.

(After this short interview, on which so much depends, if Kakaji is attracted to sister Pom and favourably impresses our family, the talk proceeds, but without sister Pom's presence. Kakaji judiciously keeps from committing himself until he has spoken to his parents. If he doesn't like her, the matter is dropped.)

Actually four days later a note arrived from his mother, asking if sister Pom could be betrothed to Kakaji. My father, with his Western attitudes, refrained from answering the letter until sister Pom was consulted. So in the drawing-room one night, Mother approached sister Pom as to what she thought of Kakaji. Before Pom said anything, sister Umi, amused by all the arrangements, remarked, 'How do you expect her to know what her mind is when all they talked about was the furniture? Could she have fallen in love already—'

'Love, Urmil,' my father answered, 'means something very different from "falling in love". It is a process rather than an act, and only time can shape it. The best we can do is give it every opportunity to succeed, and I'll admit this is hard.'

'But doesn't "every opportunity" include knowing the person better?' sister Umi asked.

'Yes, it should,' Father replied; 'but here the question is of choosing. To know a person thoroughly might take years. Now, we believe that knowing can only come through living together.'

'Do you mean, then,' said Umi, 'that knowing and love are the same thing?'

'Not quite, but understanding and respect are essential to mature love, and this deep understanding cannot come from friendship alone. Even serious conversations can't fully reveal a person's character. That can only come through experience, through sharing each other's problems. No amount of talking will bring about full understanding. It is only when you consider each other's problems as one and the same that you can hope for true understanding.'

'But, Father,' said Nimi, who was the political rebel in the family, 'look at the risk that's involved.'

'We minimize the risk as far as possible,' he explained. 'We try to find a home which is most like ours. Take Kakaji. He's a dentist. His life will not be too different from mine. Now, if I were to marry Promila in the Brahman caste, I would be increasing the gamble. They might not eat meat; they would pray two or three times a day; and their professions would be on totally different lines. These things are small, perhaps, but they have far-reaching effects.'

Nimi spoke again. 'Then you are perpetuating a caste, because this presupposes that Pom would have to be married in the Kshatriya caste of professional people. For myself, I'd willingly marry a Bania shopkeeper or even a Sundra untouchable, and help break down these barriers.'

'That day might come. But you will admit, Nirmil, that you are increasing the gamble.'

'But for a cause I believe in,' said Nimi.

'Yes,' he answered, 'but that's another matter.'

'You say,' Umi broke in, 'that understanding and respect are necessary for a happy marriage. I don't see why you would respect a person more because you lived with him and shared his problems.'

'In our society,' said Father, 'we think of respect as coming only through sacrifice.'

'Then,' said Umi, 'you're advocating the subservience of women. Because it's not Kakaji who will sacrifice, but sister Pom. And why should that be? And how is it that sister Pom will respect Kakaji because she sacrificed for him?'

'No, Urmil, it is the other way around. It is he who will respect her for her sacrifice.'

'Does that mean that sister Pom will respect Kakaji, though?'

'Not necessarily. But if Kakaji is moved by Promila's sacrifices he will show more consideration and growing concern for her. I know in my own case I was moved to the depths to see your mother, Shanti, suffer so. It took me long enough, too long, I believe, to reach that understanding, perhaps because I had broken away from the old traditions, and had given in to the Western influences. You can hope, then, for this respect to be reciprocal between Promila and Kakaji; and don't forget that all this time they are getting to understand each other better.'

Umi persisted. 'This may take years, and is sister Pom to be unhappy all this time?'

'Perhaps so. But she is striving for ultimate happiness and love. These are precious gifts which can only be cultivated in time.'

'Hard only for Pom,' sister Umi insisted. 'Aren't you struck by the injustice of this? Shouldn't Kakaji sacrifice for their happiness too?'

'There has to be a start. Remember, it's her life that's joined with his. She will forsake her past to build a new future, and you may call this a complete beginning of absolutely new experience. If both Promila and Kakaji were to be obstinate and wait to see who will take the first step, what hope do you have of their ever getting together?'

'That's evading my question, Father. Why shouldn't he take the initiative?'

'He would, perhaps, be expected to if Promila were working too, and leading another life which would be equal to his. I suppose more than this I really can't say, and there may be some injustice at that.'

'What is this happiness you speak of?' said sister Umi. 'I only vaguely understand it.'

'It is a uniting of ideals and purposes, and making them blend into one. Love grows gradually. This is the tradition of our society, and these are the means we have adopted to make our marriage successful and beautiful. We must have faith in the goodness of the individuals, and rely on the strength of this sacred bond. In the West they have solved the problem in a different way, because their conditions vary from ours. I cannot say if it has worked any better.'

'But I love my independence,' said sister Umi, 'for that is my ideal.'

'Remember always,' said Father, 'that the ideals must be resolved by placing values on every one of them, for you must choose among them.'

Then to sister Pom he said, 'I have done my best, and my responsibility for you is not over. I will always be there to help, and continue to find satisfaction in your happiness. I have lived and worked for these values.'

'And I respect your values and your judgement,' replied sister Pom. 'I have faith in your choice. Even if I do suffer, I can hope that some day our marriage will be as happy as yours.'

Then, with Umi and Nimi chattering and Father and I following along behind, we went to bed, leaving Mother and sister Pom together in the drawing-room.

The engagement ceremony is a simple one and was performed a few days after our conversation in the drawing-room by a learned *pandit,* who recited the *Gayatri Mantra* from the *Rig-Veda* and invoked the blessings of the gods for the future happiness of the couple. A ring was placed on Pom's finger by Kakaji's sister, who brought a brocade *sari* and a veil and sweets along with the ring. The platter of fresh-baked sweetmeats was a big one and a servant began passing it to the friends and relatives who had been invited for the ceremony.

While sister Pom sat in the corner with her face completely covered by the veil, her intimate friends and our near relatives sang the songs which have been sung on similar occasions for generations – to the simple beat of the *dholki,* a small drum. No man is permitted to be present at this ceremony, but curious brothers are sometimes able to hide near the door and listen to the ladies sing. Now and then they stopped to make jokes at the expense of the bride-to-be, who is supposed to smile and cry beneath her veil, for the words and moods of the songs vary from utter sadness at the girl's leaving her family, to jubilant singing over the new life awaiting the bride.

As I listened I wondered what must be going on in sister Pom's mind, and I was glad that she had the privacy of the veil.

As brother Om, Cousin Yog and I crouched by the closed door, we could hardly make out the remarks, for the ladies all chattered at the same time. Shortly before midnight a supper was served, and then the older ladies departed, giving sister Pom solemn advice about preparation for marriage. Soon her teasing girl-friends left also, promising to be back for the wedding, which was still two months away.

If the wedding was going to be on time, all the preparations had to be squeezed into the interim. Actually they would have been well under way, even without the prospect of a groom, had it not been for the time spent on the finishing touches for our house.

The first step was to begin collecting the dowry. Originally, in Vedic times, the bride was adorned simply and affectionately and the dowry consisted of no more than a few presents from the family at the wedding. I soon learned how different it was now. Sister Pom's dowry must include clothes, jewellery, bedding, a sewing machine, cooking utensils and cutlery – in fact, everything for a home save a car and the house itself, which might have been included had it not been for the three younger sisters, whose dowry had to match sister Pom's. The splendour of this dowry might well determine the subsequent offers to my other three sisters, and my grandmother carefully canvassed many of our relatives as to the presents they would give to the bride, so that there might be no duplication.

Although a few of the relatives thought the number of twenty-two *saris* was rather few, most consented. Long days were spent by Mother and sister Pom going to crowded bazaars and choosing the *saris*, which had to differ in materials, colours and borders. No two could be alike, and even though the expensive ones of Benares brocade cost hundreds of *rupees,* the wardrobe was supposed to be so rich in variety that the bride could have a *sari* for each and every occasion for many years to come. Actually, *saris* are very practical garments. Always six yards in length, they fit every size of woman, be she short or tall, slender or stout, merely with a few subtle adjustments of the folds.

Jewellery, matching the *saris*, had to be made to order. Because until recently the laws of inheritance in India favoured the male members of the family at the expense of the widow, a woman's most valued possessions were her gold and diamonds. These jewels alone formed her *istri-dhan*, her inheritance, which could not be taken away from her after her husband's death, according to Manu, the great Hindu lawgiver. My mother had recited to me the law of Manu sometime before: 'The ornaments which may have been worn by women during their husband's lifetime his heirs shall not divide. Those who divide them shall be outcasts.'

However many packages Mother and sister Pom brought home from their frequent trips to the bazaar, the bundles did not tell the whole story. There was the constant hum from the veranda of the two sewing machines, operated by friendly tailors who had been engaged to help with the preparations. They sewed pillowcases, embroidered borders for a few *saris* which had been purchased plain, and made blouses, jumpers and gowns. Since in India hardly anything can be bought readymade, the tailors also helped hem tablecloths and bedspreads, which my sisters and their friends were kept busy embroidering. There were also the regular visits of the jewellers, who brought with them bags full of necklaces, rings and bracelets, in order that my other sisters and Father could be consulted before a final selection was made. The house was full of new odours – of threads and linen, of flowers and cosmetics. It was chaos. I found it difficult to move about without stumbling over one bundle after another, and the beds and chairs were piled up with dozens of half-unwrapped packages.

While the ladies made these preparations for the dowry, the men were busy arranging for the *barat,* the bridegroom's party, which consists of his many relatives and friends. Although the bridegroom's family is burdened with the expenses of their transportation, it falls upon the family of the bride to be the hosts during the three-day marriage ceremony. It was fortunate for us that the distance of three hundred miles between Dehra Dun and Lahore would prevent Kakaji from bringing a party of two hundred, which, although the highest number permitted in any marriage, was quite appropriate to his social status. Besides, because of the famine in Bengal at that time (which took a toll of two million lives), the government did not allow a *barat* of more than fifty to be entertained.

Here and there, there were surreptitious suggestions, although never from the *barat*, that my father could easily circumvent this ruling, but he stubbornly refused. It was well for our pocketbook that my father would not break the ruling of the very government which he served, because, had the number of the *barat* exceeded fifty, we would probably have been forced to hire, at great expense, a *janj-ghar*, a community building for their housing. As it was, by doubling up some of the families in the Mehta *Gullie*, the vacated houses could be used for the barat. Burlap sacks of ground wheat for *puris*, the little pancakes, fruit and spices, chickens, legs of mutton, mounds of rice were lugged in – enough to feed a regiment. Arrangements were made for pooling servants of the Mehta and Mehra (my mother's) families, and shoeshine boys and barbers were engaged from May 10 through May 13.

Along with the housing of the *barat*, there were also two hundred of our relations expected from all over India who had to be looked after. Each of the Mehta and Mehra families in Lahore promised to make available a few beds for those who came from longer distances and floor space for those who were coming from the neighbourhood. Thus for the two months between the engagement and the actual wedding ceremony the house was taken up with frantic preparations. Everyone took an interest in each step, and what I did not feel or hear or stumble over was carefully explained to me, as, indeed, was the whole wedding ceremony, with all its pomp, colour and splendour.

On the morning of the tenth, brother Om and I stood across the street from the Mehta *Gullie*. I heard car after car, some borrowed, some hired, pull away for the station. Neither Father nor brother Om nor I could go to the station because we had to wait for the formal meeting, the *milni*. It was a long while before the cars started streaming back into the Mehta *Gullie*, filled, as brother Om told me, with 'bright but tired-looking people'. The shoeshine boys were in a more fortunate position than we, for at least they could be close to Kakaji right then, and we would have to wait until the evening. The servants and my cousins were at great premium at home because they brought snatches of news about the *barat*. Now three of the *barat* were having haircuts. Kakaji had just breakfasted, and two barbers were quarrelling as to who would shave him. Now all the *barat* was out in the cars for sight-seeing. They had lunched already. Our cooks were gratified because they had eaten heartily. Tea was over, one servant reported, and Kakaji had eaten three pastries. Now all were getting dressed for the *ghori*, the marriage procession.

No sooner did we hear about the *ghori* than all the necklaces of lights which were strung around our house were lighted up. From the Mehta *Gullie*, less than a block away from our home, I heard the band strike up, the blending of trumpets and clarinets, drums and cymbals, into one of the popular cinema tunes, and I knew the *ghori* was on its way. I slipped rapidly into my long, coat-like *achkan*, and had my father tie my turban up, and ran out on the street with brother Om. The turban and *achkan* felt awkward, and the *achkan* rustled like a *sari*.

'I have never worn an *achkan* before,' I said.

'I never would,' brother Om said, 'if it were not for Mother's insistence upon observing the tradition.'

From the gate of our house I listened to the gay music of the band, and in my mind I pictured Kakaji mounted on a *ghori*, a well-bred and trained mare. From Kakaji's waist there was undoubtedly a sword, symbolizing his readiness to defend the woman against his enemies and to ensure the inviolability of the home to which he would bring his bride. I thought about the horse with all its ornamental trappings and wondered, amidst the loud music, whether Kakaji or the *ghori* was the more nervous. Probably Kakaji, since the *ghori* had gone through similar experiences. The band music got slightly muffled.

'They have probably taken a detour,' brother Om said, 'to show off the groom.'

'And advertise sister Pom's marriage,' I said.

Thus far it was Kakiji's evening. He rode on the horse because he was a knight coming to get his bride. As of old, it was a chivalrous and heroic thing, and like all knights, he possessed moral and physical courage.

As soon as the *ghori* turned into our street, brother Om described to me Kakaji's pink silk turban and its gilded crown, loaded with garlands of flowers.

'Here he is,' I shouted, and my father, his friends and relations and the *pandit* gathered by the gate for the *milni*. By now all the guests had alighted from their cars, and they stood facing us, each one of them having been garlanded. Some of my sister's friends were inside, engaged in the ceremony of dressing her in the traditional red brocaded wedding *sari* which I had seen earlier, while other friends were evaluating the worth of the dowry which was set out on exhibition in the drawing-room.

The *barat* procession, with Kakaji on his horse at the head, approached closer and closer, but slowly, very slowly, as though to give us time for every last arrangement. The band kept up its fury, playing medley after medley, blanketing all other sound. Kakaji's horse halted right in the passageway formed between the row of guests on one side and all of us on the other. The band immediately stopped playing, and a chapel-like quiet reigned as the *pandit* stepped forward. He recited Vedic hymns invoking blessings from the Almighty. The *pandit* then called my father for the *milni,* the ceremony of introduction between the fathers of the bride and the bridegroom. As Kakaji's father had died years ago, the embrace was exchanged between his uncle, Dr Prakash, and my father. After my father's introduction, important male relations of the bridegroom were called to meet the respective relations of the bride. We made presents, for the most part in cash, to our opposite number in the *barat*. Kakaji had no younger brother or a substitute for my *milni*, so I thrust my present back into my pocket.

Kakaji, who had remained on horseback during the ceremony, now moved forward to the steps leading to our house, where my sisters and their girl-friends were waiting with buckets full of flower petals. The servants were running around, spraying people with scented water and helping my sisters hurl the petals. Kakaji was surrounded by the teasing girls, and brother Om and I helped him to alight. Presumably, sister Pom had a choice, until that moment, to refuse Kakaji, because it was she who had to garland him as a sign of her acceptance. The *jaimala* she did shyly, without a word.

As the band struck up again, brother Om and I led Kakaji to an empty room. Here we had a chance to chat with him for a little while. This time he was in a freer mood than we had seen him at our tea table, and he even jested about the elaborate arrangements we had made. Soon after, sisters Nimi and Umi came in, and they started arranging for Kakaji's dinner. I went out and listened to the colourful sounds which filled the air and brought excitement to a fever pitch. Servants were running to and fro, serving the twenty-piece band. My uncles were leading the whole procession of the *barat* upstairs, where they were to have their dinner.

On our back porch, a row of *halwaiis* sat preparing large cauldrons of food in makeshift fireplaces. There was the ceaseless noise of their stirring something in the cauldrons, and the noise of clapping as they shaped *puris*. They must be making a *puri* a second, I thought, and I remembered the famine in Bengal. I walked up and down the rows of *halwaiis*, guests and orchestra members, feeling in my unfamiliar *achkan* as though I were another wedding ornament – with legs on. Friends of my father greeted me warmly. Servants asked me to go inside and rest, and the drum player showed me his tight coat belt, with an ornamental buckle. All our two hundred guests were there *en masse*, milling about, waiting to be fed. For them there was a long wait ahead, however, because the *barat*, as our honoured guests, would be served first, and only then our relatives. And I would have to wait until the very end.

'I have been looking for you,' brother Om shouted above the din of voices. 'We have to go upstairs and meet the *barat*.'

The feasting was over by midnight, the band had been dismissed, and some of our relatives had gone to bed, with full stomachs. Other relatives, close friends and the *barat* gathered around the *vedi* and took their places on the floor for the actual wedding ceremony. Earlier, I had helped with the decoration of the *vedi*, the wedding arch which had been built in the centre of the courtyard. Four posts of banana trunks had been firmly set in the ground to form an eight-foot square. Twigs with green leaves formed the arcades, around which were hung fruit and flowers, balloons and strings of coloured lights. A brass cauldron was placed in the centre for the sacramental fire, which in Vedic rites is considered the purifier.

The *pandit*, who was to perform the ceremony, cleared his throat repeatedly, and silence grew to suspense. Sister Nimi whispered to me that Kakaji and sister Pom were sitting on low stools with cushions next to my mother and father, looking very grave. Now the *pandit* walked into the arcade and started the *havan*, the lighting of the sacred *agni*. The fire crackled as the *pandit* fed it with butter, chips of scented wood and incense. A huge platter of perfumed salts was passed around the circle and I took a handful.

'A pinch will do,' sister Nimi whispered.

I tried to aim my fistful at the flame and prayed that I would miss the *pandit*'s head. The fire sizzled, and the whole courtyard was filled with the strong aromatic scent. The *pandit* began chanting the Vedic hymns in Sanskrit in his soft, melancholy voice. He paused now and then for Kakaji and sister Pom to repeat the Sanskrit vows after him. Compared to the *pandit*'s delivery, theirs seemed hesitant and uncertain, but the voices of both of them, pitched together for the first time, sounded good.

After the vows had been taken, he translated them for the benefit of the bride and groom. Both of them had promised to live according to the Hindu creed, to be true to each other, share each other's burdens, propagate the race, beget sons, remain firm and faithful like a rock.

'They are putting their feet on a piece of stone side by side,' sister Nimi explained, 'and now they have started circling the *vedi*.'

I knew they would have to circle seven times, symbolizing the invocation of the seven planets. Having gone around the ceremonial fire, the bridegroom addressed my sister in a hymn:

'Become thou my partner as thou hast paced all the seven steps with me. Apart from thee I cannot live. Apart from me do thou not live. We shall share alike all goods and power combined. Over my house you shall bear full sway.'

The first day of the three-day ceremony was ended when Kakaji took sister Pom over to the Mehta *Gullie* for a few minutes, so that she might be introduced to the members of the *barat* who had not attended the wedding. This was an exercise of his will which symbolized that the bride was his, and that she was no longer a part of her own family. But the formal departure of my sister was to come after another two days of feasting the *barat*. For each meal the party came with a band, but a small one consisting of only five people.

The pageant came to an end on the third evening, with the *doli*, when in a car bedecked simply with flowers, the bride and groom drove away from our house with the whole caravan of the *barat* on their heels. None of our relatives were in the caravan; only Father, Mother, Nimi, Umi, Om, Usha, Ashok and myself drove in the last car. This was the first time in those three days that all of us had been together, and then, too, alone. The whole caravan moved at a camel's pace, and I remember feeling hot and uncomfortable as though the *havan* itself was burning inside that car. I felt sorry for Kakaji and sister Pom, who would have almost no time alone together before facing the ordeal of still another reception upon their arrival in Dehra Dun, this time given by the *barat*.

Even though we had left our relatives behind, I could still hear their voices as they saw sister Pom off, voices which seemed tense with suppressed emotion. They're probably looking back to their own bridal days, I thought.

'All the ladies must be discussing the dowry and its worth in real gold.' Umi broke the silence.

'After a wedding like that for your first daughter, Daddyji, you'll never have to worry about proposals for us.'

Kakaji and sister Pom were to ride alone in a small compartment, in which the coolie was now stacking buckets of ice. Calling Kakaji aside, I heard my father tell him to take the journey gently. The train pulled away, and we returned home, alone.

All the relatives had dispersed, and without sister Pom, the house seemed very lonely. The close family for the first time was broken. I wondered how the house would be when sisters Umi and Nimi were married, and it heightened my sense of loss.

Sister Umi said, 'I am going to get married quietly in a church, as Westerners do, with no crowds of relatives.' My mother listened to her patiently, too tired to argue or contradict. Brother Om and I, however, were content. We could live for weeks on the sweetmeats left over from the feasts.

2

PAKISTAN & TRANSITION

ELEVEN

'Divide et ...'

In February 1947 my father prohibited me from attending
R.S.S.S. meetings, which had now become militant. Children
of civil servants, he reminded us, like their parents, could not
join political organizations.

Whereas before our house had been filled with happy excitement over wedding plans, now it had the tenseness of uncer-
tainty. On the streets could be heard slogans of processions:
'*Leyke rahengy Pakistan, jaise liya tha Hindustan*' – 'We will
take Pakistan just as we once took Hindustan'; and 'Unionist
Ministry *murdabad*' – 'Death to the Unionist Ministry.'

At first we climbed to our terrace and silently listened to the
shouts of hate. We would all stand side by side, with our hands
resting on the railing, leaning forward to catch every word. They
sounded too threatening, too unreal for belief. Whereas before,
my sisters had always explained what they saw, now they remained quiet. As these processions grew in frequency and were
no longer a curiosity, we stopped going to the terrace. Whereas
before we had discussed politics and the fast-approaching day of
independence with great enthusiasm, now we avoided it. We
felt uncomfortable in one another's company, and the conversation ceased to come spontaneously. Often we spoke too loudly,
our voices jarring each other's nerves, in the hope of drowning
out the cries for blood outside.

Jhanda, whose husky voice each day called, '*Phal, bibiji?*' –
'Fruit, madam?' was heard no more. For twenty years he had
carried fruit to the Mehta family, and had often distributed free
mangoes or pears to the children on the street. All that now was
in the past, for he was a Muslim, and might be denied burial
rights if he sold food to Hindus.

At school, Mr Baqir had stopped cursing Muslim students. His punishments were reserved for Hindus.

What had happened to disrupt the tenor of life and revive this long-dead religious fanaticism? This question was debated time and again by the experts in every newspaper, and while they disputed what would be the outcome of the present pitch of emotion, they did have some basic agreements as to its causes.

It was a matter of common knowledge that Hindus and Muslims had lived together for a thousand years like brothers; they had toiled together in the fields, feasted together at each other's religious celebrations, and even fought together against the British in 1857. In the twenties, under the leadership of Gandhiji and the Congress Party, they had launched the struggle for independence with equal fervour. They had marched with Gandhiji on his salt march, demonstrating to the British people the force of Gandhi's non-violent and *Satyagraha* methods.

Gandhiji and the Congress Party represented an India where different cultures had flourished side by side until all the various strands of diversity had been woven into one fabric to clothe the subcontinent, and each religion had borrowed from the others until the texture seemed indivisible.

This fabric had been systematically strained to the breaking point by the British policy of divide and rule. As early as 1859, Mount-Stuart Elphinstone, the English governor of Bombay, had precisely outlined the course British policy was to take in an official dispatch: '*Divide et impera* was the old Roman motto and it should be ours.' This policy was expedited by the fact that the Muslims did not take to Western customs as readily as the Hindus, and since the blame for the mutiny of 1857 had been placed on the Muslims, the British Government gave preferential treatment in handing high civil-service posts to Hindus. Then, too, more Hindus than Muslims owned property, and more of them formed the professional and middle classes.

Thus in time it was not too hard for the British Government to stir up resentment among the Muslims against the Hindus. They shifted the blame for the Muslim's lack of enterprise to the Hindus and thus furthered economic rivalry between them.

The British posed as the only guardians of Muslim rights, and some Muslims did not waste any time in playing up to them. Sir Sayed Ahmad, an outstanding educationist, advised the Muslims that their hope rested with the British, and they must remain loyal to the government.

Aligarh College, which the British helped to found, became a sort of headquarters for promoting this divide-and-rule policy. The college was for Muslims only, and in 1906 Mr Archbold, the British principal of Aligarh College, played a decisive role in encouraging a few dependable Muslims to ask for a separate electorate. According to plan, the British hailed this demand of the deputation as representative of the Muslim sentiment throughout the country, and separate electorates for Hindus and Muslims were granted. This was the first time that an outright distinction was drawn between the two communities.

This policy was well timed, for it prevented all Muslims from throwing their lot in with the Congress Party. Aligarh was to train leaders who preached a doctrine of the separate identity of Muslim and Hindu. Englishmen could not have asked for better agents for executing their designs, since these leaders were Muslims themselves, educated and trained orators whose words had more impact on the masses than if an outsider had tried to persuade them of their right to an Islamic state.

Thus, gradually but skilfully, the emotions of the masses were manipulated until the wave of nationalistic feeling culminated in the formation of the Muslim League. Historians concur that if religion had not been used to drive a wedge between the two communities, no amount of effort by the British or the Muslim leaders in Aligarh, striving for personal power, could have torn them asunder.

Even so, many distinguished Muslims did not desert the Congress Party but remained true to its goal of independence without partition. Yet these leaders, who at the most crucial moment might have checked the growing number of adherents to the Muslim League, were placed in jail with other Congress leaders during the Second World War, while the Muslim League was at liberty to carry on its activity with unabated zeal. At the end of World War II, Congress leaders came out of prison utterly baffled at the momentum the cry for a separate state had gathered and at how obstinate the leaders of the Muslim League had become. They were amazed to find, too, that the league did not have any definite plan as to the bases on which this state was to be formed.

The Muslims were spread out all over India, and while they did have a majority in some sections, a state for all Muslims was impractical, for wherever there was a Muslim majority there were Hindus as well. When this dilemma was presented to Mohammed Ali Jinnah, a rising star of the Muslim League, he flippantly evaded the question. He adopted an uncompromising attitude, and the pleading of Gandhiji and Jawaharlal Nehru for a coalition government where all the rights of minorities would be respected was ignored.*

For some time my father had been under no illusions as to what was in the making. To be sure, he could not predict the extent of brutality and riots, but throughout the preceding months, the emotional tide had been swelling, to reach its breaking point in the Punjab district in the first week of March 1947. It was the swift rise of this tide which baffled Chachaji, our elder who had lived in Lahore longer than anyone in the Mehta or Mehra families. Chachaji stubbornly held on to his belief that these leaders were fanatics who had no great impact on the masses. His devotion to the past prevented him from sensing the pulse of the time. It was almost as if he lived in another world.

One evening as we lingered sombrely in the dining-room, my father said to my mother, 'I tell you, there is hardly any time to prepare for the bloodshed. I have listened to Chachaji long enough, and respect his wisdom, but I cannot reconcile myself to his lack of preparation. If he cannot look after himself, then it is our duty to do so for him.'

It was common knowledge that most of the police were Muslims who would stand passively by or even take an active part in carrying out the destructive designs of the Muslim mob. If the

---

* In this survey I have drawn from the findings in *Stern Reckoning* by Gopal Das Khosla, Bhawnani & Sons, New Delhi, 1950.

Hindus retaliated by rousing their own people they were sure to be ruthlessly fired upon. We knew, for instance, that whenever there was a procession of Muslims and the police were called out to disperse it, they never used tear bombs, *lathee* charge, or gas, as had been used by their predecessors. They would simply arrest the Muslim leaders heading the procession and carry them a few miles distant to where Muslim League cars were waiting to bring them back to regroup and remobilize their forces. We knew all this, and more. But whereas my father took this as a sign of the darkest evil to follow, Chachaji took it more lightly than the situation demanded.

'Let's walk over to Chachaji's,' my father said, and all of us went to Chachaji's house. As usual, he was seated on the veranda, surrounded with papers and books, carefully reading them and meticulously taking notes. I could imagine his frown on our arrival even though I could not see it. He was happy enough to see us, but he knew that on our arrival the whole issue would be opened again, and confident as he was of the esteem in which he was held by the younger members of the family, he did not cherish an argument.

'So do we have to go over it all again, Amolak Ram?' he asked my father.

'Chachaji, you've got to listen to us. In your house there are ten women, and one of them is pregnant. There is no sense in taking chances. Now I beg of you, either send these women to our house and let us try to improvise some kind of shelter or hiding place there, or let me bring my daughters here. I still feel that my house is safer.'

'Don't you understand,' Chachaji interrupted him, 'that I feel just as responsible, if not more so, as you do about the women in the family?'

'I don't deny that.' My father tried to justify himself.

'Then leave it to me, and let me handle it my way.'

The upshot of the two-hour session was that we returned home no nearer to convincing Chachaji than we had been when we left. As we walked home, my father remarked, 'If he won't listen to me, Shanti, I must act on my own responsibility. I have talked this over with Bishan Das' (our next door neighbour with whom we shared a common wall) 'and he tells me that all the Hindu families in this neighbourhood can gather in his home without going into the streets, while we men can guard the terrace with guns. That's the only solution.'

'Whatever you say, *jio*.'

My father closed with the remark, 'This may mean abandoning our home, but the times have changed, and it is not going to be property that's at stake, but life.'

Next morning, even before I was up, I heard a soft knock on the door.

'Who is it?' I asked.

'Sohan,' answered my friend from the R.S.S.S., who was eighteen, five years older than I.

My room was on the far side of the house, and Sohan had been able to reach it unobserved. My father had strictly forbidden me to entertain guests from the R.S.S.S., for rumour had it that houses of members of the *sangh* were topmost on the lists of Muslim League leaders who incited the mobs.

I opened the door. 'It is so good to see you, Sohan! Tell me what has happened. I heard that the *sangh* was banned three days ago. What is happening?'

'Wait a minute, boy – keep a cool head,' he said. 'This is not like yourself. Yes, the situation is very serious. It seems everywhere I go people are jittery. I am convinced that the time is approaching for the Muslim League plan to be put into action. They say even Mayor Mian-Amir-ud-Din has a supply of firearms in his home and is distributing them free to Muslims, and sending each day for more.'

'I heard of that,' I told him. 'My sisters were speaking about it only yesterday.'

'Yes, he's not making any secret of it.'

'What are we going to do, Sohan?'

'It's what can we do? In the meetings when I brought up this subject, and talked about the leadership of Gandhi, they took me seriously enough, but they didn't do anything. I tell you, leaders like Gandhi are outmoded. They have done their work for India. They are too idealistic to cope with these hooligans.'

'You know what you're saying, Sohan?'

'I know – it's heresy. I mean it, though.'

I could not dispute his earnestness. This feeling had been at the back of our minds for many months, yet no one had put it as bluntly as Sohan. He was always calm and collected, and his words were well chosen. They were keen and sharp, and yet delivered with the greatest confidence. How many times I had heard him at the *sangh* talking with such fervour that even the most devoted members of the Congress Party could not resist his arguments.

'I believe you,' I said. 'You are almost always right, Sohan.'

'Well, I don't know about that, but I think I'm right this time. Look here, we must begin to plan. I love your sisters and family as though they were my own.' (His family was out of the so-called danger zone.) 'You can't wait any longer.'

'That's what Father told us yesterday; he has a plan and, Sohan, I think it's still secret.'

'I respect your father. Have no fear on that score. By the way, what does Chachaji say?'

'He's still immovable as ever.'

'I thought so. You know, I wish I were old enough to go and talk to that man.'

'I'm not sure even you could convince him of anything. I saw him last night in action. He certainly seems to have good arguments.'

'What are they?'

'You know, he talked about history, and how amicably Hindus and Muslims have lived together.'

'Yes, he's just as archaic as the rest of the Congress people. Why don't they understand the changing times? They speak of history, but what about the British history, I ask you? These times haven't changed overnight, you know. They are the steady work of a century. Or does he just skip that hundred years?'

'Don't be harsh on him, Sohan. He thinks differently. He can't see how some foreign power can disrupt the good relations of centuries. He sees all this in a larger perspective.'

'I wonder sometimes, Ved, if he understands the power of the British people. They are no fools. They understand what their left hand is doing. But what is this plan you speak of?'

'My father has agreed that we should all gather in Bishan Das's house.'

'You won't have time to do that. The street will be sealed off.'

'Well, he said we would avoid the streets.'

'I wonder how. You surely couldn't jump from terrace to terrace. That's too dangerous, and impractical besides. You could, of course, make a hole in your common wall and go through it.'

'That might be what he's planning.'

'But the mob will just come through your house, see you're not there, find the hole, and that's it. They'll know your hiding place.'

'But my father said all the men will go to the terrace with guns. In fact, we got one only yesterday.'

'Do be sensible! Can guns stop herds of people? You might kill a few of them, but you won't stop them from taking the women and butchering the men. Your father must realize that. He must have a better plan, though I can't think of one offhand.'

'What are you going to do, Sohan? Where are you going to be?'

'I'll manage. I'm here by myself, and even if they kill me, I'll surely take a few of them with me.'

'Please don't talk like that.'

'You might as well get used to hearing about bloodshed, and about your friends being killed. Well, I must go now.'

'Will I see you again, Sohan?'

'I'll come in tomorrow morning – the same time. You are not afraid, are you?'

'About my father and you?'

'Yes, you know what I mean. I'd hate him to think I'm disobeying him.'

'I must see you, Sohan, to find out what's going on.'

'Well, I'll be here tomorrow.'

And then he left as it was nearing the time for my parents to get up. What a wonderful and determined fellow, I thought. Sohan's courage was contagious, and I waited eagerly for his next visit.

TWELVE

Ideals and Irony

THAT day was to bring an even more puzzling event than Sohan's visit of the morning.

Shekh Sahib, a Muslim whose house was across from ours, came to call. As he rang the bell I opened the door for him.

'Is your father here?' he asked.

'I think so. Won't you sit down?' I left to get my father.

Following him back to the drawing-room and hiding behind the curtains, I listened to what Shekh Sahib had to say.

'Ah, Doctorji. I'm so happy to see you.'

'It's a pleasure to see you,' Father greeted him.

Such a long while had passed since I had heard Hindu and Muslim address one another like that! Even my sisters' best friends had stopped coming to the house; and whenever we met them on the street they avoided us.

'Well, Doctorji,' Shekh Sahib continued, 'I'll come right to the point. Trouble is in the air and you're not too safe here. The neighbours to your left are Sikhs and you know what that means. I don't want to interfere, but my wife and I both want you to know that we will be happy to accommodate your children.'

I was suspicious. Only three months earlier Shekh Sahib had offered *lakh rupees* for our house and my father had refused. I wished he had taken it, for the value of Hindu property was on the decline. Now Shekh Sahib was offering to get us all out of the house. Maybe he would have us all killed. Then he would have the house to himself. What audacity, I thought.

I was overjoyed to hear my father's words. They were just as forthright as Shekh Sahib's.

'I don't think that will be necessary, Shekh Sahib.'

'Be reasonable, Doctorji. Your daughters are as dear to me as my own, and I'd hate to see anything happen to them. This is a dangerous situation!'

'I'm very grateful to you, Shekh Sahib, for your kindness.'

'Well, I told my wife perhaps you'd feel the way you do, but she still wanted me to come and tell you, and I'm glad for that. I can't say I blame you.'

'I'm glad you are understanding.'

'For thirty-seven years, Doctorji, we've known one another. I've seen your children grow up with mine. My daughters love yours like their own sisters. But however that may be –'

'I'm sure my daughters feel the same way.'

'I wish all this didn't have to happen, but then wishing won't do any good. I'm sorry, yes, I'm sorry.'

I was almost moved by the sincerity of this man. Even Sohan, I thought, couldn't scoff at this; but then again, maybe he could. Hadn't he told me how clever these Muslims were, and how all of them were being asked to form Pakistan in the name of Mohammed?

'Very kind of you, Shekh Sahib,' my father said, 'and I would always trust you, but –'

'I know what you mean, Doctorji. You don't have to explain it any further. Let's leave it at that.'

My father, whose presence of mind was admirable, fumbled for words. I wondered if he, too, was experiencing the same conflict to believe or not to believe. After an uneasy pause Shekh Sahib began again.

'Well, if you won't let me do any more, Doctorji, one thing I hope you'll permit me to do. It will give me great satisfaction. As you know, I have my own well, and I'd like to have you draw your water from there.'

What an absurd idea this was, I thought. Surely they couldn't contaminate the reservoir, for that would poison Hindus and Muslims alike.

'Why will I need water?' my father asked.

'It may be that your house will be set on fire, and if you had water, plenty of it, you might be able to save part of it. You know the fire brigade won't come to your call.'

'I suppose not. At least, not to save a Hindu's house.'

'Well, then,' Shekh Sahib continued, 'I expect that we could run a pipeline from my tank under the street and connect it with your water line. I've heard you talk about how low your water pressure is; it would not be sufficient in case of an emergency. You see, if your house were on fire, I couldn't stretch a hose from my house to help you. For then I'd be a traitor, and my fate wouldn't be any better than yours.'

I was even more confused and baffled. That would mean risking our lives; for if the reservoir couldn't be contaminated, Shekh Sahib could put poison in his tank. That was just as bad as going to their house.

'That is very generous of you, Shekh Sahib. I'd like to talk it over with my wife.'

'Well, I leave you, Doctorji.'

Then I heard my father show him to the door. This was such a different visit from Sohan's, and I was so completely lost in thought trying to discover the meaning of it all, that I forgot to keep my place behind the curtain, and soon my father found me.

'You heard it all?'

'Yes, Daddyji.'

'And what did you think of it?'

This was always his way. He respected everybody's opinion. We both sat down on the couch.

'I don't think I should like to go there,' I told him. 'I'd rather be burned here, and I'd prefer if we didn't accept his water either. If the house has to burn down, it must, but we shouldn't risk our lives by drinking their water.'

'I think the same way, son. But I wish you could have seen his face. He was in earnest.'

'I could tell it from his voice, but even so –'

'Even so!' he said. 'That's the question, isn't it?'

We sat there for a long while without saying anything to one another. At last my father said, 'I must go and talk it over with your mother. I don't care as much about the property as I care about hurting Shekh Sahib's feelings. You have only known him as our good neighbour, but to me he is a *guru*. I started my college education with him. For thirty-seven years I have known him, and he is like a father to me. You can't understand the veneration I feel for him. Even today he is one of those Muslims who believe in one India. Indeed, he is publishing letters pleading for calmness and for one nation.'

He left me sitting there by myself just as Sohan had in the morning. How paradoxical it was, to trust yet not to trust. I was glad that the decision rested with my father, not with me. But I was mistaken about that. He called us all into the bedroom, and repeating the scene to my sisters, asked us what we thought should be done.

My youngest sister, Usha, didn't have much to say; brother Om was definitely opposed to trusting Shekh Sahib. He would rather risk antagonizing him than forsake the safety of our home for the whim of one man. Sister Umi commented on the nerve of the man, and was amused that he was earnest or seemed sincere. Nimi, however, took a different position.

'Daddyji, we'll have to trust someone. If we don't have faith or trust, what is to become of us? The mature people will have to keep their heads and not succumb to the temper of the times. This is our test. I'm not afraid of dying, and I'd as soon die from poisoned water as commit suicide.'

She was right, I thought, and very convincing. This was our test and we must meet it squarely. Then my father interjected. 'Your mother feels the same way as sister Nimi. I will keep myself neutral and put the question once again to all of you now that everyone has commented. I don't want to influence you, and I'll take responsibility for the final action. But I want to know exactly how you feel. Yes or no?' he asked me first.

'I think sister Nimi is right.'

Brother Om was lost for words. 'I still think that we oughtn't to do it. But sister Nimi has a very strong point. I'm not sure.'

Sister Umi was more thoughtful now and we had to wait some time for an answer. Finally she spoke, and in one breath. 'I'm willing to go ahead with Shekh Sahib's idea.'

Then my father addressed Om. 'Do you still feel very strongly about your contention?'

'No, I do not. I suppose it's pretty clear that we'll have to go through with it.' There was something discouraging in brother Om's voice. It must have taken a lot of courage for him to abandon his high spirits.

'I think it's the right decision,' Mother said. 'It's a gamble, but, then, all's at stake.'

'Everyone is agreed, then,' said Father. 'I will go over to Shekh Sahib's and tell him so.'

'Take brother Om with you,' I said without thinking. I had concurred only because of the business about a test and mature people.

'Don't worry,' my father said to me. 'What will happen will happen, and if we're going as far as drinking their water —' And he left.

He returned after what seemed an interminable time. 'We'll have to install the pipes tomorrow night, and with Hindu labourers. And I don't think we should say anything to our other Hindu and Sikh neighbours about it. We know what they'll think. But now I want to return to a much more important matter. I told you last night that we had a plan. See if you agree with it.

'We will all go to Bishan Das's house. It's the most centrally located one and it can be made accessible to almost all Hindu-Sikh houses in this block. For our family we'll have to build a heavy steel door and install it in the wall. It can be painted the same colour as the wall, and at night, if a good job is done, the mob might miss it. As soon as we've entered Bishan Das's house we can lock the door, and even if the mob discovers it, it would be almost impossible to break through.'

There was a sigh of relief, and this was acknowledged a good plan.

Now the problem, of course,' my father continued, 'is to find a steel door. Bishan Das tells me that he knows a reliable firm which can be trusted with the job. We still haven't worked out a quiet way of installing it.' And so details were discussed.

'We must keep this plan completely secret from everyone or it's no good,' said my mother.

When I went to bed that night, so much had come to pass that the thoughts of Shekh Sahib, Bishan Das, Chachaji, Sohan and sister Nimi all tossed in my mind. I waited for Sohan's return; to me, he was not an outsider.

I was up next morning early and Sohan did not disappoint me. I heard his gentle rap on the door and I hastened to open it.

'Come in, Sohan. Am I glad to see you!'

This time, rather than my being impatient, it was he who could not wait to hear the happenings of the day before. I told him all.

For a long time he was thoughtful. Finally he said, 'All this, Ved, is so ironic, so incongruous! Here you are, making preparations to escape, and then you hand over your lives to the mercy of one Muslim. You tell me about faith and trust, but do not lose sight that it's the bugle of religion that the Muslim League leaders have sounded.'

'Stop, Sohan. Don't go on! I don't wish to be disillusioned. You say ironic; you comment about irony in our home. But what about history?'

'Precisely so, Ved. Like life, history is nothing but a tragic irony. Take the British, for instance. You and I both admire them, think of them as the greatest people on earth, sometimes, even over our nationals. These calculating Britishers were positive almost until the end of the Second World War when the Conservative ministry felt that they had played their cards with good care, and that finally their divide-and-rule policy had reached its climax. They were going to prove to the world how unfit we were to rule ourselves. Well, then, even they miscalculated. Don't you see that? Do you see the irony?'

'I see it too well.'

'Yes, they failed to discern the impact of the Congress Party and Gandhiji. They turned out to be much more stupid than you and I could have thought possible. I have been thinking about Chachaji and perhaps this morning I understand him better than I did yesterday. You see,' he continued, 'perhaps Chachaji is too much of a historian. He cannot see the irony and the contradictions.'

'But for all your bold statements about history, I still don't see what's wrong with having ideals.'

'Perhaps that's all we have, and by this talk I'm not trying to detract from what your sister Nimi said. I admire her very much, and I think your father did the right thing.'

Just then I heard the confident tapping which I readily recognized as my father's. Just for a flicker of a moment I was frightened. But then Sohan was one step ahead of me.

'He'll understand, Ved.'

I opened the door. 'Good morning, Daddyji.' He came in.

'I have been looking forward to seeing you, Sohan,' he said. 'You were here yesterday, weren't you?'

'Yes, I was.'

'I thought as much.'

This calm tone of my father's voice, which was understanding enough, sent chills down my spine. By having Sohan come to see me, I had jeopardized the future of the whole family. If my father was correct in assuming that the seizure of many of the *sangh* records by the police had resulted in their being handed over to the Muslim League leaders, as indeed even Sohan admitted, then to have a member of the *sangh* at our home was foolhardy. I did not know if my name had appeared in the register. I thought not, or so I chose to think, anyway. My father sat down on the bed and started talking to Sohan.

'I'm glad Ved has a chance to talk to you,' he said. 'I want all my children to understand what is happening. Then only will they be prepared to meet any emergency courageously.'

My father continued talking for a long while, and Sohan spoke candidly of his fears and his philosophy of history. My father and he found much common ground, and I was happy for that. I was relieved that in these times, some minds agreed. At last Sohan left. 'He's a good fellow,' my father said to me. 'Very intelligent. You have picked a good friend in him.'

THIRTEEN

The Bugle Sounds

ON the night of the first of March, the few trusted Hindu labourers who had helped build our home were called in, and the pipes were installed, leading to Shekh Sahib's house. Whatever attempts had been made to hide the nature of this project, the night had not been dark enough, the labourers not silent enough to prevent the neighbours from discovering that something was going on. They probably dismissed it as something wrong with our water system, for the project on which we were launched was so inexplicable that no one in his right mind would have suspected it. From that night on, we started drinking the water of Shekh Sahib, and even relishing our own trepidation.

The same Hindu labourers were retained for the night of the second of March to install the steel door which had been smuggled in in a closed van. But they did not show up, for the Khizar ministry of Punjab – a coalition of Congress and Unionist parties – resigned that day, touching off a powder keg.

Khizar, the Prime Minister of Punjab, had earned the ill-will of Muslims and non-Muslims alike. The Muslims considered him disloyal, because he did not cater to all the demands of the Muslim League; the non-Muslims found his indecision unpalatable. He was a man caught in the vice of trying to please two opposing groups, with the result that he antagonized both.

On the next day, the third of March, all the non-Muslim parties, Congress, Hindu and Sikh, held a meeting in the Assembly Chamber in Lahore. They knew that while they could not form a new ministry without the co-operation of the Muslim League, so the league could not form a ministry without their support. Although frightened at the thought of a Muslim League ministry, they decided to withhold their support.

While they were reaching this decision within the chamber,

outside a crowd of Muslims, instigated by the Muslim League Party, stood shouting that they would take Pakistan by force if necessary. Their meaning was clear. If the Congress Party would not support the Muslim League Party, then the mob would take matters into their own hands. But if that prospect was ominous to the Congress Party, the prospect of a Muslim League ministry was no more pleasing; the non-Muslim parties therefore decided to launch upon a firm policy.

Tara Singh, the Akali Sikh leader, rushed out of the Assembly Chamber, pulled out his *kirpan*, the blade carried by all Sikhs as a symbol of their force and power, and shouted back at the pressing and threatening crowd, '*Kat ke dainge apni jan magar nahin dainge Pakistan*' – 'We shall give our lives and be killed but will never concede Pakistan.'

Although the rage of Tara Singh was understandable, the timing of his words was bad. Had the police not intervened, the temper of the mob would have resulted in a nasty incident. But the police did come to the rescue, this for the very last time, and the crowd was dispersed.

That evening, a meeting of the non-Muslims was held in Kapurthala House, and I asked my father if I might attend. He did not give a straightforward answer.

'Processions are prohibited,' he said, 'meetings banned, speeches of leaders outlawed in public gatherings. This meeting is illegal, and anything could happen.' He went on, 'The *lathees* of the Muslim police might be heaped upon the non-Muslim gathering. They might fire, and where would be the escape?' But for all this, he did not say no. 'Think for yourself,' he said characteristically.

But I had become too impassioned to resist the temptation of hearing leaders like Tara Singh. Sohan came for me in the evening and we set out together. Mother stopped us at the door. She said '*Namaste*' to us half-heartedly. Then we left. Our walk to Kapurthala House was in itself full of peril, but the fresh air of the evening revived us. I was thrilled at the prospect of hearing Tara Singh, who was reputed in the Punjab to be the most daring leader of the non-Muslims.

The house was packed, and still the people kept on coming until we were pressed together body to body. Then the leaders appeared. The very presence of Congress Party leaders on the same stage with men like Tara Singh who felt no compulsion to use non-violent means to stop the bloodshed seemed to imply the victory of the strong-heads and their attitude that, let the Muslims start something, the Hindus and Sikhs would retaliate. The leading question was, however, what would they retaliate with? To be sure, at the waist of each Sikh hung a *kirpan*, but they were primitive compared to the guns and bombs which had been distributed to the Muslims.

Men like Giani Karter Singh spoke in enraged voices. The crowd responded in unison. With perfect cadence they roared, they cheered, they shouted slogans. Their voices clashed against the walls, and echoed back to amplify the ferocious cries.

Then, instantaneously, as Tara Singh came forward, the cries of the crowd were smothered as though by a great blanket, and the air became heavy and thick with hot, moist breathing. Tara Singh delivered his famous words with resolution and heat.

'Oh, Hindus and Sikhs! Be ready for self-destruction like the Japanese and the Nazis. Our motherland is calling for blood and we shall satiate the thirst of our mother with blood. By crushing Moghulistan we shall trample Pakistan. I have been feeling for many a day now that mischief has been brewing in the province and for that reason I started reorganizing the Akali Party. If we can snatch the government from the Britishers, no one can stop us from snatching the government from the Muslims. We have in our hold the limbs and legs of the Muslim League and we shall break them. Disperse from here on the solemn affirmation that we shall not allow the league to exist. The world has always been ruled by minorities. The Muslims snatched the kingdom from the Hindus, and the Sikhs grabbed it from the hands of the Muslims, and the Sikhs will even now rule over them. We shall rule over them and shall get the government, fighting. I have sounded the bugle. Finish the Muslim League!'

The malice of Tara Singh's words was contagious, and it gripped one and all. Men curled their fists and clenched them tightly. These people seemed able to walk together down the streets and defy any force with their solidarity. Were these the people, I thought, that the Muslims called meek, servile and decadent? Just as the Muslim League had sounded a bugle months before, so now Tara Singh sounded his. But unfortunately for Hindus and Sikhs, it was a belated sound, with no preparation or force behind it. It was tragic that the emotions of the crowd had been inflamed to such a point, for the warmed crowd could not but be slaughtered, and whatever strength or daring they might possess, it was useless when computed against the armed mob's.

Sobered by the walk and deserted by the contagious spirit of the crowd, we foresaw too clearly the consequences of that meeting. We knew that Tara Singh had made a mistake, even though whether he had spoken or not, the bloodshed would probably be the same.

The third of March passed and still the steel door had not been installed, and we were uneasy about remaining in our house. We longed for the community of other Hindu families. The evening of the fourth we walked over to Chachaji's, but he was nowhere to be found.

We were too apathetic to return home right away. Then the night drew on, and we could not risk going back. We waited, our hearts palpitating. The grandfather clock, as old as the house, ticked undeviatingly. The chimes which had previously sounded resonantly with rich sweetness now seemed jangled and discordant. Ten, ten-fifteen, ten-thirty; and then it all happened at once. The cries of the procession, thirsting for blood and lured by the prospect of loot, marched closer. Their cries resounded and reverberated through the streets.

How was it that the fire was described to me? A yellow-grey glow in the sky? The smoke tickled my nostrils, and I was reminded of Dadar. My father and brother were on the terrace of the house by now. They came down hurriedly.

'I think you had better leave the house. The fires seem not too far away from here.'

We all went around Chachaji's garden and towards the servants' quarters, where we crouched between the back of the servants' quarters and the wall. Dazed with the action of the preceding days, I stopped listening. There was nothing different to hear, no different smells, and I sensed nothing. My breathing steadied, and my heart stopped throbbing. Was it resignation? Or was it that too much had happened to sort out?

I wondered what was this Hindu religion which had marked us for an ignominious death. Religion, my father had told us, was an individual matter. Hindu religion was a way of life, enriched by centuries.

Who were Muslims? For them, religion meant complete abandonment of individual personality. In the villages, I had seen them sometimes all eating and drinking from the same containers to show the extent of their brotherly love. Their eyes turned five times a day towards Mecca, and they kneeled and prayed to Mohammed. They swore by the *Koran*.

But in Hinduism, no prophet, no one dogma, no one sacred book bound believers together. Our beliefs were as diverse and various as the climate, geography and culture of the country. We as individuals might even venerate Mohammed or Christ, as prophets, and still remain Hindus. That was the power and pride of Hinduism, for it tolerated all religions and embraced all ways of life. Muslims, however, knew no diversity. They were united by one God, one prophet, one book – proselytism was their creed.

Was I really a Hindu? I asked myself. During childhood I had been profoundly influenced, insofar as a child can be, by the Christian love. Since then we had sung hymns at 'Pindi and at the *sangh*, discussed values and ideals, and tried to conform to those. But the values and ideals were of a society where Hindus and Muslims lived side by side, toiled in the fields shoulder to shoulder. What was it that set us apart from the Muslims? Our old servant Gian Chand said the Muslim religion taught cruelty.

'The Muslim children, Ved Sahib,' he said, 'are taught to break Hindu statues.' Then Sohan said that most Muslims in the Punjab were weavers, cobblers, herdsmen, potters and black-smiths, that their mentality was low. They were labourers in cities, and among them vice and poverty bred more vice and more poverty. Then another of our servants, Sukh Dev, who had recently returned from his village, said the Hindus' houses were much cleaner than the Muslims'. While Hindus never brought shoes into their homes, the Muslims wore them everywhere. Their manner of eating he considered filthy and repulsive. He wanted a separate plate; he did not care to dip into one big bowl with a large spoon.

Yet for all this, Hindus and Muslims had lived on together for centuries. Had Gian Chand always considered Muslims cruel, and had Sukh Dev always thought of them as unclean and filthy? I could not help wondering.

At the arrival of dawn, around four or five, when the cow coughed in the stable next to the servants' quarters, we staggered back to the home of Chachaji. He greeted us, a shattered and broken man, and we realized instantly how much the happenings of the last few days had affected him.

'I am sorry, my children,' he said as we all surrounded him. 'Forgive me.'

Our hearts went out to him, but we knew he would have to overcome his anguish alone. Quietly we went back to our own home.

That whole day, rumours filtered in. Hindu college students had been fired upon by the police unjustly; a British governor, whom the Hindus regarded as sympathetic to the Muslims, was put in charge of Lahore. Martial law was declared; curfews ordered; riots had broken out everywhere; scores of fires lit the sky. Men and women were leaving home, turning their houses over to the whims of the mob. Pedestrians were stabbed; shops looted.

Another night drew on, and all was dark again.

terrace of Bishan Das's house to keep watch. The rest of us silently walked to the room which was to be the refuge of all women and children. I felt self-conscious. If only I could see so that I, too, might keep watch on the terrace instead of retreating to a hiding place.

We all had been calm behind the servants' quarters at Chachaji's, without a roof over our heads, but here, where fifty persons crowded into a small room, things were different. The women shrieked and moaned, each bewailing her own misfortune. This was the despair of women who might never behold their husbands or sons again. They might be abducted or brutally raped like the women in the other parts of Punjab. We children did not cry, but found a place in the corner where we might huddle unobserved.

I wanted something to happen, something to put an end to the suspense. But it was not to be that night, and the next morning we returned to the uncertain safety of our home.

Even during the daytime there was no security. The shouting and outcries continued unabated, and rumours of murderous raids throughout the city and West Punjab filtered in. Without a doubt, the Muslims had the upper hand, and the Muslim League leaders might well relish their triumph, for it was complete. Some Sikhs tried to mar the glory of their victory by plunging *kirpans* into a few Muslims, but these casualties were too few in number for notice.

We accustomed ourselves to the routine of the terror. We listened to the news on the radio, and that was our sole contact with the outer world. Even at midday it was considered unsafe to leave the security of home. Each afternoon Gian Chand would make the rounds of the Mehta and Mehra families and announce to us that another night had left them unharmed. No one in the family went to school, or to shop. My father alone ventured out to go to his office. He was a doctor, and a government servant. No riots could be allowed to interfere with that obligation. When he left, the question would he return repeatedly haunted us.

If this was the state in one home, which in the distant past had experienced happiness and gaiety, then what was the

condition of the outlying villages which had no steel doors between them and death? The news reached us that the Hindu and
Sikh women in villages around Rawalpindi, a dominantly Muslim area, and in other sections as well, had piled up their beds,
clothes and fuel to make a great bonfire and courageously hurled
themselves into the flames, for they wanted to die with their
honour, and a pure soul. They preferred the torturous death by
fire to the fury of the mob, and the tradition that all Hindus who
commit suicide are reincarnated in the form of a crow, to caw
for the rest of that life cycle, did not stop them.

The Punjab rocked, and with each shock perished the lives
of thousands and the beliefs of hundreds of thousands. The
scars of this religious strife would persist long after the fury of
the bugle had faded. Would the Muslims and Hindus ever live
amicably again? There seemed no hope.

In the inferno of strife, the pleas of the Congress leaders and
Gandhiji for non-violent resistance, exhorting the people to
prefer death to conversion to Islam, sounded ridiculous. The
idealism of non-violence seemed as archaic as Buddha himself,
who had been the first to formulate this doctrine, and to us it
seemed the same disaster which had let men like Aurangzeb
forcibly convert many Hindus, while others remained passive,
was ahead.

Now it seemed that it was not necessarily the non-violence
that had driven out British government, but, as Sohan said,
'their decency in not letting men like Gandhi starve,' the decency which respected some prerogatives of leaders; and I thought,
if it had not been for their humanity, they might have remained
for ever ruling non-violent India. Faith in the Congress Party
was shaken, the faith on which the struggle for independence
had thrived; and the respect for leaders had disappeared. The
disillusionment which had characterized Chachaji on the fifth
of March seemed to afflict one and all living in the dismal reality
of human inadequacies.

On the fourteenth of March, Pandit Nehru arrived in Lahore
and was greeted by expectant and excited men who still thought

him capable of halting the destruction. Surely, I thought, Sohan would come now to discuss the import of Panditji's visit, but he did not. The twenty-first of March, my thirteenth birthday, came and went unnoticed, and still he did not come.

When Pandit Nehru returned to Delhi, the leaders of the Congress Party and the Muslim League began once again to debate around the conference table in Delhi, while widespread destruction overtook the whole of West Punjab. Trains were looted, houses razed, villages destroyed with their herds, crops and inhabitants. Stabbings multiplied in the cities, and rapes and abductions continued in the dominantly Muslim areas.

It was not surprising that the Hindus and Sikhs in West Punjab were growing impatient with the ineffectual haggling around the Delhi conference table, and were crying for the Hindu and Sikh brothers in India to act, not talk, and come to their aid immediately.

Yet what could the Congress Party do? They had been devoted to the cause of independence for united India too long to abandon it now. History and logic were on their side, for the cultural and economic ties bound India as one nation.

Worn out by tedious negotiation, fatigued by continuous rebukes from the Muslim League, frustrated to find that their years of long labour were to be rendered futile, unable to bear the prolonged pressure for action from Hindus and Sikhs in West Punjab, and, finally, convinced that almost all Muslims in West Punjab had responded to the call of religion and Jinnah, the Congress leaders conceded Pakistan in May 1947. But if they had any hopes that this concession would end the chaos and anarchy, they were very much mistaken, for the Muslims in the Punjab hailed this as another indication of their strength and power against the servility of the Hindus. They were not satisfied with this first victory, and they thought that by spurring their mobs on to fresh riots they could secure all of Punjab and Bengal for Pakistan. But the Congress was under no misapprehensions that once Pakistan was formed, the cries for Hindu and Sikh blood would subside. They faced the grim possibility that all the Hindus and Sikhs in West Punjab would have to be evacuated, and if all of Punjab were lost, this task could never be performed.

For once an Englishman, Lord Mountbatten, sided against the Muslims, and considered their demand for all of Punjab and all of Bengal exorbitant and unreasonable. So the Congress leaders stood firm, with Lord Mountbatten as their backbone, on the ground that the provinces of Punjab and Bengal would be divided rather than ceded in their entirety. Subsequently, boundary commissions were set up to determine the exact lines of demarcation.

All these negotiations did not stop the atrocities of the Muslims in West Punjab; and even though in Lahore there was a momentary lull after the hectic days of early March, we were never able to resume the natural course of life. There was always a steel door, torches flashing, rumours of where the mob would strike next, and news of another stabbing to remind us of altered times.

But all the struggle was not destructive. On 16 April a child was born to Pom, a fine, healthy boy. Yet the times had their due, for no festivity, no celebration greeted him, even though he was the first grandson. Our concern for sister Pom increased. She was too weak, and the child too young, to permit us to execute our plan of escape safely.

About the middle of May, the riots in Lahore broke out with the same intensity as they had during the March days. For four consecutive nights we had to abandon our home, each night more convinced than before that it would be for the last time. Now it was the fifth night, and as always we were standing on the terrace where we could keep in touch with the other houses, and take full advantage of the view. Sister Pom, tired of standing, was sitting on the steps with her baby, only a month old, with Ashok now silently moving to sister Pom, now returning to his other brothers and sisters. Soon he fell asleep on the small bed which had been moved there earlier for sister Pom's use.

My sisters kept watch, breaking the silence only to estimate the exact location of the various fires. Some of them seemed no more than half a mile from our home. The vile shrieks and sounds to which we should by now have grown accustomed, though we had not, vibrated through the sultry night. As always in the month of May, there was no noticeable movement of air; the days had been stifling, the temperature running as high as 115 degrees. Finally, once again clasping hands, we slowly descended the stairs, brother Om and Father following.

Within the four walls where once sobs and moans had given vent to the terror of women, we were now surrounded by the quietude of enervated women too spent, too resigned to cry out. Never was the scene of our first night's exodus repeated. Drill after drill had made these women trained and proficient.

For a quick death each one of them carried poison, firearm, or razor-edged blade. If anything remained to sustain them, it was the value of honour and courage, the principles of renunciation and suffering practised by untold centuries of Hindus.

As I held Ashok, I thought of the day he had arrived, then his near loss with meningitis; how he had tugged at my mother's *sari* and crawled on the carpets. Many a time I had scolded him for entering my room and tinkering with my electrical equipment. I had always been afraid in case I forgot to unplug all of it and Ashok, unable to resist the urge to copy his brother, would try to make it hum.

Being the youngest, he was pampered by everyone, and almost nothing was denied him. Whereas before he had been noisy and full of life, ever since the March days he had tried to make himself invisible, or so it seemed. Now he lay still, and he had even returned to sucking his thumb.

Bombs exploded outside. The mob sounded no farther away than the gate of Bishan Das's house, and at any moment we expected to hear shooting break out which might deter their onrush for a time. But fate was not to end our existence that night either; and once again at dawn we passed through the steel door.

Next day, Shekh Sahib came and earnestly told us that our house had barely escaped the mob. If we would not relent in sending my sisters to his house, we had better get them out of Lahore. He said it enigmatically, as though he knew more than we did, and was aware of the mob's next move.

His visit, combined with the fresh assaults on Lahore since the conceding of Pakistan, determined my father to send us away, and for once he did not ask for a vote, or heed my sisters' attempts to dissuade him. That day he would go to Uncle Daulat Ram and ask him to send his daughters away also. My sisters pleaded with Mother, once he had left, that they would be more apprehensive away from Lahore, not knowing what had happened to her and Father. But it seemed Mother and Father had reached this decision together, and she was just as firm as he.

All this time I did not know that their decision affected me as well. But when my father returned, he said Uncle Daulat Ram wanted to send his son away, and they had determined that Ravi and I should leave, too. My father seemed taken up with the idea that he wanted everyone to leave but him, but Mother stubbornly persisted that she would hear none of it, and if Mother remained, Ashok must stay also. Sister Pom was to leave that night for Dehra Dun, and the rest of us were to board the train for Bombay the next day, even though trains were sporadically stopped by the mobs and the passengers robbed and slain.

Despite the dire predictions of all those who learned that we were to cross the border by train, our journey was uninterrupted by the Muslim mobs. But the emotional state of us all made the trip anything but peaceful. An old woman near us kept up a ceaseless stream of invectives and forebodings, and the wailings and outcries of the frightened and lonely and bereaved only served to augment our own sense of loss.

All through the journey, the journey across the hot and dry plains back towards Bombay, I kept thinking about Sohan, who had always treated me as though I were his brother, equal to understanding the shades of his opinions and moods. I kept wishing that the *sangh* boy who had brought me word of Sohan's death the night of our departure had been wrong. But in that train, reality was too much with me.

FIFTEEN

'Hindi, Hindu, Hindustan'

THE drum rolled outside, and the band tuned up to greet the eve of independence, but the spirited music was flat to our ears. For us, on that 15 August, Independence Day meant that we could never return to Lahore.

We had spent two months in Bombay with my father's nephew, Cousin Anand. There was almost nothing for us to do except remain in the house, and since we had no idea how prolonged our stay would be, we could make no plans for the future. In peaceful Bombay, business went on as usual, but when conditions took a turn for the worse in West Punjab, other relatives came to stay in the four-room apartment, until the number swelled to seventeen. In spite of these cramped quarters where we had to sleep on the floor, we were reasonably happy, for regularly streams of letters arrived from Mother, assuring us of the safety of those at home.

In Lahore, she said, things had improved slightly since our departure in May, though the situation in West Punjab had progressively grown worse. But now and again we would detect a note in her letters which revealed that their position was increasingly precarious. It was only a matter of days, she said in one of her later letters, before the massacres which were sweeping the countryside would reach Lahore, but they hoped to get out soon.

Her last letter, written on the third of August, left us with grave concern. My father, as head of the department, was charged with dividing the assets between East and West Punjab. This responsibility, she thought, would delay him beyond the tenth of August, the date by which all Hindu officers and the Hindu police had been told to be across the border.

We knew this would delay them beyond the safety of the present lull, even though the boundary commission had not drawn the exact line of demarcation, and many inhabitants believed that Lahore still might be included in India. Whether awarded to Pakistan or India, however, the fate of Lahore would be the same, for the Muslims would launch another onslaught which would surpass all human conception. Lured by the prospect of becoming wealthy overnight, once the Hindus were ejected, the Muslims would express their resentment in a frenzy of destruction. As in the past, the fact that middle-class Hindus and Sikhs owned most of the property would be used by the Muslim League leaders to give added incentive to the anger of the masses.

Our anxiety was increased when Mother wrote that Chachaji refused to leave Lahore, and that all my father's attempts to dissuade him were meeting with rebuffs. He believed that once the state of Pakistan was formed, normal conditions would resume, and all Hindus would be able to return to their homes. He had entirely regained his confidence during the two months since our departure, and assured himself that he was right after all in believing that ultimately Hindus and Muslims would come to terms. Chachaji had seen every conference betrayed, yet he continued to believe in sanity and to give more credit to human nature than it deserved.

Now as we sat in the apartment on Marine Drive, on the Arabian Sea, we learned that Lahore was ablaze, and the fateful predictions had come true. We tried to call our parents, but the telephone lines had been severed. Indeed, there was no communication even between East and West Punjab. We tried to call at Amritsar, the first city across the border in East Punjab, to check for their arrival, but found that the circuits were overloaded with calls booked days before.

Night after night we had sat up waiting for the telephone to ring or the telegraph messenger to knock. In a fitful doze I dreamed I was back in Lahore and escaping through the steel door only to reach another wall. This waiting in mournful silence with mind filled with happy and tragic memories seemed more painful than any physical torture we might have experienced at the hands of the Muslims.

The glorious music of the triumphant band blared on in martial concert, lifting emotions until people shouted jubilantly and danced to its rhythm while the Army marched with its guns on shoulder and shoes polished. An hour away was independence for the country, but it seemed a hollow celebration. We had seen too much of freedom in Lahore, the freedom to loot and to kill.

The only comfort I could derive from all this was that we still had hope, but I was soon melancholy again when I thought of how many hundreds of thousands were meeting the day without hope, and the words of my father flashed through my mind: 'What will matter in these times is not property, but life.'

We gave no second thoughts to the house or the luxury of having separate rooms and beds to sleep in, though I recalled with grief my loss of friendship with Sohan and Mr Khanna.

But to this melancholy mood was added anger when I thought about the recent utterances of Gandhiji. He was asking Hindus and Sikhs to remain where they were and be strong, and strength to him meant resistance to conversion unto death, stoicism and non-violence even as you saw your daughters abducted, your wife murdered. He was demanding spiritual strength from people tortured beyond endurance.

I knew my repudiation of Gandhi's ideals was a rejection of those I too had held, and had I not been so overwhelmed by personal emotion, I might have reproached myself. Now I felt a slight exhilaration return as I thought that the long cries for action by the suffering non-Muslims in West Punjab had finally been heeded. It took five months of systematic annihilation in West Punjab before the Hindus and Sikhs abandoned their policy of non-violence and fought back. By the end of July, enough refugees had begun drifting in to dramatize vividly the reports which had preceded them. Their harrowing tales and their mere presence moved their previously passive Sikh and Hindu brothers to ruthless retaliation. Eager for revenge, I was happy to read in the papers that Hindus and Sikhs, with the Muslims, had started taking pride in the number each personally had slain. If I had been lucky enough to kill two or three Muslims, I, too, would have boasted with pride of the accomplishment. Gandhiji's ideals were dated.

The fifteenth of August came and went. Now the new India was a day old, and still there was no word from our parents. Then the thick, heavy silence was pierced with the sharp ringing of the telephone. It was our parents. They, with Om and Ashok, had crossed the border, but had not been able to persuade Chachaji to leave Lahore. They had barely escaped, and told us that few if any had been able to get away from the city after the twelfth of August, though many had tried and lost their lives. They had spent the last three nights in Amritsar, as had many other thousands of destitute refugees, and they asked us to come to Delhi to meet them as soon as possible.

Ever since I had started attending R.S.S.S., and had come to know Sohan, I had begun to doubt whether Hindus and Muslims could ever live together amicably as they had in times past. There was always a possibility that another man like Jinnah would start out by making his cause one with Hindus, but would later make a clean break from them, and using religion as his basis, would start once again the circle of religious strife. The whole bloody story would be repeated once more, and it seemed to me at the time that the only way to avoid another tragedy was never to give Muslims the chance to abuse leadership.

Knowing Sohan, brave and vigorous, ready to sacrifice his life in the name of the new Hindu India, had moved me deeply, and his blunt assertions that the work of Gandhiji and other Congress leaders was done had not left me untouched. During those four restless days when we waited for the telephone to ring, I had become increasingly convinced by Sohan's logic. I, too, could then have shouted, 'India for Hindus' – 'Hindi, Hindu, Hindustan.'

Yet now that my fears about my parents had been arrested, I felt more sober thoughts returning, reproaching me for my change of heart. On the one hand I felt that Hindus and Muslims could live side by side, and on the other, that the only way the religious strife could resolve itself was by the formation of a state where Hindus, the majority, ruled.

Disturbed by these contradictory thoughts, I finally went to sister Nimi, who was an ardent supporter of Gandhi. The words of Sohan came back to me, that it was not the non-violence of Gandhi, but the decency of the British Government, which respected his methods, that had led to independence, and I wondered if she agreed with this.

Her response was immediate. 'British people decent? My foot! Was it their decency that made them imprison the leaders who protested against their enslavement? Was it their sense of decency that turned Muslims against Hindus? If Gandhiji had died fasting, even Britishers with all their might could not have ruled India any longer. They let him continue his hunger strike as long as they did simply because they did not realize its effectiveness. They always kept a close eye on Gandhiji so that they might come to the rescue before anything happened to him.'

'Granting that's so, couldn't it be said that Gandhiji has done his work? He's too idealistic to face the Muslim threat. You and I have seen their orgy in the name of religion.'

'But you can't condemn all Muslims for the work of their leaders. What would you have us do? Wipe out all Muslims? That would mean we Hindus would launch an orgy as bad as the Muslims'.'

'No, but you could deny them a share in the Indian Government. Hindus have no voice in the Pakistan Government, so why should the Muslims have any in India? You would also rule out the possibility of another leader like Jinnah.'

'Just the opposite might happen,' sister Nimi replied. 'You can't ever subjugate a race of people. Eventually they would rebel, and under a leader probably much more ruthless than Jinnah. Besides, when you subjugate Muslims, you are enslaving some of your own kind. No. Gandhiji's work is far from done. There are too many people like you who are beginning to waver, and are being more emotional than reasonable. Unless we are careful we shall prove the British right, that India is too unstable to rule herself.'

'Do you think that we should not even avenge some of the things that happened in Pakistan? What do you plan to do with the millions of refugees that come across the border? If no Muslims leave, they certainly won't have any place to go.'

'If you let them start on revenge, where would you ever stop? Before you knew it these fanatics would have carried the war all over India, and the result would be the same, for the Hindu nationalists who demand India for Hindus would replace the more sober leadership in the Congress Party. If there ever was a need for non-violence, it is now.'

'Buddha taught the same non-violence and you see what happened to India. The Muslims conquered her and ruled her until the British came. Why couldn't it happen again?'

'By that argument, what has ever happened when people used violence? Wars have been one of the chief causes for the decline of many a nation. Non-violence has never been given a try. It alone will rescue the world.

'The Muslims have become too much a part of us. Their traditions have become ours, and I dare say that an Indian Muslim bears little resemblance to the Muslims of other countries. He has an Indian character which marks him as our brother, and part of our culture.'

'Tell me, sister Nimi, honestly, have you always thought like this? Haven't you ever doubted your faith in one united India?'

She was quiet, and did not answer immediately. 'I sometimes feel very bitter about losing everything we ever had, and more than that, about the thousands of innocent people who were killed. My faith in non-violence —'

She was quiet, and did not answer immediately. 'I sometimes us to trust Shekh Sahib, if she, idealistic as she was, could waver, what about the rest of us?

'We must derive strength,' she said, 'from Gandhiji. He suffers most of all.'

SIXTEEN

Refugees

A WEEK or two after our parents' call, we returned from Bombay to Delhi. The same atmosphere which had prevailed in Lahore during the March and May days seemed to have gripped Delhi, too. During our two-week stay there, the city was convulsed with outrages patterned after the too-successful methods of West Punjab, and we were once again caught up in a climate of nervous tension and anxiety.

While in Delhi, we learned that all the Mehta and Mehra families had escaped from Lahore without casualty. Even Chachaji, who had been the last to leave Lahore, had miraculously reached Delhi. We heard, however, that our distant relatives in Sheikhupura district had not been so fortunate; they had met death at the hands of the Muslims.

Almost every one of those who escaped from Lahore came without their possessions, and those who had once enjoyed large homes now lived in one room. We were staying with one of our uncles in Delhi, where thirty people were crammed into only four rooms.

Meanwhile my father had been asked to proceed immediately to Simla, the capital of East Punjab, so our parents did not meet us at Delhi. At last, when it was considered relatively safe, we left our uncle's house and went to Simla.

Our parents had not been able to bring anything with them from Lahore, and the small official house which was allotted to us stayed unfurnished for nearly three months. The cold nights of this hill station forced us all to stay in, wrapped in our bedclothes, for at the time we could not get fuel. Even during the daytime, we scarcely left home, for we had only summer clothes.

My father was now posted as a director, and had taken over the whole Public Health Department in East Punjab. He spent

some time in Simla, grappling with the dimensionless problems which had come into being as more and more refugees
poured across the border in convoys miles long, each bearing
the marks of the tragedy in his family, and without an *anna* or
a promise of shelter ahead. By December 1947, three months
after the independence, no less than four million people had
been evacuated from what was now Pakistan.

A considerable part of Father's work, consequently, was done
in the plains, where the refugee camps spread miles square. The
Hindu and Sikh retaliation was still continuing with great
ferocity, and so it was not considered safe for my sisters to leave
Simla. I was allowed, however, to accompany my father a few
times. We travelled with a police escort and stopped at various
refugee camps, where he made detailed inspections in order to
plan further attacks on the problems of sanitation and epidemic
diseases. Day in and day out, powdered milk, packaged foods
and vaccines were flown or brought to these camps. All the
services co-operated to meet this desperate problem of providing
for and rehabilitating these refugees.

I remember my first impression of a refugee camp. It was a
huge, sprawling encampment near Ambala, and we reached
there in the early part of the afternoon. Two of my father's
assistants joined us there, and we began the tour. While my
father conversed with the inspectors and other health officers,
I sensed the appalling surroundings; if there was ever a pathetic
sight I imagined this was it.

The foul smell of human filth and the odour of the sick and
dying were overpowering. Flies droned and crawled; children
begged for food and mothers tried to distract them from their
hunger. Medical attendants followed the flies and jabbed needles
into the arms of children too weary to wince or cry, then inoculated women and men. The men who had once worked their
own land, ploughed and sowed through long days, and pro-
visioned their families for longer winters, now sat idle, so apathetic that we stumbled across them and still they did not move.

Everywhere one turned there were stories of unbelievable
atrocities. Even if margin were allowed for refugees' exaggera-

ting their own misfortunes, their treatment had been hideous.
Some talked more readily than others, but many of them were
too dazed to speak. As one of the inspectors was inoculating,
we approached him. My father, pressing my hand, said quietly
that the man being inoculated had no hands.

As the inspector rapidly moved away to another refugee, I
stood by the man and tried to speak to him. From his first few
softly spoken words, I gathered that he was a Sikh, and like all
Sikhs, had been marked by his long hair and beard as sure prey
for the Muslims. He asked, 'Where did it happen to you?' –
my blindness had often been mistaken by the refugees as one
more inhuman act of the Muslims.

'We lived in Lahore,' I answered, 'but it wasn't the Muslims.'
There was a long pause. 'Your hands – how did that happen?'

'In a *gurudwara*. We expected them. We had been sleeping
there for four nights. The fifth night they came. They told us
to come out and they wouldn't make trouble. "Become Muslims," they said, "and return to your homes." But we would
never change our faith.'

I had heard of some Hindu villages where the villagers had
embraced Islam. Even their daughters had been forcibly married to Muslim hooligans. But most never considered changing
their faith, even though it meant losing all their possessions and
seeing their families tortured and slain.

'They besieged the *gurudwara* for two nights and a day. Our
ammunition ran out the first night. Our supplies were gone,
too.'

From there the story was no different from that of a hundred
other villages where the temple had been forced by the mob.
The men had begun killing their own women to save them from
torture and rape.

This Sikh was able to kill his daughter, but had hesitated a
moment and was overpowered before he could put his wife to
death. He resisted, and thought he had killed one Muslim before they hacked off his hands, then slashed his ears. They would
have tortured him to death, but through some impossible

strength born of rage, he broke from their hands to follow the men who were carrying his wife. In the thick of the mob he had lost them, but escaped himself. He had hidden for a week without food, until a lorry of Sikh police had carried him to the convoy.

But all refugees were not so stunned as this Sikh. Their misery had made them vow to avenge the deaths of their loved ones. Whenever you talked to them about non-violence and Gandhi, their response was immediate.

'Gandhiji did not see his daughter raped.'

'Gandhiji didn't lose his wife.'

Some went even further, accusing him of cowardice, and saying that he was afraid to come to Punjab. But only one prayer meeting with Gandhiji in the Delhi refugee camps was enough to convince one that he suffered even more than those who had experienced violence and bloodshed first-hand, and that his world was above cowardice or consideration of self.

The heavy snow had not yet begun to fall, to fill the streets and shut each family up around the hearth for the long Simla winter. By now, in early December, we began to have a small fire, since the fireplace provided our sole warmth against the frosts and winds that chilled the hill station. We clustered around it on comfortable chairs which the government finally provided. Mother knitted, my sisters read, even Ashok was busy rattling his crayons a little as he worked over a colour book. I alone was doing nothing.

This routine of idleness had never preyed so heavily on my mind as it did now. Before, in 'Pindi, there had been spacious compounds, the friendship of Saran, chickens and fish to distract me from the continuous reminder that I was doing nothing. Then, too, in 'Pindi the thought that one day I would return to school, perhaps go to America with all our family packed into a lorry, had been there to sustain me in my idle moments. Now even that was in the past.

In less than three years the government's plan of compulsory retirement at fifty-five would force my father to give up his job, our government home, and all the privileges of service. As we had lost all our property and belongings in Lahore, every bit of his present salary had to be saved to make provision for this retirement. We no longer spoke of America.

While in 'Pindi and Lahore, at least a music teacher had been engaged to take up some slack in the time, here in Simla even that could not be done. All my musical instruments, *tabla, tambura, sitar* and harmonium had been left behind, and no teacher here could add to my progress. The few Braille books I had started collecting in Lahore on my return to school had been lost to Pakistan also. Even my electric transformers and carpentry tools were gone.

Day after day for two months I passed the time in this state of inaction, each day contributing to the depression of the next. I longed for something, anything, to do, but in this forsaken hill station there was no distraction. I was now approaching my fourteenth birthday. Brother Om at the age of fourteen had started attending college. I had had, altogether, three years of school, a little over two and a half of which had been spent in Bombay when I was very young.

One day I had asked sister Nimi if she might not read to me from a book, as Mr Khanna had suggested; but she did all her reading in English, and being educated in a convent, had not even learned to read Hindi. This from the very outset barred me from any pleasure I might have derived from reading, for my English vocabulary was comparable to that of a nine-year-old Indian child attending school.

There was as yet no standard Hindi Braille, and everything for the use of the blind was written in English. I had written to the National Institute for the Blind in England for some books so that I could start studying English on my own, but they had not yet arrived. Besides, I had not been able to learn grade-two Braille, in which most good writing was transcribed.

Even though I said nothing about my state of mind to my parents, it was too obvious to go unnoticed. They saw me sitting continually in one chair at the end of the semi-circle, occasionally interrupted by Ashok to help him with his Meccano set, to tighten a screw or bend a strip for his home-made windmill. But they, like myself, refrained from discussing what seemed hopeless.

One evening while we sat as usual in the drawing-room, Father, who had been away in the plains, returned unexpectedly with welcome news for me. Through Lady Mountbatten (with whom he was looking after the refugee camps and convoys) he had come to know Sir Clutha Mackenzie, a totally blind Englishman who was directing St Dunstan's Hostel for the war-blinded in Dehra Dun. He was the first highly educated blind person that my father had ever met, and he had been much impressed by his learning and abilities.

Father had talked to him about me, and asked if I might be admitted to St Dunstan's, as that was considered the best training centre for the blind in India. Sir Clutha Mackenzie considered this most improbable, as no civilian had ever been admitted to this hostel for the war-blinded.

My father had insisted upon my at least meeting him, if for no other reason than that he would be an inspiration. So when he returned to the plains, I accompanied him and was introduced to Sir Clutha. While I could not understand all he said in English, I did converse with him, my father prompting. Though I told very little of my state of mind, it seemed to me he comprehended amazingly well how I felt. He promised to take up my case with the government.

Within a week's time I was told that a special exception had been made, and I could attend morning classes in Braille and typing at St Dunstan's. I had not been separated from my family since the time I had spent in Bombay, and my mother remarked that I seemed too happy to leave them.

St Dunstan's was so much of a contrast from Dadar and Emerson schools that at first I felt completely lost. It was a beautiful place which had once been a residence for the bodyguard force of the English governor-general, and like most army encampments, was located at the outskirts of the city. Since those who lose their sight late in life have a difficult time with mobility, long wires were stretched across the sprawling campus from barracks to barracks, the buildings that were now dormitories and classrooms.

The classroom atmosphere was as wholesome as that of the huge compound with its scores of lichee trees. There were no boys standing at the door of a class swinging a fan, or instructors with wet canes. I came in contact with only two teachers, Mr Cameron, the typing instructor, and Mr Advani, who taught Braille, both of whom were blind.

I remember the first day I walked into typing class. Mr Cameron greeted me. He was an Anglo-Saxon and spoke with a strong Scottish accent. His handshake was nervous but hearty. He introduced me to the only other student then in the classroom. I remember my shock at putting my hand forward and meeting a steel hook. The man had lost both his arms at the elbows. He used this steel hook to type, and I believe his speed was twenty or twenty-five words a minute. Later on as I grew to know him better, I often unscrewed his steel hook to insert other instruments, such as a knife or fork.

There was an unexpected advantage in being taught by Mr Cameron. He could only speak English, and since I spent one hour with him alone, he had ample time to tutor me in that language as well as teach me typing. Mr Advani taught me grade-two Braille, the more complex Braille which includes contractions and abbreviations. I became quite adept and was even chosen as one of the students to read when Lady Mountbatten visited the school.

My stay in Dehra Dun was not only fruitful but happy. I was allowed to take out Braille books and magazines from their small library, and for the first time I was able to do some reading. While I missed my family, I did value my independence and my serious studies which for the first time could be considered as academic progress.

I had almost no friends there, for all the students were beyond my age, full-grown men, the majority of whom had been recently blinded in the Second World War. They were not well adjusted to their blindness, and it was considered best that I come in close contact with them as little as possible. Indeed, if it had not been for Kakaji and sister Pom, who lived in Dehra Dun, or the Braille books which occupied my time, I would have been quite homesick.

I stayed at St Dunstan's Hostel only eight months, for Captain Mortimer, who had taken command from Sir Clutha Mackenzie, wrote to my father in September 1948, telling him that he felt I had learned all St Dunstan's had to offer and that I should now pursue the possibility of higher education. He added that I had done well, on occasion substituting for the Braille master, but that however much they welcomed me 'the company of resentful and discouraged servicemen was not good for an impressionable young boy'. He felt that I, who did not regard my blindness as a visitation of the gods, was ready for the next step. Since India could offer me nothing more in the way of education, 'next step' meant the West – a step in a sense made easier for me by the inspiring examples of Mr Cameron and Sir Clutha Mackenzie.

On a Sunday morning in the month of October 1948, my father and I left our cottage in Simla for Clarke's Hotel. We had started out early so that we might take a leisurely walk, and so that I might have ample time to relax from my excitement.

On our way we talked about the forthcoming interview with Mr Baldwin, a representative of a large American corporation.

'Americans generally are easy-going people. They're understanding and even if you make a mistake it won't matter. Just don't be nervous.'

Yet I was nervous. All night I had tossed in my bed, thinking about the next day with fear and excitement. So much depended on this interview, for Mr Baldwin had promised to try to make some arrangements through his company for financial assistance, as his corporation was considering awarding scholarships to Indian students in America, in recognition of its expanding business in new India.

'Suppose,' my father continued, 'suppose Mr Baldwin is not impressed. It doesn't matter. Remember, I am always there. We'll manage somehow.'

'I don't want it to be that way,' I answered him. 'You have too many responsibilities.'

'But if my children aren't my responsibility, what is? From the very day you lost your sight I set my heart on giving you as good an education, or a better one, as the rest of my children. You have waited a long time.'

'Yes, but you had no idea about Pakistan and all its consequences.'

'Remember your grandfather's circumstances. No man in his position could have dreamed of sending his children to England. Yet he did. The sacrifices I made to send you children to school are nothing compared to his. I tell you, son, education is in our blood.'

That phrase from his diary, 'I would sell my soul to give Ved an education,' came back to me, and I was moved to tears.

We finally reached Clarke's Hotel, and my father sent his card up to Mr Baldwin's room before we climbed the stairs ourselves.

'Is this the young fellow,' Mr Baldwin began, taking my hand, 'that you talked about, Doctor?'

'This is he, sir.'

'Come on, take a seat, son,' and he led me to a chair.

I had not met many Americans, for most of my father's friends before independence had been British. The mere sound of a British accent, and English spoken in that crisp, firm way, had delighted me.

Mr Baldwin, however, spoke fast, less deliberately, and with a nasal twang to his voice. At first I was taken aback, for I could not understand what he was saying, but his friendliness put me at ease. After chatting with my father for a while, he came to me and stood behind my chair.

'I understand you want to go to America.'

I nodded.

'You know that's a long way from your home.'

He asked me to sketch what education I had received in India. I was ashamed to tell him that altogether my studies had occupied less than four years. Hearing my answers, he was silent, and I sensed his disappointment.

'You have a *Reader's Digest* there,' he finally began. 'Would you read an article for me?' His easy-going manner had become brisk and businesslike. He searched through his desk and found a printed copy of the same month.

I had rehearsed one article and had learned the meaning of the words, hoping that he would ask me to read an article of my choice. But to my dismay and great nervousness, he said:

'There's a good article here about American youth and the effect of comic books. I think you'll find that interesting. Can you find it here?'

With my unsteady fingers I ran through the contents once without success, and then again, this time more slowly, but I could hardly recognize the words beneath my fingers. At last I found it. All this time he had remained behind the chair and I felt very uneasy, thinking he must be watching my trembling fingers. As I turned to that article, I pressed my fingers down on the dots, trying to steady them, and held my arms close to my sides. At the very first sentence I stumbled, but neither my father nor he came to my rescue. When I came to words like 'manifested,' 'juvenile,' 'delinquency,' I could hardly pronounce them, let alone understand their meaning. Rather than reading fluently, with understanding, I isolated words from their sentences, paying no heed to punctuation. He stopped me at one place and asked if I understood what a particular sentence meant. I did not.

Then a typewriter was brought in, and he started dictating to me from the same article. If I could only steady my fingers, I thought. I typed the first sentence using the third row instead of the middle one as the home row. I never did get my bearings after that. I typed and back-spaced, then typed over again. By the end of forty-five minutes the interview was over, and I knew I had failed miserably.

My head was heavy from the sleepless night before, and I did not follow all the exchanges between my father and Mr

Baldwin, but I did understand one sentence which dashed all my hopes and plunged me into despair.

'I want to be frank, Doctor. I think this boy should stay here.'

Then he went on to say that my language handicap and the very mediocre quality of my educational foundation would stand me in poor stead when I competed with students who had been at school since the age of six.

'But I'll write to a friend in my company back home, acquaint him with your unusual circumstances, and try to find out what can be done.'

With this sentence, which was added more as a courtesy than a guarantee that some future arrangements would be made, my father and I left.

As we descended the stairs, I experienced a keen sense of frustration. Students who had been in school since they were six years old, he had said. They would be the ones I would compete against. What was my education as compared with theirs? I knew almost nothing about arithmetic. My English, though considerably improved during my stay at St Dunstan's, was poor. My experience in Braille reading was slight. All the talking of Mr Khanna about the vagueness of my ambitions for education had not disconcerted me as much as this one interview.

'Success,' my father was saying, 'depends on determination and perseverance, and disappointments should strengthen rather than shake them. I will stand behind you, and you will go to England or America even if you have no financial assistance, or as far as that goes, no admission. Don't forget, child, that I myself went to England without promise of admission. Once you are there, they won't send you back.'

His words were not without effect. His voice betrayed no sign of disappointment, and he spoke as confidently as he always had. As I walked beside him, holding his large surgeon's hand, I revived a bit. There was something contagious about his confidence, and in spite of all my reservations about my own

inadequacy to pursue education abroad, and the depressing interview just concluded, I vowed not to give up hope. I decided to
open correspondence with the educational authorities abroad
and redouble my efforts to study there.

In my desperation I also typed out a long letter to Pandit
Nehru. I wrote to him about our losses in Pakistan, about my
search for education, and about my growing frustration. I begged his help and guidance. I gave the letter to one of my father's
clerks, to correct for spelling mistakes and to mail.

'What is this ambition of yours, sahib?' he asked. 'Why do
you want to leave home and go to places where no one will take
care of you? You can get all the education you need here, by
going to schools for the seeing children.'

I felt too discouraged to tell him that I had tried this, too.
In the seven schools I approached I was greeted by compassionate teachers who, rather than having faith in the capabilities of
the blind, pitied them. They seemed to lack the gift of imagination to replace their complete inexperience in handling blind
students, and they seemed fearful that we would disrupt the
routine of their classes.

'Please mail this letter,' I said, drawing myself up. 'Register
it. I want to see the receipt.'

I got the receipt and two weeks later a perfunctory acknow-
ledgement from the Ministry of Education. They could do nothing.

SEVENTEEN

'We all agree . . .'

'WE both agree that it would be a mistake to bring your son over to England during the most formative years of his life. We have had two Indian students at our secondary school for blind boys in Worcester and both of them on their return have found themselves ill adjusted to Indian life, and out of touch with the interests of their people.'

'. . . bringing these boys to England appears not altogether to be doing them a kindness.'

'. . . it is essential that he should not be too early subjected to Western influence.'

These were answers given by education authorities in Europe and the United States to letters seeking my admission to a school of higher education. They were echoed with monotonous exactitude until one might have thought they were written with one pen.

There was yet another question they asked, for which neither my father nor I had an answer. What does he want to do with his education; does he want to specialize in anything? The only reply approaching a satisfactory answer that we could give them was perhaps learning Western music. Ever since I had left Dadar I had been tutored in Indian music, in which direction I had shown considerable talent. Since my sisters' music teacher in Lahore, Master Kohli, was, although blind, one of the most successful musicians in Punjab, it was thought this would be a good means of livelihood for me.

This possibility had gained weight with my father when he noticed that songs coloured with Western touches which were composed for the film industry were received with enthusiastic applause by Indian audiences. He thought I might well be a pioneer in improving Indian music, which is almost solely melody, by bringing about a fusion of Eastern melody and Western harmony.

I had reservations about pursuing this career. I knew nothing about Western music, and I might not be at all talented by Western standards. So I was honest in admitting to the Western authorities that I had not the slightest notion as to what type of education I wanted or for what purpose. Needless to say, this did not improve my chances of enlisting their support. I longed for a good, solid academic education equal to the one my sisters and brother were receiving. If I did not know what I should do with it, it was simply because I was young and because very few blind people in India had ever possessed it.

When I had first decided to start seeking admission to one of the institutions in the West, the first practical hurdle was where to begin, whom to approach. Perkins was the only institution of which I had previously heard, so my first letter was written to them. Next I looked through the fly-leaves of my Braille books for addresses of publishers, for I had been told at St. Dunstan's that these institutions not only published but took an active part in promoting education for the blind.

So I wrote to the National Institute for the Blind in London and the American Printing House in Louisville, Kentucky. It was to these letters that I received answers like those quoted above. Thereafter, any attempt to dissuade them only increased their conviction that I should not leave India.

I searched feverishly for more addresses in my Braille books and magazines. I found only two others, one in Edinburgh and one in Paris. The one in Edinburgh turned out to be an asylum and referred me back to the National Institute. In my letter to Paris I said that my lasting desire was to study in France, though I knew not a word of that language, which they were quick to point out. So I reached a dead end until another idea occurred to me.

I wrote to the American Printing House for the Blind asking them to send me a list of the literature published so that I might select some more magazines to read. This list I knew would include the addresses of various schools in the United States which had their Braille newspapers published at the Printing House. On its arrival, indiscriminately I hammered out letters to almost every place listed, claiming that their school alone would meet my need. Within two months I had written to thirty people and awaited expectantly their answers. I made the postman promise to deliver our mail first, and each time I would take the letters to sister Nimi with my hands trembling. She would open and read them to herself quickly, and the silence which followed made me understand that one more unfavourable reply had come. At first she tried to console me by saying that all was not over yet, but by and by she gave up and began to cry; and I would be the one to keep a brave face in her presence, only to return to my room and break down.

This universal opinion of the authorities should have convinced anyone, but it did not change our course much. Even if I were too subjective, too consumed by my own ambition and could not appreciate their argument, my father, objective as he was, should have encouraged me to abandon for the present my desire to go. But he did the opposite. He himself wrote to many authorities entreating them to reconsider.

I tried to occupy the empty, anxious days and in some measure check my growing disappointment by reading whatever Braille material I could get my hands on, from St Dunstan's or England or America. If my correspondence was indiscriminate, my reading was no better directed. I read religious magazines like the *Braille Baptist* and the *Discovery*, various digests and some fiction. Thus I had the consolation of not resuming my fireside seat at the end of the semi-circle with empty hands.

Three months of uninterrupted waiting and disappointment seemed finally approaching an end, for my addresses were being exhausted. About then, Cousin Anand, under whose protection we had spent the months after leaving Lahore, visited us.

Though he was my father's nephew, to us he had been like a brother. My father had played an important role in helping him receive his education. He had just returned from America and I felt a keen sense of satisfaction in talking to someone who had recently been to a place where I so longed to go. It was the same type of satisfaction, sweet melancholy, which I used to experience sitting by the radio listening to (and not always understanding) a broadcast in English from the B.B.C., Australia, or India.

One day the topic of my going to America came up, and my father asked him his opinion.

'You want my honest opinion?' he began.

'Yes.'

'I don't think he ought to go. Supposing he did get all the education he wants. What will he do with it? You know yourself how many young people there are in this country today with B.A.s and M.A.s who can't get a job. And they can see.

'The long absence from his own people at this age would be most harmful. Their world, their way of life, is very different. Conflicting cultural backgrounds will make him a misfit. He will belong neither here nor there. I think he would be happier if he stayed in India, got what little education he could, and took up music more seriously. He will be more than self-supporting, derive satisfaction from his music, and be close to all of us so that we can give him help when he needs it.'

My heart sank. I knew how much my father respected Cousin Anand's opinion. What he said seemed so sensible and true. All the letters agreed. He had just returned from America, and even visited the American Printing House. I knew his opinion was held by almost all our relatives, but they were not as candid, knowing my wilfulness and my father's determination. All the workers in the field of education for the blind gave the same arguments.

Yet there was one thing. He spoke of happiness. At night when I lay in bed I had often wondered about it. Could I ever be happy just teaching music like Panditji? Could I bear to abandon for ever my desire to seek further learning? Perhaps if I had not been brought up in a family where everyone talked of nothing but education, making me feel always apart from them, and perhaps if there had been no talk of going West for me, I would probably have been happy being a music teacher like Master Kohli.

As I had expected, the next day my father opened the subject with me when we were alone.

'You know,' he said, 'what little money I've saved for you can be used any way you wish. You could continue to study Indian music and still have enough left over perhaps to open a small shop. There is no doubt in my mind that this way you will be self-supporting and independent.

'Besides, as Cousin Anand says, you would be close to all of us. Leaving home, son, is no easy matter. I did it in my younger days, and it was hard enough. In your case it would be even harder.

'Going West is, at best, a most hazardous undertaking. We do not know how your small education compares with that of other boys there. You may have to start from the fifth or sixth grade, and the longest I could support you would be three to four years, perhaps another year if we borrowed money. But you wouldn't have even finished high school by then. Meanwhile all the money would be gone, and you would not be able to pursue your Indian music. Nor would I have anything left for you to open a shop. If Pakistan hadn't happened I could have given you as much education as you might have wished, but now it's quite different. Beyond anything else, there can be nothing more miserable than to be a misfit in your own home and country.'

I remembered the refugee camps. The image of the handless refugee with his ear slashed passed across my mind. So many had lost so much! What was my ambition compared to the land and lives sacrificed to the birth of Pakistan?

'I can reconcile myself,' I said swallowing hard, 'to anything.'

Father put his hand on my shoulder. 'Something may work out, but right now it looks pretty hopeless,' he said.

'Can I still go on writing to foreign schools, just on the chance of some encouragement?' I asked.

'Of course,' he said.

'I promise, Daddyji,' I said, 'I will try to learn to be happy here.'

EIGHTEEN

'Yes'

It was seven in the morning, and I was awakened by brother Om, who was leaning over my bed looking through the frosty window. Soon my sisters joined him in searching the sky for the balloon which would indicate safe skating.

'I suppose it didn't freeze last night,' Umi said in a disappointed voice.

'There!' brother Om shouted, and there were exclamations of pleasure as they caught sight of the signal.

They left my room, the partitioned-off end of our sun porch. Brother Om could not find his skates, so I got up to help him. The house was bitterly cold, and some icy air came in through the cracks around the window. At last all paraphernalia were collected and everyone dressed in heavy coats and left the house.

Almost every day now the weather was clear and cold enough to freeze the ice, and my sisters and brother Om spent three hours in the morning, three in the evening ice skating. I alone could not take part in this treat of the Simla hill station. At first they took me to the rink, and I stood at the edge listening to the blaring music and shouts of the skaters. But I had put a stop to that. I preferred staying home to standing alone at the edge with now and then someone skating up to talk to me.

I stood for a while now, shivering at the open door, listening to the voices fade as they hurried up the hill towards the ice-skating rink. Finally I shut the door and returned to bed – the only place where I could keep warm – but I could not go to sleep again. With everyone gone and Mother and Ashok not up yet, the house seemed dreary indeed.

I tried to pick up my Braille book to read, but my fingers were stiff with cold and I gave up. For almost two hours I lay there, thinking what school to write next.

I had missed several schools on the list, most of them in the southern part of the United States. As I had not even heard the names of the states they were located in, I felt no particular desire to go there. I wanted to go to Boston, New York, Chicago or San Francisco. For me, that was the United States. Nevertheless I decided to try them all.

I wrote a letter to Arkansas School for the Blind, presenting my meagre qualifications as impressively as I could.

Simla.
31st January, 1949.

To
   The Manager,
     Arkansas School for the Blind,
      Little Rock,
       Ark.
Dear Sir,
   Unfortunately I am a Blind boy of nearly 15 years of age. I beg to state that I would like to come over to America for my further studies, I know the following subjects.
   English.
   Mathematics.
I can read Braille and can write Braille and I know sighted Typing with touch system. I know contraction and abrivations. I have colified from the following Instituation :—
   1. Dadar Blind School fr the Blind.
   2. Emerson Instituation for the Blind.
Lahore Pakistan.
   3. St Dunstan's for the War Blinded. Dehra dun.
India.

I have been studying in Dadar Blind School Bombay for nearly four years. I learnt Braille reading and Writing and English. I was sent there by my father when I was only five and a half. I got Blind when I was Four Years old, I lost eyesight with Manigitis. I studied in Emerson Instituation For the Blind Lahore for one year, where XXI learnt only AXXMathematics. And little bit of my Country Language. Then I was sent over to St Dunstan's for the War Blinded. As this Instituation was only ment for War Blind Soldiers then even as I was Civilian I had to come across many difficulties before I could get myself admitted in St. Dunstan's. I was taken there as a extra ordinary case. I stayed there for only one year but I must CX confess that I made very good progress in St. Dunstan's. I stayed in St. Dunstan's Hostel for eight months and rest with my relation. I am herewith enclosing a copy of a Certificate from St. Dunstan's from which I think that you will be able to judge that what is my position at present. St Dunstan's is the biggest Instituation going in India. And there is no more scope in India for my studies as I have gained from St. Dunstan's what they could teach me. However, I shall feel obliged if you could send me your Application Form & Particulars. Anyhow I would like to possess your form & Particulars even if you do not think or if such question arises that with which you would like to know some information. As this matter has been already been extremely delayed I won't like the matter to be more delayed. I am very sure that you will help me in this matter. I am typing this letter myself. The typing and Braille gr 2 was taught me in st Dunstan's My Father won't mind spending any thing as far I can be admitted in your School. I would like to completeX your full course. I am herewith enclosing a Picture of mine I hope you will appreciate it. Do you have university Examination?

I do hope to get a reply in affirmative.

An early reply is requested.

Thanking you.

Yours faithfully,
S/O Dr. A. R. Mehta,
Deputy Diector of Health services,
Erneston, (Upper Flat),
Simla, East,
East Punjab.
(India).

I wrote the letter with no expectation that this school would respond more favourably than any other. Then, in the last week of February, I received a letter from them, and as usual took it to sister Nimi to read.

February 16, 1949

Mr. V. P. Mehta
c/o Dr A. R. Mehta
Deputy Director of Health Services
Erneston,
Simla—E.
East Punjab, India

Dear Mr. Mehta:

I have your letter of January 31, in which you state you would like to attend the Arkansas School for the Blind.

In reply, I will say that we shall be happy to have you if details can be arranged. By this I mean, entrance into the United States, which I presume can be arranged on a student basis, financial details, length of time you will want to stay, course, or courses you will want to pursue and perhaps other details.

The usual fee charged for out of state pupils is $600.00 per school year of nine months. I am not sure that $600.00 would be the fee charged you, but certainly no more than that.

We offer an academic course which prepares you for University entrance. This consists of the usual courses offered in most American public schools. In addition we offer broad courses in music, many vocations and athletics.

I am not enclosing an application form, but will send one later if you are still interested. We are sending you a Braille copy of the Arkansas Braille News so that you may read for yourself something of our educational programme here.

May we hear from you again, if you are still interested in our school.

Sincerely yours,
J. M. Woolly, Superintendent

JMW/lh

I was ecstatic. I could scarcely believe sister Nimi's voice. *They would be happy to have me.*

She read it fast and then re-read it. There was no doubt of its contents. Had it not been that every letter before this had refused me, perhaps I would have run to my mother and cried jubilantly that finally I was going to America, and asked her blessings. But disappointment after disappointment had made me wary.

'Tell me something about the school,' she said.

'I don't know anything about it.' There was a pause, a pause long enough to sober me.

'I think you better keep this letter and show it only to Dad-dyji,' she said in an expressionless voice.

So it was that in the evening, before handing the letter to my father, I told him, 'I know absolutely nothing about the school.' Heretofore I had not taken any letter to him that was not written by a great and famous school like Perkins, or Worcester College, or a printing house like the National Institute. All my other correspondence with less known schools I had considered too unimportant to trouble him with. The contents of those letters, which indeed varied little from one to the next, remained between sister Nimi and myself.

'That's encouraging, all right,' he began. He said it with perfect composure, with no sign of any particular feelings.

I sensed the same hesitations that I had imagined he would feel at sending me to a school ten thousand miles away which, for all we knew, might be no more than two classrooms.

'It could, you know,' he said, 'be a school for Negroes. Anyway, I shall follow this lead through and write to Mr Woolly, but I warn you in advance not to bank too much on this.'

For three more weeks, a childish but quiet hope lingered on, and I fancied, sometimes, that maybe all was not over. As March came and passed, however, and then April, I resolved to forget about it completely, for no word had come from Mr Woolly, nor indeed had the *Arkansas Braille News* arrived.

Then finally late in April, I received the *Braille News*. I started reading it more as a chore than with any great expectation; but as I read on and learned of their social-adjustment programme which made blind people independent, able to go about the streets themselves, and read something about their curriculum, my hope was aroused, though it was a cautious hope, for I did not wish to be disappointed again. I waited in a somewhat expectant mood until the middle of May, when my father brought home a letter informing him that I was admitted at Arkansas School for the Blind.

'Are you going to send me there?'

'That depends. Anyway, this letter can be used to get you a visa and dollars. After you are once in the United States, if you find that Arkansas School is not suited to you, you can always change.'

I could tell by his warm voice, in spite of its caution that I might never really attend Arkansas School, that he was happy for me. Yet I felt a certain remorse, for I was going to America over the protest of all educational authorities, and against the opinion of all my relatives. Suppose I had been wrong all this time and I were to fail, what then? Would I be able to bear the disappointment?

Such was the paradox of my reaction that I could see nothing but utter disaster ahead. Perhaps I had waited so long it seemed an anti-climax. I wanted to discuss these anxieties with someone, someone who could understand all my contradictory sensations. My father was the one person who had seen what my struggle meant to me, and when he told me that he had decided to take his accumulated leave before retirement and journey with me as far as Britain, where he had some special business, and perhaps as far as America if dollars could be obtained, I felt very much relieved. During the long sea voyage I would be able to discuss my fears with him and seek his guidance.

With this security in mind, I gave myself over to the enthusiastic preparations of the family, Mother in particular. The state of my clothes, always her preoccupation and my annoyance, was now to be remedied, for she could at last convince me to adopt her standards. All my sisters fell into a fever of knitting, as each was determined to present me with a sweater before I left; sister Nimi wanted to take me to a record shop where I could choose music to remind me of home. Ashok began to paint me a picture.

The confusion and excitement left me in complete indecision as to where to begin. But that problem was soon settled. Preparation went on, but I lay in bed, suffering from the effects of half a dozen inoculations.

One day, when all the arrangements for my father and me to sail together for England had been made, passports and visas secured, Father returned home to say that his leave had been cancelled. He had been promoted to Deputy Director General of Health Services in the Federal Government and had been asked to stay on for another year, because he was 'indispensable'.

He said, 'My first duty is to the nation, then to my family.' He added in the same breath, however, 'It isn't all altruism. If you are going to America, I must continue earning. If you can wait another year, I will take you. Otherwise you will have to go alone. It is all up to you.'

'I will go alone now,' I returned, and for all my eagerness, the word 'alone' jarred.

My father took me at my word, and since ship companies would not take me on by myself, it took as much money as two sea passages to get me accommodations on the plane. Through one of our relatives we heard that a certain *pandit* preferred the date of 14 August for my departure to any other, and I, being indifferent, agreed to go then, although I was sorry to miss, on the day following, the celebration of the second anniversary of India's independence.

One important detail still remained to be settled. The *pandit*'s decision was going to put me in the United States a month before the opening of my school. What was I to do in that time? I wanted, of course, to see the country and meet people, but going alone with meagre command of the English language and without an introduction to a single American hardly seemed feasible. I began to feel frightened. Father encouraged me.

'You can take a taxi to a small hotel in New York and you will meet lots of people right away, because America is the friendliest country in the world. Even the taxi driver will become your friend.'

Despite the comforting words, I knew he was really worried about me. He wrote to one of his old friends in the United States who lived in Ohio, asking if he knew any family in New York who could take me on as a paying guest. The friend responded by saying that a distant relative of his in New York had married a blind musician and that he had talked to the DeFrancos, who would be glad to have me as a paying guest for fifteen dollars a week. Everything was perfect.

My father's new job required a move to New Delhi, so the preparations for my departure were interrupted while we packed our meagre belongings.

I did not really feel I was going until three days before my flight, when I had an interview with Pandit Nehru. I was the first blind boy, it seemed, who had ever left home to go to America. Panditji therefore wanted to see me.

It was a hot and sultry August day in New Delhi, and I felt uncomfortable in my new long pants and oversized coat. My interview with Pandit Nehru was still a few minutes away, and to pass the time we rode around the streets, which were unusually quiet for India. Father was driving the car and brother Om was sitting beside me, opening and shutting the camera nervously. I consulted my Braille watch again and again, and the hands seemed to move at once too fast and too slow.

'I just hope,' Om said, 'when I take your picture with Pandit Nehru my hands are steady. Otherwise it will come out blurred.'

We finally pulled up at the house of the Prime Minister of new free India. I took my father's large hand, and with brother Om carrying my typewriter, the *Arkansas Braille News* and his camera, we went in.

'Do you think, Daddyji, that Pandit Nehru will ever remember this visit?'

'I think he will,' he said, but I wondered. I was one fifteen-year-old boy out of a mass of three hundred and fifty million people to whom Panditji was both servant and lord.

'I hope he'll let me take pictures,' brother Om said.

I opened my typewriter, inserted a page, and prepared to type and read Braille for Panditji, to show him how well equipped I was for going to America. I thought about finding a passage in the Arkansas school paper which I knew especially well, so that I would not falter when asked to read, but that seemed dishonest.

Just then Panditji walked in. His step seemed to me gentle but firm, just as I had imagined it. Instantaneously all three of us stood up. Father, putting his arm round my waist, said, 'This is my blind son, of whom I spoke to you, Panditji,' and after brother Om was presented, we all sat down.

Many a time I had heard the voice of the Prime Minister

over the radio, or listened to his dramatic political speeches in a public square packed so tight with people that it was hard to breathe or move one's elbows. Now I was sitting at his right hand in his own house. I wanted to tell him that I loved him as I did my father, that during the cruel days of partition I had really believed in him and that I would even give up going to America for him if he wanted me to, but all this seemed to me like baby talk, compared to his few carefully chosen words of encouragement.

He dictated a few sentences which he then read aloud and signed. Before I had read even a paragraph from the *Arkansas Braille News,* he interrupted, 'Why Arkansas?'

'That is the only place in America which would have me,' I said. He did not pursue the question, and asked me how I had lost my sight.

'With meningitis,' I replied, 'when I was three and a half years old.'

After a slight pause, Panditji reminisced, 'I was almost your age when I went to England. That was a long while ago.'

All of a sudden I felt closer to him.

'My elder son,' Father proposed, 'would like to take your picture, Panditji, if you will allow it.' And with this we all rose together and went to the veranda. With the two clicks of the camera, the interview was over. While Panditji gave me his blessing, brother Om collected our things.

We got into the car and made our way home. For the rest of the day, I would be the centre of interest, and the interview with Panditji, brief though it was, the topic of conversation.

3

AMERICA & LIBERATION

NINETEEN

The Centre of the Universe

I WAS in the States. In my imagination the land appeared as boundless, as infinite as the oceans themselves, and I longed for an impression, any impression, which in years to come I should be able to remember. At home one could hardly go half a mile straight – there were curves, turns, alleys and back streets, and with the windows of the car rolled down, you could hear the rhythmic tread of a horse harnessed to a *tonga,* the occasional cracking of the whip of the *tonga* man as he tried to get his clients quickly to their destinations. There were the tinkling bells of the bicycles and the curses of the ever-present bicycle riders, who swore at the *tonga* men for blocking their way, and the sepoys, who cursed the bicycle men for cursing and blew whistles at the *tonga* men at every corner for going so fast. Yes, the streets I remembered in India were streets of unmistakable life, with colourful sounds and profane language, with bends and turns. But the street that I was now riding on seemed to stretch before me wide and straight, and it was quiet. The taxi driver had not yet used his horn and carried on no conversations with his fellow drivers. In these streets, I thought, you could travel fast and you could always get places, and smoothly, too.

On my right in the back seat sat Mrs DeFranco, saying, 'Oh, you simply had a dreadful trip, poor boy. What a terrible way to arrive.'

'I didn't mind it,' I said.

'Oh, but just imagine having all the contents of your bags stolen.'

'I have two bags, Mrs DeFranco,' I said, 'and one of them is still full.'

'I know, but what a bad introduction to America.' She took both my hands in hers. Then suddenly she broke into laughter.

There was something that seemed open and unrestrained about her laugh. I had heard women laugh in India but never quite that way.

'Why do you laugh?' I asked, baffled.

'I just realized that all this time you've had your hand inside your jacket. Are you afraid of losing your wallet, too?'

'I hadn't meant to,' I muttered. I could feel the blood rising in my cheeks.

The taxi driver had joined in the laughter by now and was eagerly awaiting the details of the theft. He was almost as curious as a *tonga* man, I thought to myself, and the muscles of my jaw relaxed. Mrs DeFranco described to the driver how I had come up to the baggage counter to collect my bags and found that one of them had been broken into, and how we had had to remain at the airport for two hours, filling up forms and cataloguing the articles lost for the insurance people. The driver kept on exclaiming, intermittently, 'Oh, too bad. So sorry to hear that. What a bum way to enter the country.' I kept on wishing all the while that Mrs DeFranco would stop. After all, as the baggageman had told me, it was the first robbery from a passenger's bags that he could remember.

But the inquisitive driver persisted. 'How did it happen?'

'It seems,' I explained, 'that someone broke into my bag while it was being taken from the airplane to the terminal.'

'Well, it shouldn't have happened to you, sir,' the driver said, and Mrs DeFranco added, 'It shouldn't have happened at all.'

I kept waiting for the driver to take a turn (I remember that when he finally did, it was a sharp right turn, and not the half-bend to which I had been accustomed). I broke into their conversation. 'Where do you live, Mrs DeFranco?'

'On Broadway,' she said.

'Is Broadway a wide street?' I asked.

She laughed. 'Oh, it is the centre of the universe.'

'No, Times Square is,' the driver said.

'But Times Square is on Broadway,' Mrs DeFranco reminded the driver, and laughed again.

The centre of the universe, that's where I was, I thought, a centre of the universe without the circumference which I'd always imagined the universe to have. In India the universe was an endless circle and there it was a horizontal line. I wanted to tell this to my two companions, but I did not know how to begin or how I could make it clear to them.

In India my life had been routine, a circle of routine from which there was no escape. It was like being on a merry-go-round, always in the midst of colourful things but nevertheless circumscribed by the monotonous movement of the merry-go-round. Being in America seemed like being on a swift train, and the life was full, indeed bursting, with incidents, like your bag being broken into.

It was too early to tell which of the two I preferred.

'How was your plane ride otherwise, sir?' asked the inquisitive driver.

'Yes,' Mrs DeFranco said, 'tell us about it; it must have been very exciting indeed.'

I wondered what I could tell them. Could I tell them what my father had said just before I boarded the plane?

'You will have to learn not to be so shy and sensitive,' he had said. 'You'll have to become thick-skinned.'

And my sister Umi had remarked in her usually light manner, 'Daddyji, you certainly can't expect him to be thick-skinned when he only weighs six and a half stone.'

'What do you mean?' I had retorted. 'I'm almost five foot five.'

Sister Nimi had tried to console me by saying, 'He looks like a man. What are you saying, Umi?'

Sitting in the airplane, I had tried very hard to put this conversation from my mind. I said to myself that I was a man. After all, I was almost fifteen and a half; and with my overcoat on, no one could tell how slender my 'boyish body' was. That was another of the phrases sister Umi used when she talked about me, and however much I tried to console myself, still the phrase had caught like a thorn in my mind. That first night on the plane I slept a little while, only to dream of a full-sized mirror. For the first time I was seeing my reflection in the mirror, and I was beating it, saying, 'I am a man, not a boy, a man.'

I jolted awake, breathing hard. I supposed it was morning, although inside the plane it was hard to tell. I'd never been closeted like that before, and the senses of sound, smell and even touch were dulled by the incessant roar of the machine so that to a blind man night and day merged into one. I surmised it was morning, because shortly the air hostess gently tapped my shoulder and said, 'Sir, care for some breakfast now?'

My first inclination was to say yes, because my stomach did feel empty, but in a moment I remembered that my father wasn't there, and how would I eat breakfast? All my life I'd eaten with my hands. A spoon was the only implement I had ever used, and that very rarely. A week before leaving home my father had tried to give me quick lessons in eating with a knife and fork, but I felt as clumsy with them as I would have trying to read Braille with gloves on. The effort required to cut the meat from the bone of a lamb chop was frustrating and terrifying for me.

'Not yet,' I said to the hostess, 'but I should like some orange juice.'

That morning I felt more keenly than ever the need of that support I had left behind me. I had postponed learning to eat with a knife and fork in the hope that I would learn it from my father on the way. Then my father had not been able to come with me.

'Are you on a diet?' the hostess asked me once.

'No,' I said. 'I am just trying to follow Gandhiji.'

'Ah,' she said, 'but he fasted for twenty-one days, and I understand he didn't even drink orange juice.'

'I, too, may have to,' I said, and although I said this with a forced smile I took my words more seriously than did the ironic hostess.

'Please don't go on a hunger strike, sir,' she said, 'against our airline.'

'It's not the airline,' I said, biting my tongue, 'but there are some religious reasons.' And by this statement I knew I had raised myself in her estimation, for when we stopped in Brussels she had special flasks of orange juice ordered for me, and I had an ample supply to last me across the Atlantic.

More than once I wished that Mother had let me carry the chocolates in my handbag rather than stuffing them into a laundry bag along with socks and underwear, and then sewing it to my overcoat. 'You can carry more with you like this,' she said, 'for they won't weigh your overcoat.'

Often I was on the verge of asking the hostess to bring me my overcoat, but the fear of being shamed because of the laundry bag kept my mouth shut and my stomach empty. I tried to minimize the sensation of hunger as much as possible by blowing up my stomach with frequent glasses of orange juice. The more I thought about the predicament of the knife and fork, which the sensation of hunger never let me forget, and the more I reflected upon my puny size, the more gloomy I became. I despaired at how long I could keep up the pretence and my pride.

I was about to phrase a sentence including the words 'pretence' and 'pride,' describing my trip for the benefit of my two companions in the taxi, when Mrs DeFranco gently pressed my hand and said, 'Poor boy, you still have difficulty with the language, don't you?'

'Yes, it is a language difficulty,' I said, belatedly.

The driver remarked, 'Sure enough, I have difficulty speaking English. I could never learn to speak Hindu.'

'Hindi, you mean,' I corrected.

'You see?' he said, with another jolly laugh. Mrs DeFranco and I joined him, and laughing, we turned on to Broadway.

'Ved, we'll soon be home,' Mrs Defranco told me, 'and then you and my husband can have great fun together. I know you will have a lot in common.' He was blind and I was blind and she thought, therefore, that we would of course enjoy one another's company.

'Here we are,' the driver said, coming to a stop, and I hastily pulled out the two dollars an American friend of my mother's had given her and handed it to the driver.

'That won't be enough,' Mrs DeFranco said.

'But it is ten *rupees*!' I said. 'One could hire a *tonga* in India for a whole day for that.'

'This is America,' she said.

'All I have is a cheque for eighty dollars,' I said, with embarrassment. Mrs DeFranco paid the balance, and the taxi driver put both my bags on the kerb, shook my hand and said, 'If I go to India, I will remember not to become a *tonga* hustler.' Then he drove away. Uncertain as to what to do next, I stood there while I heard Mrs DeFranco click her purse shut. She grabbed the empty bag and asked, 'Can you carry the other one?'

'Of course,' I said, and lifted it up. Then, with a quick motion, she tucked my hand under her arm and led me to the apartment building. As we climbed the four flights of stairs up to the apartment, I wondered what a woman in India would have done to lead a blind man. She probably would have cringed at such an immediate contact of flesh with a strange man, even as my hand was instinctively pulling away from Mrs DeFranco's arm. But this thought did not prevent me from being conscious of her well-developed muscles and thinking that America itself, at least, did not hold blind men at arm's length.

Had a bomb exploded in that quiet apartment, I could not have been more surprised than I was when Mr DeFranco exchanged a loud kiss with his wife upon our entrance. I wondered if my mother would have permitted me to spend my first days in America with the DeFrancos, had she known that my hosts kissed in public.

I was already frightened of Mr DeFranco. His handshake was firm and masculine, his voice unmistakably that of a trained musician, and the casual way he took my shoulder and led me to the living-room revealed a confidence which I had never known among the blind in India.

'Muriel tells me you have some bad luck,' he said, bringing my bags after me into the living-room.

'Not bad enough to prevent me from coming,' I said.

He laughed. 'You were delayed so long that I started preparing your dinner.'

'Oh, you cook?' I asked, unable to contain the astonishment I felt.

'Sometimes,' he remarked casually, 'I help Muriel.' He started apologizing for not coming to the airport. 'Your arrival time coincided with the lesson of one of my pupils.'

'Don't mention it,' I said.

'Besides,' he continued, 'I knew you wouldn't mind being greeted first by a charming lady.'

'We had a delightful ride from the airport,' I said.

His pacing up and down the living-room was distracting for his footfalls were heavy on the floor.

Mrs DeFranco asked from the kitchen if I ate meat.

'I do,' I said. I had been about to say no, for I did not welcome the ordeal of cutting it, but my hunger got the best of my shame.

She sighed with relief. 'John and I have been playing guessing games about it.'

'I promised my mother I would gain some weight and my father that I would eat any and everything in America.'

'Even beef?' she asked in astonishment, and I mechanically recited the sentence from my grammar book, 'When in Rome do as the Romans do.'

Then Mrs DeFranco served the dinner and while she was filling our glasses, she casually remarked, 'The peas are at twelve o'clock, the meat balls at six, and spaghetti is in the middle.'

'Do you understand that code?' asked Mr DeFranco.

'No,' I said.

'We use the clock dial to locate the food on the plate.'

'It is an ingenious way of doing it,' Mrs DeFranco remarked, 'and you would hardly find any blind in America who would not understand it. I was sure that blind everywhere knew it.'

'Darling, you forget,' Mr DeFranco interrupted, 'that India has many primitive conditions, and without a doubt work for the blind there is very backward.'

'There is nothing in India,' I snapped, 'primitive or back-ward.'

The quiet sound of Mr DeFranco drinking his water stopped, and after a pause he said, 'I didn't mean it that way.'

'I'm sorry,' I said, lifting my water to drink. We began to eat.

I was glad that meat balls did not need to be cut, and during Mrs DeFranco's trips to the kitchen I took my largest bites of spaghetti. The stubborn peas, which kept sliding off the plate, and my constant wishing Mrs DeFranco away in the kitchen prevented the conversation at the table from being more than desultory.

My fast, which had lasted forty-eight hours from India to America, had left me weak and dizzy, but the absence of the vigilant airline hostess and the frequent runs to the kitchen by Mrs DeFranco finally permitted me to fill myself comfortably so that I was ready after dinner to explore the lives of my new acquaintances. Once we had finished our apple pie and settled into easy-chairs, I asked Mr DeFranco if he would tell me about himself.

'My life,' he began, 'is simple and rather unromantic.'

'Oh,' I persisted, 'you are being modest.'

'No,' he said in a matter-of-fact way. 'I spent twelve years at Perkins Institute for the Blind. I entered when I was six, left when I was eighteen. After some college work I came to New York, started giving music lessons and appearing on radio now and then to sing, married Muriel, and here I am.'

As he spoke I pictured to myself how similar a life to his I might have had. Dr Halder had tried to get me to Perkins as early as my seventh birthday. I might very well have studied music there, and then like Mr DeFranco settled in New York as an accomplished musician, to live by my talents. But marriage?

As it was, he had education, grace and independence, and I had none of these.

'How was your life at Perkins?' I asked, suppressing the awe and envy I felt for him.

'Not too different from that of millions of other kids,' he said matter-of-factly. 'It was normal and uneventful. We played and studied like all other children.'

'What was it really like?' I persisted.

'A great deal of fun,' he added absently. 'Fun, that's what it was.'

I projected into the word 'fun' all the imagined qualities that I attributed to his life. But I did not want him to say any more about his life at Perkins, because I had a vague feeling he might spoil it for me.

'Now that you know all about me,' he said, 'tell me about yourself.'

'Yes, do,' Mrs DeFranco added. 'We have heard so much about India. It must be a very exciting place.'

While I was silently wondering whether my hosts would be interested in the Panditji, my music teacher, the division of India, or Ram Saran's comment on Partition – 'it was all in the cards' – Mrs DeFranco asked if I would mind very much if she finished the dishes.

'Not at all,' I said. 'I am rather tired now, but perhaps some day we can have a long talk about my past in India.'

'Soon, I hope,' she said, touching me on my knee, and added with a smile which I could hear, 'Don't worry, your English will improve very rapidly.' And then in a moment from the kitchen I could hear the plates clattering as Mrs DeFranco washed them swiftly.

No matter how tired I felt, I knew I could not go to sleep until I had the answer to one more question from Mr DeFranco. 'How did you happen to get married like this?' I asked bluntly.

'What do you mean?' he said laughingly.

'I mean how did it come about? How did you meet her?'

'Very simple,' he said. 'When I came to New York, she was living in the same apartment house that I was. We met at the door coming and going, I asked her out one night and we came to know each other better, and there you are.'

'Just like that?' I asked, for my curiosity was barely whetted.

'Of course,' he said.

'Incredible,' I could not resist adding.

Only a week before coming to the States I had sat with my father in New Delhi and we had talked about marriage. His manner was candid, his tone serious and compassionate.

'You are old enough so that whether you want it or not, you will think about marriage. You will, of course, not get married for some years, but you will start thinking about it.'

'I won't,' I said determinedly.

'Don't be shy – it is biological. I wanted to talk with you about this now, as I don't know how long you will be away from home, or when I will see you again.'

I waited, all the time thinking about the sea voyage we had planned together. I was sad for him and for me, because the views which he might have imparted to me in two or three weeks had now to be squeezed into the drab hours late in the night.

'My thoughts are wandering,' he said, fumbling for words. 'You think you might marry a Westerner?' he asked dryly.

'Of course not!' I said emphatically, overcoming the initial shock of the question.

'I have seen a lot of Anglo-Indians,' he continued, the pace of his speech increasing, 'Anglo-Indians who are fathered by some nameless Englishman and have for their mother some poor Indian. You know what their condition is like?'

But he did not pause for an answer.

'They are ashamed of their mothers because they are black women. These exalted Anglo-Indian children consider themselves white, and superior to their Indian mothers. They have the audacity to speak of England as home. They speak of a country they will never see as their home. Home, indeed!' he said contemptuously.

'The truth is they have no home, no land they can call their own, no father who will own them and no mother whom they will respect. I – I would remain a bachelor, before I would father such a lot.' He added reflectively, 'In India, at least.

'It hurts me to say this,' he continued, with his voice returning to its normal pitch, 'because the irony is that I believe in one world, and I have never believed in the nonsense of superiority of nationalities and races.'

There was a calm, a fertile moment of communication which I did not choose to break with any response.

'Remember,' he went on slowly, 'I am speaking of the most degenerate of the Anglo-Indians. They are to be pitied rather than condemned, and again do not forget there are exceptions upon exceptions who do become assimilated into our society.

'There is more than a mere connexion between what I have been saying about the Anglo-Indians and what everyone has been saying about your becoming a misfit in both India and America because of your leaving home so young. Fifteen is a young, a very young, age to be going away.'

He paused, and the straining silence was enough to emphasize the danger and gravity of the situation.

'Marriage,' he began again, 'is, I believe, crucial to a full and rich life, and perhaps even more so in your case. I am fifty-five – an old age for India,' and then slowly he repeated, 'a very old age. So far you have lived through the eyes of our family. But your leaving home now, my death and the marriage of your sisters and brothers will change it all. Neither your mother and father nor your sisters and brothers can be there all your life to help you live it fully.

"I can never hope to marry you in India well. I am going to be cruel and realistic. To marry you in India would be like trying to marry your sister without her face. I bring this terrifying image to mind because I want you to understand fully how important people think eyes are in any kind of sexual relationship. Men and women fall in love and make love with their eyes. Again, the irony is that I don't believe that blindness cripples a man sexually, and I think there exists no psychological evidence for it, but you don't read psychological textbooks to people when you are asking them to give their girl in marriage.

'Oh, you could get married in India all right, but not well, not happily, because the kind of girl you would want could not be found here. Once you have seen the other side of the coin, I mean a Western marriage, you will want a life companion equal to yourself.

'India is a harsh land. Marriage here is like a business trans-action and people weigh and measure their liabilities and assets carefully. In the States, no doubt your blindness would make marriage difficult, though I believe not impossible, because there values are different and marriage is made by the two people in-volved without the agency of parents. But all this you will find out only by living there.

'One more thing I would have you remember. In the melting pot of America, the problem of the Anglo-Indian does not exist, but here it does. At the same time your duty and service will never cease calling you back to India, where your roots lie deep.'

The lonely image of my sister without her face was with me during the dinner and while Mr DeFranco and I sat in the easy-chairs.

'There must be more,' I stupidly insisted. Mr DeFranco laughed and said, 'There is really nothing more. Except,' he added, 'ours is one of those stories where they lived happily ever after.'

Mrs DeFranco came in from the kitchen and said to her husband, 'Perhaps, dear, you could show him the apartment and the bath while I make his bed on the studio couch.'

So Mr DeFranco took me around his two-room apartment with the adjoining kitchen and bath, casually putting my hand over the screen separating the living-room from their bedroom, over the double bed, his writing-desk, the radio-phonograph combination in the living-room, and then the bathtub and the refrigerator. The apartment seemed to me small, in fact crowded, with barely enough space between the dining-room table and the radio-phonograph to allow one to pass through to the kit-chen.

Mr DeFranco said, however, 'It is a very comfortable apart-ment for both of us and we are very happy in it.'

My small studio-couch bed was made, and after formally saying good night to my hosts I climbed into it. I'm not going to think about anything, I thought; nothing, not even the empty, hollow feeling. You can at least think about the air hostess. Why can't you think about your mother? She didn't give you a lecture before you left home.

Mrs DeFranco returned once more from behind the screen of their bedroom and quietly whispered, her breath warm, 'I don't know whether you have refrigerators in India or not, but I didn't want you to worry at the noise of ours. The motor of our refrigerator makes dreadful sounds all through the night. I hope you don't mind.'

'Not at all, Mrs DeFranco,' I said, turning my face up to her.

'Oh,' she said, 'I meant to tell you. Call me Muriel and my husband John.'

'Of course,' I barely said. 'Good night, Muriel.'

'Sweet dreams,' she lightly said as she walked away behind the screen.

TWENTY

Wake-up Bells in Arkansas

I PASSED my two weeks with the DeFrancos happily, and then the time came for them to leave for their summer holidays in Maine. They invited me to go with them.

'August days are the most glorious days in Maine,' they said. And Muriel remarked, 'Even if you don't see the beauty, you feel it in your bones.'

'Every time,' John said, 'I get into the boat, lower the line into the water, and feel the weight of the string on the rod, then and then only I feel I'm really alive. You like to swim?' he asked abruptly.

'I don't know how,' I said.

'We will teach you,' Muriel said.

'Yes, and there is nothing like feeling the water against your body,' John said.

'You aren't afraid of the water, are you?' Muriel asked.

'Not at all,' I responded. 'I have been in swimming pools a number of times, but no one would teach me to swim in India, because they thought I might hit my head against the pool wall.'

'Rubbish!' John snapped. 'You can feel the wall of a pool approaching with your facial vision as easily as you can sense any other object.'

'But anyway,' Muriel interrupted, 'in Maine we won't be swimming in pools.'

I noticed that John and Muriel talked about Maine as I might have talked about my bicycle in Rawalpindi. They might even have bicycles in Maine, I thought, and vast stretches of land for riding.

'On our way up to Maine, if you wish, we can stop in Watertown and you can talk to Farrell about going to Perkins, rather than to that miserable, wretched place in Arkansas,' John said.

'I don't want you to go to the South. Besides, that's no place to learn English. I just can't imagine how your parents thought of sending you to Arkansas. Why, it's a state school. You'll be the only one paying for board and tuition. Now that you are here I am certain Farrell will let you attend Perkins.'

That day one of Muriel's friends visited her and told us they were having a serious polio epidemic in Arkansas. For my benefit Muriel's friend explained, 'Polio is quite a common disease in America, especially in the summer. Muscles of your body get paralysed and sometimes you can never walk again and sometimes you die. One of my friends had polio. . . .' I was already feeling numb, for Muriel's friend was gifted with unusual imaginative powers. I decided I would not go to Arkansas after all.

But when I called Mr Woolly on long distance that evening, he said, 'Son, we're anxiously waiting for you. Don't stay in New York any longer. The school starts in another two weeks and you should come out early to get used to our set-up. What, you're afraid of polio? Fear more than anything else brings it about,' he said, laughing. 'Son, when should I expect you?'

I would go to Arkansas. After all, Mr Woolly had been the only one to invite me to America.

There was a fence, a very high fence, higher than anything one could imagine. There were sheep and sheep and more sheep, and they were lined up in an endless line. One sheep jumped the fence, and there went another and yet another and another still. The fence was getting higher, but the sheep were jumping higher.

And now I myself was a sheep and the one on my right was whispering in my ear, 'You'll never make it, I tell you, you'll never make it,' and I could feel all the eyes of the sheep watching me.

'He's frightened,' one yelled, and another said, 'Incarnated humans make bad sheep,' and they all laughed. My muscles hardened and the fence seemed higher than the Himalayan Mountains themselves. The sheep on my left said, 'You can make it. Thank the Lord you can't see, because that way you won't know how high the fence is until you fall on the other side.'

I was falling, turning, falling trying to hold on to something, but there was nothing, nothing. I was falling, turning, rolling, and it was all empty space. Then there was the floor, the bare, tableless, chairless floor of the dining-room at the Dadar School for the Blind. As usual, the boys were sitting on the floor having their tiffin. I came into the room late, and brushed my knee against Abdul's elbow. Now he was holding my bare knee and pulling vigorously at my knee pants.

'You spilled my tea,' he shouted. 'If I had a knife, I would cut your leg off for you.'

'I am sorry,' I said, 'but this place is so crowded and you are sitting in the doorway.' Why was there not enough room even to pass through the door? Why was everything so stuffy? And why did people with fat feet, feet which had never worn shoes or slippers, drink tea? Abdul was pouring the remaining tea in his cup deliberately down my long socks. The tea was scalding hot and I tried to kick Abdul and work my leg loose, but he was holding my shoe-clad foot fast, and would not let go.

I was small and Abdul was big; I was weak and Abdul was strong. The tea was hot and the pungent odour of the rotting feet strong. I wanted to run, run home to Mother and cry. I was pulling Abdul's short hair.

'I will teach you to pull big boys' hair,' he said, and abruptly got up off the floor. I was running fast, and Abdul lost me. I was running home, and Abdul would never be able to find me there.

Suddenly I tripped and fell and jolted awake with my arms tight around my steel bed, with a white sheet, clean earlier, now plastered to my back, and I was still perspiring hard. Only yesterday I had been in New York, and the two weeks I had spent with the DeFrancos seemed very delicious indeed. Now I was alone in the cramped sleeping hall of thirty beds in the Arkansas State School for the Blind. I felt my Braille watch and it was only twelve-thirty. Night had barely begun and I had not been asleep more than a half hour. I forced myself wide awake, so that I might not lapse again into that terrifying dream. What

was this school to which I had travelled ten thousand miles?
I would write home tomorrow and tell them about it, and I tried
to recollect the clear visual image which I had painstakingly
acquired of the building while going around with Mr Woolly
that morning. None of the other students had as yet arrived.

The building was utilitarian and symmetrical and not hard
to visualize. One side of the building was reserved for the girls
and the other for the boys. In the centre of the main floor was
a small corridor off which were six classrooms, each with a
capacity for ten to fifteen students, one auditorium and a two-
room office where the superintendent, the principal and the
bookkeeper had their desks.

On the second floor above the corridor was a small library
and music conservatory separating the girls' sleeping accommodations from the boys', and below the corridor, in the basement,
adjoining the kitchen and a few other classrooms, were two
dining-rooms, one for the students and the other for the faculty
members.

Like the girls', the boys' dormitories were partitioned into
three sections: one for the small boys, that is, under ten; another
for the boys ranging in age from ten to fourteen; and then there
was the section for the older boys, in which I was placed. Allotted
to me was a small locker, about six feet tall and two feet wide, in
a long room with twenty-nine similar lockers arranged in a
double row with two sinks at the end. I was assigned a bed in
the sleeping hall upstairs, a room holding thirty such beds with
hardly more than a foot of space separating one bed from the
next. Along with the older boys, I would also have the use of a
small lounge off the locker room. Scattered between various
sections of dormitories for older and younger boys and girls
were small rooms for the faculty members.

The architect had conceived and executed the buildings so
capably that the entire student body, ranging in age from five
to thirty and comprising in number a little over one hundred,
along with a dozen and a half faculty members, including the
superintendent and the principal, not to mention the mainte-
nance help, could be accommodated in a building not more than

three times the size of the cramped Dadar School for the Blind in Bombay, or my home in Lahore. The architect must have miscalculated slightly, however, for there were three small cottage-like projections at the back of the building. One of these was an industrial shop for teaching the students carpentry and chair caning; another was a gymnasium which served a dual function – it was a place for calisthenics and wrestling matches and was also used for Saturday-night dances; and the last projection absorbed the overflow of the girls from the main building.

The corridor containing the main classrooms had, on the boys' side, an attraction which obviously had not been part of the original plan and had been added only that summer. Behind a clumsily built, freshly painted counter there was a small refrigerator holding bottles of soft drinks, with a chocolate case at its side, and I was told that high school seniors were to maintain this 'concern'.

Lying in my bed, I surveyed the building as I had gone over it, room by room, that morning. Each time I reconstructed the building in my imagination it seemed smaller and smaller, and I wondered how this empty building would feel once the one hundred students returned to the school and life was restored to the empty halls. Even in my bedroom, the farthest extremity of the building, with my door shut, I could hear the disquieting sound of the freezer motor, and I also remembered hearing the bookkeeper's typewriter that morning in my locker room. It would not be at all impossible, I thought, to hear, in the boys' lounge, girls conversing at the other end of the building.

But it would be two weeks before any students would return. Why had I been dreaming of Abdul? Were there to be Abduls to harass me here also? But I was big now, twice, no, maybe three times the size I had been in the Dadar School, and I was sleeping in the older boys' dormitory. The freezer motor had stopped running. I knew it would start back again as it always did, and I listened. Everything was absolutely still.

At the head of my bed there was a window, but nothing rustled outside. The air was still in that hot August night, and the building seemed hollow and deserted. I could not bear the silence. All of a sudden something started to rattle loudly. I was paralysed with fright, for the sound was threatening and it seemed to fill the whole building. I jumped out of my bed and ran down the stairs, shouting, 'Is anyone here, is anyone here?' My words echoed from hall to hall. Listen, what was that sound? Someone was hammering. Where? But the sound could not be placed, for it was irregular and reverberating. I was shouting frantically. Then I heard footsteps starting from the other end of the building, the girls' end, and shuffling rapidly on the floor. I waited; then I heard the muffled voice of an elderly, a very elderly, man call out, 'Anything the matter?'

I did not answer.

He stopped right in front of me, looking the other way, asking still, 'Where are you? Anything the matter?'

'Listen,' I barely articulated, and then his body brushed against mine as he swiftly turned about.

'Oh, there you are,' he said, putting his hand on my shoulder. 'What's the matter? Are you homesick? Calm yourself, sir.'

'But that sound, that sound, can't you hear it? Are you deaf?'

'Oh, that,' he said. 'Those are the steam pipes.'

'Steam pipes?' I repeated questioningly.

'Steam pipes with which we heat the building in the winter. They were working on them today, and they must have left them on, or something.'

'I hate it,' I said, 'I hate every bit of it. I want to go home.'

His hand was trembling on my shoulder. I heard him gulp loudly. Then he said, 'I am only the night watchman here, can I help you?'

'Leave me alone!' I snapped.

Then I heard his retreating footsteps, and I wanted to run after him and tell him I was sorry. Old men were always kind and understanding. They left you alone when you asked them to – maybe there were other such old men at the school who would put their hand on your shoulder and would not say anything to you that embarrassed you.

I went outside and sat down on the ledge next to the side door. When my heart returned to its normal tempo, and I stopped feeling it was going to leap out of me, I decided to do some exploring. I wanted to see what else there was besides the building, and I started walking around. First I started circling the main building. I timed myself. I could do it in ten minutes if I walked fast. There were many grass patches around the building which I had not encountered that morning. Later that night I also found behind the cottages what seemed to be a large wooded area. I walked a little way in the woods and found the ground to be rough and piled up with a few inches of thick dry leaves, which crackled under my bare feet. I did not want to go back inside, so I found an even stretch carpeted with leaves and sprawled down, smoothing the leaves under me.

I slept soundly, but when I awoke, the morning had set in and it was pleasantly cold. I walked to the front door of the building and found the watchman sitting inside the door. As I entered, he asked, 'Are you feeling better, sir?'

'Very well,' I said.

He got up and brushed the back of my shirt.

'Promise you won't tell anyone about –'

'Of course not,' he said. 'I understand perfectly. Well, it's almost five-thirty,' he continued, 'and it's time for me to leave. Will you be all right?'

'Yes, of course,' I said confidently, and walked through the centre of the corridor to the boys' end of the building.

Everything was strange, strange and incomprehensible. School had been going for some time before I grew accustomed to the routine, and all the babble of voices in the locker room, the comments and the jokes made in the classroom seemed as irrelevant to my education as the noise of the subway station in New York. With my head bent slightly forward, I would carefully listen to the name of the student introduced to me and would try to remember his voice and the shape of his hand. Gradually, almost at a snail's pace, people, by the very repetition of their mannerisms and thanks to my growing familiarity with the English language, began to imprint their personalities upon my mind. To the students I was, in the beginning, an object of curiosity, but once they found out that I had neither long hair nor a beard, as many Sikhs do, nor any other distinctive characteristic, they accepted me as just another boy. Indeed, after the first week, they never asked me any questions about India.

The avalanche of impressions at the beginning of school had so overwhelmed me that my senses had been deadened. Now, as I became firmly entrenched in the routine, my senses of sound, smell and touch came alive.

It was a Saturday night, and such was the din in the locker room that it was all I could do to stay in it and continue dressing; a boy called Other was jovially whistling as he shaved, the hot water running in a steady stream. Kenneth was desperately trying to get hold of one of the half-sighted fellows to choose a tie for him. 'Is George in the room? George? Where did Pat go?' he was shouting in his high cracking voice. Bill, who had evidently finished dressing, was practising on his clarinet, with Max, who had once said, 'I can't stand Billy's playing,' trying to drown out the music by singing at the top of his lungs.

Big Jim had his shoe propped on the long bench which separated the two rows of lockers, and he was complaining that Joe was not giving him a good enough shine. 'What the hell do you expect for a nickel?' Joe retorted loudly, apparently trying to enlist the sympathies of the other students in the locker room.

'Joe,' said Big Jim in an earnest voice, 'if that blind Kenneth there isn't able to see his face in the toes of my shoes, I'll beat your brains out, and you'll never be able to think for the rest of your life.'

'Can Joe think?' queried a boy in passing.

By now the line had formed behind Other and a number of voices were prodding him to finish his shave. 'You've been shaving for all of ten minutes now.'

'Just be grateful you don't have a stubble like mine,' Other said.

'But, Other,' pleaded another boy in a more urgent tone, 'the dance is only half an hour away.'

'Patience is a virtue,' Other teased, but he was through and was walking merrily away from the sink.

I was bent down trying to sort out socks from the bottom of my locker, and his knee caught me right in my back. Immediately, Other flung his bare, hairy arm around my neck and laughingly apologized. His face smelled clean, of shaving soap, and his wet hands were pawing my new white shirt, which I had just put on. His hands were ruining the front of my shirt, but I did not say anything because I was nervous about the dance, and I knew there was no way of avoiding the ordeal. I was already getting dizzy. The long narrow room was hot and stuffy; tobacco and toothpaste, shoe polish and deodorants, hair oil and shaving cream formed a pervasive atmosphere which hung over the room suffocatingly, and the odour got thicker and heavier as the feverish preparations progressed for the Saturday night dance.

Fat Charlie returned from the shower, announcing his presence by thumping on the swinging door loudly in his customary way.

As he entered, Other and Kenneth both shouted to him to come and inspect their clothes.

Arlie called him next, by his nickname. 'Come here, you One-Eyed Bull.'

Joe said good-naturedly, 'Let the poor boy get himself dressed.'

'You are stupid, Joe,' Arlie snapped. 'Have you ever heard of bulls getting dressed? You don't have to show your blindness so obviously.'

Jim was still arguing with Joe, but this time about the dance. 'What plagues you, Joe? You never show up at any of the dances. Is it because you don't have enough money to buy your girl a Coke there?'

Other joined in from the far end of the locker room. 'Big Jim, if you can get Joe to go to the dance, I'll give him a nickel, maybe even a dime, so there will be enough for both of them.'

'Oh, hell, what would I do at the dance?' Joe said, discouraged, and although Big Jim still sneered loudly, Other didn't say anything.

Fat Charlie continued dressing and simultaneously walking from locker to locker inspecting the boys' clothes. He was standing next to my locker, tying Kenneth's necktie. I waited. I knew his one eye would scan me next.

'You seem set to kill,' he said, turning towards me.

'I hope not,' I answered with an instantaneous smile. He straightened my tie, put a few strands of hair in place on the back of my head with his comb, and with no ceremony was gone. For the first time, that evening, all the muscles in my body relaxed. The din and the gaudy smell were transformed into a hilarious gaiety and colourful scent. I felt like a person totally inexperienced forced to audition and then accepted to play a part which was contrary to his character. To be sure, I was still in the dressing-room, but the mere attention of Fat Charlie was as encouraging as the attention of an accomplished actor to the nervous and inexperienced novice. Being fully dressed, I stayed by my locker, anxiously awaiting the dress rehearsal. The boys were gradually filing out of the room, and it was clear they were going to the end of the building for their 'girlfriends'. At last the clock outside struck eight, and I followed the boys who called themselves members of a 'club with bachelor tendencies', the word 'tendencies' being used, it was explained, to indicate the dynamic, hence changing, attitudes of the members.

The walk from the main building to the gymnasium was hardly more than a fraction of a block, and by the time we entered, the music was blaring, and at least half of the high school were gathered in the hall, which was hardly twice the size of our drawing-room at home. Having never held a girl, or danced a step, I stood back against the wall, listening to the bustling activity on the floor, activity which seemed all the more lively as the room was small and the floor so crowded; even where I stood someone would brush against me now and then. Standing there alone, amidst this light-hearted gaiety, I felt exposed to the full view of all, until I reminded myself that some at least were totally blind, and the others had no time to care.

'My name is Ann Lambert, Ved,' I heard. 'Would you like to dance?'

'No,' I barely brought out, and after some confusion added, 'I don't know how.'

'I'll teach you,' she said simply.

'I'd rather not,' I said, and then she was gone.

Ray was standing next to me now. 'You are an idiot, a fool. Do you know who asked to dance with you?'

'I don't care, Ray,' I said.

'The most gorgeous and the smartest girl in school, and that, too, at the first dance. Don't you know anything about manners? You *are* an idiot.'

I did not stay for the rest of the evening. I went back to the locker room and started undressing. Joe was sitting on the bench, humming 'Home, Sweet Home.'

'Who is it?'

'It's me,' I said.

'Oh, you back already?' he asked.

'I'm not feeling very well,' I said, and Joe went back to humming. When I left for the sleeping-hall, his humming was the only sound in that long and narrow locker room.

Invariably the school day opened with the voice of the housemaster. He was an old, a very old, man. His lackadaisical attitude and slow, almost mocking, way of speaking frightened hardly anyone. Even by the first morning of school, everyone had met the housemaster and had recognized the type. He always stood in the door calling loudly, 'Good morning, gents. It's time to face the world. As you well know, because you can hear the birds chirping outside, the world isn't all very cruel. Wake up, men. Can't you hear the church music?'

But there was never church music. There was only the tolling of the loud, whining bells.

'Ting-a-ling-a-ling, ting-a-ling-a-ling,' he would repeat rapturously with the stroke of the bells. 'The wake-up bells call you, men.'

No one stirred, but there was a round of mocking snores. 'Rise up men,' the housemaster would go on. 'The cook is cooking ham and eggs and is going to serve you a large glass of orange juice with pep-up cereal.'

The ham and eggs brought varied responses. Sometimes the lips of high-voiced Kenneth smacked, and sometimes Chubby Ernie, as everyone called him, said in a muffled voice, with his head, it seemed, buried in his blanket, 'I haven't had ham and eggs for years, and I've been at this here school for nine already, nine times longer than you've been. And there's nothing but dried-up toast and sloppy eggs once in a while for breakfast, and maybe starchy cereal.'

Ignoring all this, the housemaster would say, 'On your feet. March, my Christian soldiers.' And he would leave with, 'This is the last call to breakfast,' just as the clock downstairs began to strike six forty-five. There was always the sound of feet scraping, groping for slippers. Those few who still slept got the customary treatment from George and Pat. There were screams and shouts as the two turned someone's bed over, swung it from side to side, or propped it precariously on creaking wicker chairs which stood by every bed. Some boys were cursing them for tipping them over. Others were protesting that they were awake. The housemaster was back in the hall, scolding George and Pat, inspecting the beds, and prodding the boys.

Downstairs, two or three people were sharing one sink in the locker room. Eight people were crowded into the small cubicle with only three shower spouts. Boys half awake were singing, whistling, splashing water, running from locker to sink and back to their lockers. The housemaster had come down by now, and standing in the half-ajar locker-room door, called, 'Three minutes to line up; two minutes and fifty-eight seconds to line up,' and so on. As the clock struck seven-fifteen, there was a rush at the locker-room door, everyone hustling to be marshalled into line in whatever state of dress, provided, of course, that by the time we reached the door of the dining-room, our shirts were buttoned and our pants zipped. Grace pronounced, we would take our assigned places at tables seating six.

Hurriedly munching the dry toast, we helped it down by drinking cold milk, which had the same effect on the palate as the splashing of cold water had on the eyes. Waitresses dashed to and fro, and I remember feeling helpless when they would rush past me, shouting, 'Do you want some milk? Do you want some cereal?' Still steeped in Indian manners, where gentlemen never accepted anything at first offering and sometimes not until the third or fourth, I would invariably say no, but unlike the Indian hostess, the waitress never returned to press. And so I went hungry until I got used to their curt ways.

We returned from breakfast with a margin of three-quarters of an hour before classes. The locker room was still the centre of gravity, and boys still waited at the bathroom to get their turn at the shower cubicle or the toilet. Some took refuge in the barren and windowless basement, the only place where big boys were permitted to smoke or chew tobacco. Others did their K.P. duty, the housemaster judiciously avoiding assigning totally blind to the mopping of the floors. *They* were reserved for the cleaning and dusting of windows, bedsteads, and such. I remember the week I was on duty. The housemaster, trying to show me how to do my job properly, which was perhaps the simplest part of the routine, did all the dusting himself for the whole week, as he did, indeed, for many others, who explained, 'Why not let the old man do it when he really enjoys it?'

At eight-fifteen we all scattered to our classrooms, classrooms filled with the musty, gluey smell of the shelves of thick Braille books which lined the walls. I was arbitrarily placed in the ninth grade, although my total formal education in India had been less than five years, and that sketchy and interrupted, marred by illness. In arithmetic I had not got beyond mere addition, subtraction, multiplication, and long division. For the sake of learning more arithmetic, especially fractions, I had to attend classes of fifth- and sixth-grade students and sit with children half my size. I used to sneak into their classroom a few minutes before the beginning of the period and sit in the back as inconspicuously as possible. But I still had to put up with little blind Kenneth, who, before the starting of class on the very first day, wanted to feel my face, and Sue, who could figure out arithmetic problems rapidly in her head, and seemed always to be waiting for someone, especially me, to miss a question so that she might promptly answer.

After I had been in Miss Harper's English class for two weeks, she asked me, 'Ved, what is "the third ingredient" in the O. Henry short story I have just finished reading?'

This was the first direct question that any teacher had put to me, although none of my classes had more than four students. I was about to say, 'I don't know,' but instead said, 'Why, the third ingredient, Miss Harper? Surely the heroine's name.'

There was a pause, laughter, a rapid rushing of blood up to my cheeks.

So it went. Miss Harper read fast in her class, too fast for me to follow, and on the first quiz we had on the short stories, I got a zero.

The civics class of Mr Chiles was in some ways the easiest for me, although he had the reputation of being the hardest teacher at the school. It was a subject which did not require accumulated knowledge, as did arithmetic, and it dealt with current political issues, in, however, a dull, textual way. Ray, Lois and Evelyn were my three ninth-grade classmates, and all three had attended the Arkansas School from kindergarten up. Once, in Mr Chiles's class, I asked what he thought about the status of Negroes in the States. Ray, who was half-sighted, and already a preacher in one of the local churches although only sixteen, did not wait for Mr Chiles's answer. He snapped, 'The only nigger I have use for is a dead nigger, and if I were you I'd keep my nose out of the nigger business.' And going out of that class, after a heated exchange between Mr Chiles and him, he told me, 'Look here, I want to do you a favour.' And then slowly, emphasizing each syllable, he said, 'If you rub your nose in the nigger business too much, you'll become one yourself, and remember, whatever else you Indians are, you aren't white.' Having said this, he walked away rapidly, not waiting for my reactions.

I walked down the narrow corridor of classrooms, around the crowded vending stand, and went outside. Mr Chiles's was my last class that afternoon. I wandered out behind the gymnasium to the wooded area where I had gone my first night at school. There was a smell of dry stubble grass and rotting leaves, which crunched and wouldn't let me move quietly and just think.

I thought about home, home with six brothers and sisters, and seven very long years of idleness, when I would sit at the dining-table, listening to the lively chatter of my sisters about their school, their friends, a new book they had read. Now and then, when they couldn't find a Panjabi word for a new idea, they would use a long, rolling English word, like 'ideology', 'nationalization', 'democracy'. I would be filled with awe and remorse. It was as though people with education had their own vocabulary, and if you did not know it, you could never talk to them. And I remembered the horror and pain I felt sometimes, thinking that such conversations would soon be denied me, and I would not even be able to talk to my own family. School and education represented to me all that was good, true and beautiful in the world.

My father had let me come to Arkansas even though he had wondered whether or not it was a school for Negroes – whether that was why they accepted me when the other schools wouldn't.

Now I was at school, with books, classrooms and teachers. Why had Ray spoken to me that way? I repeated to myself, 'White, black.' It registered nothing. 'White is clean; black, dirty,' I said to myself, but 'clean' and 'dirty' meant nothing, not, at least, in that way. If I could only remember how the world had been before my sickness. If I could only remember the colours. I'd always heard that the blind lived in a world of darkness, but that couldn't be, because I didn't know what darkness was, except maybe the smell and the quiet of the night. Two birds fluttered over my head. I wondered how dark I was, how much I looked like a Negro, and what my kinship was with him.

Outside in that empty space among the fallen leaves and the sporadic flight of the birds, I wanted somehow or other to relate myself to the rest of the human race, to find out where I stood in the shadings from white to black. Maybe seeing was illusion, but I wanted to have that illusion, if only for a moment, to find out where and how I fitted into the social crossword puzzle.

There were more bells, bells beckoning to gymnasium classes. I went down to the damp and murky gym, grabbed a suit from a pile of gym clothes, and, hastily putting it on, ran upstairs. There were sounds of boys punching the punching-bag, and the unbearable smell of sweating bodies on the worn-out mats. The teacher blew the whistle, went around the small wooden floor placing everyone in position on the mats, and a session of calisthenics began, with his rasping voice calling the numbers. We instantaneously responded by bending our bodies, stretching our muscles and hopping to the drone of his voice.

I dreaded making mistakes, because I never liked the bending body of my gym teacher, his naked and bulging stomach greasy with perspiration – the body which would crawl all over me, trying to show me how to hold my ankles as I swayed from side to side, or how to touch my toes without bending my knees.

After the calisthenics we returned to the dressing-room once more, with three or four trickling shower spouts for all the boys, and then we were marched off to the dining-room for dinner, where two sighted teachers continuously kept their watchful eyes on the 'dining-table etiquette' of the students. Ever since Miss Harper had taught me how to find the end of a piece of meat with my fork and then saw it off with my knife, or how to find the bone of a pork chop to cut it out, I could manipulate these implements with a great deal of facility, and I did not have to go hungry any more.

After dinner there was a study hall, and all the students in the upper grades were crowded into the small library. Then at eight o'clock there was another session of gymnastics, and finally an hour free, just before bedtime. The housemaster, whom every student mimicked effectively, put us to bed just as he got us out of bed. He would wander in and say haltingly, 'Gents, nighty-nighty. You are all old and wise men, and know the rules, that all must be asleep, fast asleep, by ten-thirty.' But we were neither old nor wise, and it was some time before all were asleep.

TWENTY-ONE

A Donkey in a World of Horses

AFTER the initial few weeks of school, when everything seemed gloomy and I still brooded a great deal about having left home, things started to get easier. I stopped going to the elementary-grade arithmetic class, and with a little coaching from our high school maths teacher now and then, I could keep up with my own class quite handsomely. I sometimes even got better marks than Ray in English and civics. Whereas before I had spent hours on homework, I could now finish it all in thirty or forty minutes. Often, however, I felt discouraged that the classes were not hard enough, that most of the time in the classrooms was spent just talking rather than learning.

Big Jim once remarked, 'What good does it do us to keep on learning about adjustment, when we are with blind people in school all the time and might even end up working in work-shops for the blind, where no one could tell whether you ate with hands or silverware, wiped your mouth with a shirt sleeve or a napkin, or wore a navy-blue shirt with brown pants.' Indeed, the programme for 'social adjustment' got more attention than our academic education. We met in classes, sometimes twice, sometimes four times a week, to learn about social graces and adjustments to a sighted society, which, at least at our school for the blind, would not have been represented at all, were it not for some of our seeing teachers.

Mr Chiles, almost totally blind himself, introducing one of the social-adjustment classes, had remarked, 'To be blind is an up-hill struggle. You've got to sell yourself to every seeing man. You've got to show him that you can do things that he thinks you can't possibly do.'

It was true enough – if you were a donkey in a world of

horses, you had to justify your worth and existence to the horses. You had, somehow, to prove to them that you could carry as much weight as they could, and if you couldn't move as fast, you at least were willing to work harder and put in longer hours.

'Anything you do wrong in the world of the seeing,' Mr Chiles had said, 'like dressing untidily or putting your elbows on the table while eating, even if half the sighted world themselves commit these sins, people around you will chalk it up to your blindness. They'll call you poor wretches, feel sorry for you, and they will commit the worst sin of all by excusing it because you're blind.'

So we were marshalled in groups and marched into classes where we were given good common-sense lessons – that you had to introduce young to old, rather than vice versa, that it was good to avoid wearing brown and blue together, even if you did not know what brown or blue signified, and that if you could not eat an orange half with a spoon, it was better not to eat oranges at all. At the same time, we were told that, no matter how independent blind people became, they must always accept help from the sighted graciously, recognizing that the feeling for helping the blind was the result of a generous impulse.

When Ernest asked, 'If you went to a restaurant and they served you oranges in halves and you couldn't eat them and the waitress offered to feed you, should you accept the help?' he was abruptly told not to make light of serious matters.

As part of the social adjustment programme, we also had personal, private conferences with the faculty, who pointed to individual defects which they did not care to criticize in public. Ernest told us that his adviser suggested that he wash his feet more often. Joe reported that he was to start using a deodorant. Kenneth said he got a lecture to keep his mouth closed at least some of the time.

No blind person should be caught dead petting in public, and one teacher went so far as to say that it might be better to avoid kissing your wife or husband in public, just in case there might be a misunderstanding. We were carefully examined on this material in written tests, and it was a tribute to the teachers that no one failed.

The more serious side of the social-adjustment programme was concerned with facial vision and the teaching of 'mobility'. One day early in spring, all the totally blind students were herded into the gymnasium and asked to run through an obstacle course. Plastic and wooden slabs of all sizes and weights were suspended from the ceiling around the gymnasium. Some of them hung as low as the waist; others barely came down to the forehead. These slabs were rotated at varying speeds, and the blind were asked to walk through the labyrinth at as great a speed as possible without bumping into the obstacles. The purpose of keeping the slabs moving was to prevent the students from getting accustomed to their position and to force them to strain every perceptory ability to sense the presence of the obstacles. The thinner the slab and the higher its position, the harder it was to feel or hear it – that is to say, to sense the pressure of the object against the skin – a pressure felt by the myriad of pores above, below and next to our ears. Some of the slabs were of an even fainter mass than the slimmest solitary lamp-post on a street corner. This obstacle course helped gauge how well an individual could distinguish one shadow-mass from another and, having located the one closest to him, circumvent it without running into yet another. Here was where the wheat was separated from the chaff.

A person who has knocked about fearlessly – and it is a help if he was blinded in his childhood – will do much better in this test of facial vision than an individual who either lost his sight late in life, or has been restrained from developing the full range of his co-ordinated senses. Having, of course, during my childhood jumped from banister to banister, from roof to roof, and ridden my bicycle through unfamiliar places crowded with unlocated objects – and that, too, at a much faster rate of speed – for me, going through this obstacle course was child's play. The gymnasium was kept quiet so that the blind people could hear the obstacles, although I could not help feeling that I could have run through the labyrinth with a jet buzzing overhead. When someone cracked his head against one of the slabs, and the others discovered who had done it, they would laugh mercilessly, until, of course, they themselves ran smack into one.

After we had spent three or four class sessions running through this obstacle course, we were given a theoretical briefing on the importance of facial vision – that the blind ought to put the same emphasis on it as sighted do on seeing, and that the way to develop it was through abandonment of fear and through complete relaxation. We were also briefed on a few stock secrets of the trade, such as that the head should always be held high in order to more easily walk a straight line, that some found that a hardly perceptible arching of the back helped to minimize any injuries frontally received, and that compass directions – determined sometimes by the sun against the cheek – were better than remembering lefts and rights. In time, he would get the knack of such things as going into unfamiliar stores and finding the right counter or finding an elevator in a strange building.

We were also advised that in crossing streets it was safer to walk with the traffic rather than to follow pedestrians, as they might be crossing against the light. In crossing streets without lights, safety depended entirely upon the ingenuity of the blind individual in gauging the distance of the cars correctly, although it was helpful in crossing wider streets to take them in parts or in halves. Above all, one must never get panicky and run across a street.

Each instructor then was assigned two or three students, and with cane in hand, bus token in pocket, we separated for downtown. My instructor gave me a list of trifling, if not embarrassing, things to purchase from scattered counters in a Rexall drug store, and then asked me to meet him at the coffee shop of a departmental store for a milk shake, the treat being dependent upon my success in making the purchases. I was specifically told not to ask for help, and even if it were voluntarily offered, I should try to decline, provided I could do so gracefully. I did not know whether the instructor would keep his watchful eye on me, but whether he did or not, it was important to me that I should do well on this first day of independence.

I started out by tapping the cane in front of each foot before taking a step, as I had been taught. This was supposed to ward off tripping over a kerb, dropping into a manhole or meeting some other such obstacle, inclining or declining. I found that the noise of the cane made me very self-conscious and was quite distracting, so I flung it into the gutter at the end of the driveway in front of the school, and having made a mental note of the spot so that I might pick up the cane on my return, I started walking rapidly towards the bus stop, with my hands thrust into my pockets. Rather than wait at the nearest bus stop, I decided I would walk three or four blocks to the next one. Just to test my facial vision, I counted the lamp-posts and tried to guess the distance from which I first perceived them.

The sun was out in its full noon glory, although there was just the right proportion of breeze, making the heat not severe, but pleasant. In fact, the breeze was so gentle that it disturbed my facial vision not at all, and I could even perceive the curves and slight upgrades on the street, though that street was totally unfamiliar to me. However, when I unexpectedly stepped off a kerb, that fraction of a second between the kerb and the street was so frightening I almost wished I had my cane back – that cane which my instructor called the third leg of a blind man, although Big Jim had remarked that it was more like a displaced tail. I found, though, that soon my foot started registering a slight indentation before the end of the sidewalk, and that was clue enough. To my left, on the street, there was a steady stream of cars going both ways, at, I guessed, about forty miles an hour. There were sounds of Ford motors, Chevrolets, and I even remember hearing a few Buick engines. Walking on that street, I felt as confident and happy as I imagined a driver would feel with a ton of machine at the command of his feet. Then I heard the clanging vibration of the electric wire just above the traffic. My instructor had told me to listen for it as a sign of the approaching trackless trolley. Then, almost a block behind me, I distinguished the sound of the trolley motor from the rest of the traffic. The bus stop was still a block and a half ahead of me and I knew I had to catch that trolley, because it would be twenty minutes before the next one. With the ever-increasing sound of the trolley motor in my ears, I started running as fast as I could to the bus stop. I wished there were the shadow of a wall or a fence, to my right, to run by. As it was, there was empty space to my right and the hindering noise of the traffic to my left, a narrow sidewalk with a string of lamp-posts, and heaven knew what other hazards. I skirted one lamp-post by a hair's breadth, and another actually caught my shoulder, but not my head.

When I got to the next intersection, the trolley was almost abreast. If I waited to listen for the sound of the traffic, I could not possibly make it, so I dashed across the street, thinking of what I had repeated to my mother a long time ago.

'Death comes only once,' I had said.

'But,' she had said, 'what if you lose a leg?'

That had been frightening, all right.

'After that I wouldn't want to live. I don't mind being blind, but a wheel chair . . .'

Maybe if I had a white cane in my hand, I wouldn't have to worry as much about the traffic, and the bus driver would know I was blind and would wait for me. But it is better this way, I thought.

Just when I perceived the looming shadow of the bench at the bus stop, about ten or fifteen feet away from me, the trolley passed me. If only someone would be waiting there, I wished, so that the trolley will at least stop. But no one was, and I missed the trolley.

With a discouraged heart I slowly walked up to the bench, out of breath, and sat down. It would be twenty minutes more, twenty whole long minutes, and maybe I wouldn't get my milk shake after all. I took out my Braille watch and kept my fingers fixed on the hands, and I heard car after car pass by. I felt as envious of the drivers inside as a man standing in a rainstorm trying to thumb a ride, although I myself had no intention of flagging down a car.

At last there was another trolley. I heard its door open a few feet ahead of me. Walking parallel to the shadow of the trolley, I felt the gap of the door and climbed the three steps, slightly nervous, wondering if I could drop my coins in the box without having to be shown. I found the box, and the driver must have thought I could see a little, because he did not say anything about a vacant seat. The trolley was moving already. I walked down the aisle, feeling the vague shadows of the people, hearing the crackling sounds of packages or newspapers, until I felt the shadow of an empty seat and sat down. All of a sudden I was trembling all over. Arlie had been right when he said, 'I don't give a damn about being blind, but I do give a damn about being blind in a world where people have eyes.' I was glad I did not have a cane, because this way probably no one was watching me. No, I assured myself, I would rather be blind than deaf, any day. I was surer about it that time than ever before.

I did not pay any attention to the half-bends of the trolley. My instructor had told me, 'Just wait for the second right-angle turn, where the trolley goes from Markham to Main Street.' It was such an obvious turn that I could not miss it. We were going south now (I always oriented myself with the direction of one street), and the Rexall drug store was on Fifth Street. My instructor had said, 'Don't bank on the bus halting at every bus or light stop. Try to get used to the distance of a block, and that way you can't go wrong.'

I got off on Fifth all right, and crossing Main, I went into the Rexall drug store. Since it was my first time, I asked the man in the front where I could pick up some shoelaces.

'Straight to the back,' he said, 'and the second counter to the right.'

After five minutes I had bought all that my instructor had asked for, and I started walking rapidly a block up to the department store, dodging the window shoppers by using facial vision to keep a proper distance between the windows and myself, and the luncheon crowd by a watchful ear. By counting the gaps in the sustained shadow of the windows, I knew how many stores there were on that block. Next time I came to town, I would get the various stores located by keeping track of how many doors up they were from the street corner. It was as simple as that.

My instructor had said that there were a number of ways of telling when you got to the street corner. It could be done by the noise of the traffic, the draft of air, or the receding shadow of the windows. At last I was at the double doors of the department store. I went in and started walking back towards the elevator, listening for the sound of its door. Inside the elevator, I found my instructor.

As soon as we sat down in the restaurant, he said laughingly, 'You shouldn't have asked that man for the shoelace counter.'

'And how was I to know where to find it?' I retorted. 'By the smell of it?'

'You gave me the slip,' he said, 'that is, until I saw you running, from inside the trolley that you missed. But I picked you up again at the drug store.' So he had watched me!

'The first thing,' he was saying admonishingly, 'is that you've got to admit to yourself that you are blind and that there are certain things you just can't do, like throwing away your cane and crossing streets without listening for traffic.'

He was right, of course. I wouldn't make a habit of crossing streets that way, but the cane – that was another matter. I had never hooked a cane in front of my bicycle when I rode it, so I did not see why I had to carry one when walking, if I did not mind taking the chance of falling into a manhole. As for letting drivers know I was blind, I felt safer relying on myself than on their judgement. Maybe it was all rationalization, like that of Benjamin Franklin when he stopped being a vegetarian because he saw a little fish in the open stomach of a big fish about to be cooked.

'You'll carry that cane,' my instructor said threateningly. 'If not, you won't be allowed to leave campus.'

'Yes, sir,' I replied.

The milk shake was there now, and putting the straw between my teeth, I let it drain down my throat. It was cool and delicious, and I forgot about the cane. All of a sudden I felt weak and empty. 'It must have been tougher than I admitted,' I said.

'It always is the first day you are on the road by yourself,' the instructor agreed. After we had finished the milk shakes, he asked, 'Can you find your way home? I have some other business in town.'

'Yes,' I said.

We walked out of the department store together, and then separated. I could have caught the bus on that corner, but I decided I would walk all the way down to Markham (or First) Street. I must have passed a nut shop on the way, because there was the smell of roasting peanuts. And from the next open door, a fresh smell of leather. Must be a shoe store, I thought, or maybe a luggage shop. Then there was a swinging door which creaked as it was opened and closed, letting out a burst of air which breathed of dime store. At Markham Street there were three or four buses standing. I knew which was a trolley because of the motor. A number of people were getting on it, and I got in line. I felt in my pocket and there were two bus tokens. I had been given one extra for the trip, just in case I lost one or took the wrong bus. They would be good for another trip downtown, I thought, that is, if I did not use one now. So I left the line, crossed Main Street, and started walking west on Markham. I could not think of walking home, because the distance was at least a couple of miles. Besides, I did not know the way.

Half-way down the block, I stepped off the kerb and, standing about a foot away from it, tried to thumb a ride. The trolley whizzed past in front of me. Cars kept on passing me until finally a woman stopped.

'Are you going towards Stiff Station?' I asked.

'Going right there,' she said.

I climbed in.

'I bet you go to the school for the blind,' she said. Why did my eyes always give me away? I thought. Maybe if I had glass eyes and kept my eyes open all the time, no one would ever know. But that was useless. My mother wouldn't think of it, and from my left eye everyone would always know that I was blind.

'How much can you see?' she asked.

'Just enough to get around,' I replied. That way, I thought, there would be no fuss about her taking me right to the door of the school and helping me in.

'You know,' she said — we had just overtaken the trolley — 'you half-sighted people are the link between the world of the blind and the world of the seeing.'

'Yes, ma'am,' I said. That was the first time the words 'half-sighted' had ever sounded good to me.

'The blind must have a world all their own, don't you think?' she asked.

'It's just a world minus eyes,' I said. 'It's what one might call a world of four senses, instead of five.'

'But you have developed your senses so much more acutely, and to see a blind person get around is so amazing to me, until, of course, I remind myself that they have extra senses.'

'They don't have any extra senses, ma'am,' I said, 'unless you call facial vision that. Sometime try to find a door in the dark, and believe me, ma'am, you'll find even you have some facial vision.'

'They must have extra senses,' she said emphatically. She probably had not even listened to what I had said. 'If you were totally blind you would know what I am talking about.'

I was too tired to argue, and, leaning back against the seat, I relaxed while she lectured me about the extra senses of the blind, the car all the time moving swiftly through traffic.

Bringing the car to a stop, she said, 'Here we are.' I thanked her and got out of the car right in front of the long driveway leading to the school. She drove away. I found my cane where I had left it. It had a spring at the tip so that when you tapped it the cane would automatically spring up. I stood there, just springing the cane up and down, listening to the tapping sound. The more I tapped, the less I liked it. I knew I couldn't get used to it even if I wanted to. The spring made it worse rather than better.

I heard then, above the roar of the traffic, a clattering noise, beginning a block away. Clack, clack, clack, and I could almost forecast the next one. Some blind man was walking on the sidewalk, finding his way with the help of a cane. He must have very bad facial vision, I thought, to have to locate every wretched lamp-post with a cane. Clack, clack, clack. I stood there, running my hand up and down my new long, thin cane, with a fancy strap instead of a handle at the top. I took the two ends of the cane in my hands, and putting my foot at the centre, pulled hard and broke it in two. And flinging it back into the gutter, I walked rapidly towards the school building. I reached the building almost running, with 'clack, clack, clack,' still ringing in my ears.

I took the steps in front of the building two at a time and reached the lounge out of breath. As always, there was Joe, humming a tune.

'Who's there?' he asked.

'It's me,' I said. 'You ought to be able to recognize my steps by now.'

'I guess so,' he said languidly, and went back to humming his tune.

I could not shake loose the lonely image of the emptying auditorium following graduation, with a few stragglers here and there talking boisterously as though to remind themselves that the occasion was one not only of solemnity, but of happiness. And then, one by one, the parents whisked away their children for the summer holidays, and overnight the school building was empty and its halls as hollow as when I had first arrived there. The cook, the watchman, the bookkeeper and Mr Woolly with his family were the only inhabitants left in that once cramped and crowded building. For me, there was no home to go to, no parents to whisk me away. There was only the prospect of an idle and drab summer ahead.

With the setting in of the hot and humid summer, I realized how much I had been a captive of my school surroundings. Until the launching of the mobility programme in late spring,

I had been circumscribed in the building compounds like a prisoner whose every friend is a prison mate and whose every impression of the world outside is coloured by day-to-day minute observations of the happenings within the walls. For me it was like watching life in the United States with a jaundiced ear. I learned among other things that to be blind was to be jobless, because employers did not like hiring blind people, especially for temporary work. But the tireless efforts of Mr Woolly finally secured me a job working forty-eight hours a week for one hundred dollars a month at an ice-cream plant. Covering each day a distance of about four miles in trolleys and buses while going to and from work hammered home with full force the realization that the world outside by no means accepted the capabilities of the blind at face value, as we had been led to believe by the flawless understanding of the seeing members of our blind society.

I remember going out on crowded buses. To my chagrin, ladies would get up and offer, indeed force me into, their seats, and if I resisted, I ran the risk of having everyone in the bus share in the scene; it was awkward and unbearable when often two or three people tried to direct me to my seat, which I could have found quite well alone. On my first day the bus had been comparatively empty, and I had entered it without anyone's taking notice of my blindness. But now, travelling at seven-thirty and five, the morning and evening rush hours, in packed buses with scarcely any room to stand, it was hard to move in the crowded aisle without bumping into people and making my blindness apparent.

Even in the restaurants where I used to go during my lunch hour were waitresses who took me for not only blind but deaf, and who used to shout the menu, attracting sometimes the attention of the whole restaurant. If I were with someone, they would turn to my guide and say, 'What does he want?' as though I were dumb and incapable of ordering for myself. Sometimes strangers paid my bill, probably moved by pity.

When I crossed intersections, too, which I could have managed alone, two or three people would slip a hand under my arms and almost lift me across the street. When I did escape the clutches of these vigilant 'boy scouts' and was carefully working my way through the heavy traffic, someone from the sidewalk would shout, 'Watch out!' as though it were only a matter of seconds before a car would run me over. I used to get paralysed with fear and lose all sense of direction and control. Sometimes I had the distance between the car and myself so well calculated that it allowed just enough margin to get me across the street. No sooner was 'Watch out' bellowed than I would lose my nerve. From all sides I would hear the jamming of brakes so close to me that I could reach out and touch the cars. It was a wonder that I did not get hurt.

Once – I believe it was the first week of my work – I had just got off the bus and, taking the back way, was walking rapidly towards the ice-cream plant. All of a sudden I felt the firm ground under my feet give. I was falling in empty space. 'There is nothing more terrifying,' Other had remarked, 'than for a blind man to lose his footing. The only glimpse I ever had of eternity was falling into an open manhole.' And indeed, the time between walking off the edge and landing in the slushy manhole all doubled up did seem to me endless. It was not the numbing pain or the shock that I minded so much, but the screaming and fainting of an old woman, and the crowd of people who gathered immediately, clicking their tongues, some remarking that blind people should never be allowed out on the streets alone, others admonishing me for not carrying a cane, and I all the time suffused with shame – shame about what people thought.

I tried desperately to climb out of the manhole. I must escape, I kept thinking, but my clothes were wet and I was too far down. No sooner was I pulled out than I began running fast towards the ice-cream plant, with a jumble of voices shouting after me to stop.

Inside the plant, there was the ever-present choking smell of ammonia, and even when I took short, rapid gasps, I could taste the ammonia in my mouth. Forming a circle around me,

Ozella, Jean and Helen, the girls I worked with, asked, 'What happened?'

'Nothing,' I muttered, trying desperately to control the gathering tears, and after washing up, I took my place between the long table covered with an aluminium sheet and the large open freezer, which sent a draft of cold, frosty air tickling the back of my neck. While Ozella sacked the hundreds of Popsicles and Polar Bars which Helen and Jean kept dumping on trays, I boxed them and stacked the cartons one on top of another for Tommy to carry into the cold storage.

I wished Jay would let me wash pans or work the sticking machine, but, no, I was blind and Jay didn't want me to leave my place behind the table. 'If you get hurt,' he said repeatedly, 'the company is liable to sue.' But why would I be more likely to get hurt than Ozella, Jean, Helen, Tommy, or indeed Jay himself?'

'Helen, come here and box and please let me work the racks in the freezer,' I begged. 'I can do it. Believe me, I can.'

Helen did, and it felt good pulling out large, heavy freezer racks, weighed down with icy Popsicles and hardened Polar Bars, and carrying them over to Ozella. It was better than just standing eight hours a day, six days a week, boxing.

'Be careful,' Ozella said. 'The floor is wet.'

'I couldn't get any more wet than I am now,' I said happily. Then I heard the side door swinging and the footsteps of Jay in that large room. He did not say anything, but I knew he was watching. I'll show him, I kept thinking as I emptied the racks into Ozella's tray. The manhole incident seemed to fade into the background, and even the ladies who got up to give me their seats seemed good-natured and well-meaning. That was it – one had only to show the sighted people by example what one could do and they would understand. Actions always spoke louder than words ever could.

I shuttled to and fro from the freezer to the table. I heard the steady motion of Ozella's arms, lifting the ice-cream bars from the tray, putting them into crackling sacks, stop. They're watching me, I thought, all of them, every one of them. All of a sudden

I felt as though I were in the middle of the street and someone had shouted, 'watch out!' My heel caught in my wet pant leg and, rack in hand, I fell, scattering and mashing the two dozen Popsicles on the floor. It was all over. I went back to the table and resumed the boxing, what I had been doing all week – putting two Popsicles end to end and arranging them in cartons. Tommy was throwing buckets of water on the floor while Jean was scrubbing. Helen was replacing the Popsicles. Ozella and Jay were talking quietly in the other room. I heard Jay say, 'Don't let him leave the tableside.' And then, 'Keep an eye on him.' That day and the days following, Ozella did look after me, and I learned to box well. But when we were overstocked with ice-cream bars, I had to remain unoccupied while the girls were shifted to other work in the plant.

With the passing of the days, the sheer monotony of the work and the sometimes imposed idleness made me despair until I found a welcome relief that summer in learning to swim. Although whenever I went to swim in the Boys' Club it meant a trip of another four miles and shuttling from bus to bus, the physical activity of swimming made the hectic trips worth while. Swimming was like discovering a long stretch to ride my bicycle on, and it had the same beneficial effect of making me feel that, in spite of my blindness, I was free.

For the first time I could remember, I had a chance to make friends with sighted boys and girls my own age, who, after the initial awkwardness of my being blind, accepted me as one of them, ducking my head under water, pushing me off the low diving-board, sometimes trying to make me lose my directions in the swimming-pool. Ed, who always sat facing the pool and kept a watchful eye on the swimmers, at first used to scold them. 'Don't you know any better,' he used to say, 'than to treat a blind person like that?' They would leave me then, and I did not want to swim any more.

I knew I had to make friends with Ed, to make him understand that I would rather be hurt in the swimming-pool than be left alone. By and by I found out that Ed liked to play chess, so the next time I went I took my chessboard.

'You moved your queen right into the range of my bishop, so I can take it,' Ed said after one of my moves the first time we played.

The girl on my left who was watching sighed conspicuously.

'Oh,' I said, 'she's all yours,' hiding the real remorse I felt at losing the queen so early in the game, and forcing a smile as though it were a calculated move.

'No,' Ed said, 'take the move back.'

'Why?' I asked.

'You didn't know my bishop was there. You didn't see it.'

'Yes,' the watchers chimed in. 'Do let him take the queen back.'

Although I raged within, I took my move back because I knew from Ed's tone that no matter how much I persisted, he would not relent, and when one is blind, one always has to make compromises, even if they do leave a bad taste in one's mouth. Once during the game he said, 'I'm sorry. I didn't mean to move my rook there.'

'A move is a move,' I replied brutally, taking his castle.

At his next move, I was ruthless again, and he lost the game.

'You don't pull any punches,' he said, and I thought I detected a bitter note.

'I guess not,' I said, feeling sorry and glad at the same time.

After that he used to wait for me to make a mistake, and every time I did, he would break into a hearty laugh, exclaiming, 'We got the master that time,' and there would be applause all around. He stopped, too, trying to protect me in the swimming-pool, and whenever I did have a rough time, I sensed that he watched with a gleeful eye, and I was glad that I played chess with him ruthlessly.

Once when I got off the bus and was getting ready to cross the very busy street in front of the Boys' Club, Joe Red, who was the director, darted across to me from the other side.

'Am I ever glad that you showed up!'

'You knew I would,' I said carelessly, 'but why the reception?'

'Come in and I'll tell you,' he said, and I walked across the street to his office. 'The *Arkansas Democrat* would like to get your picture diving.'

My heart sank. 'Oh, Joe, you know how I hate this. They have had so many write-ups that I can hardly ride a bus without people recognizing me and greeting me. It's all very embarrassing.'

'But you've got to do it for the club's sake. And besides,' he went on, 'this is the way to educate the public about the blind and get a good story about India, and all in the Sunday paper.' He paused. 'I want you to dive off our high board for the picture.'

'But, Joe, I can't,' I said.

'Why can't you?'

'Because . . .' But I could not tell him how frightened I was of empty space.

Before I knew it I was climbing the stone steps of the high board, and trembling. The pool had been emptied of people, and everyone was standing on the side, watching. All my life, I thought, there will be eyes, staring. I wished they hadn't made so much fuss about getting everyone out of the pool.

'Do you want me to come up with you so I can help you find the edge of the board?' Joe shouted.

'I can't find it,' I said, gulping.

My knees felt weak and I did not know how long they would hold me. I was up there now, walking towards the edge. The rubber mat under my feet was sticky and wet.

'Keep in the centre,' Joe shouted. 'You don't want to fall off the side and blister yourself.' I felt as though someone had shouted, 'Watch out!' but I kept on walking towards the edge with cautious steps, wavering, unsure whether I could keep my balance. I wondered if I would miss the edge and step off into another manhole. All around me it was quiet, more quiet than it had ever been in those cheerful surroundings. I found the edge and, bringing my toes together, flung my arms up and curved my body as Joe had showed me on the lower diving-board.

'Hold it!' Van Rush, the reporter, shouted. 'Look this way.

I want to get your picture on the board first.' It was a long minute before he said, 'All right, anytime.'

I wished there were no Sunday papers, no people to educate about the blind or India. I wanted to turn back. If only I had remembered to count the steps, maybe I could have gauged how high I was. Getting back in position and taking a deep breath, I dived from the board. There was the reverberating noise of the board springing back into position, the click of the camera, and I was falling. It seemed as though I had toppled over into an elevator shaft head first. It was a long, a very long, while before the water was pressing all around me. But I was still travelling, going farther and farther down. My outstretched hands touched bottom. I wanted to breathe. Never would I come out in the air, I thought, and struggled frantically with my hands and feet, even though Joe had said, 'It's easier coming up if you just relax.' It was all terrifying. The time since I had dived from the board seemed interminable. The stretch of water from the centre of the pool towards the edge seemed long and tiring, beginner that I was. There was no woman fainting, only the steady shadow of Joe's body, swimming at my side. 'Don't work so hard. You are almost there,' he said.

'That was a beauty,' Ed said as I dragged myself out of the water.

I played chess very badly that night.

When the article did appear, the picture that was printed simply showed me posing on the board.

With growing experience in mobility, I no longer had to watch for every upgrade or downgrade in the street, count lamp-posts, or indeed look for them. I learned how to relax and how to put people at ease, even if it were just a stranger in a bus. Whenever ladies did get up to offer me their seats, I made a joke of it and gently declined. I found a way of talking to waitresses in a low voice before they even said a word, which made them speak softly too, and I discovered a certain careless manner of crossing streets and of getting on and off buses which avoided incidents – incidents which had occurred so frequently in the earlier days of my travel. Occasionally people still shouted. 'Watch out!' but if I was concentrating very hard, I never heard them. By no means was the first manhole the last manhole, but after the first I did not make as big a splash, and what splash I did make I tried to minimize by wearing a gay, rather than a glum, expression.

With the new-found freedom of movement, freedom which had been denied me in India, even on a bicycle, there opened up yet another vista which was as exhilarating to me as learning to read for the first time must be to an adult.

When I came home after putting in a long day at the ice-cream plant, and after a reviving swim at the pool, physically I would be very tired, more fatigued than I ever got during the school year. To keep my mind alive, however, I always took time off from my sleep to listen to books on records. Even though I felt discouraged because the Library of Congress recorded so much light fiction, I found enough good books to add a new dimension to the ever-expanding horizon of my activities.

For the first time now, I received novels of Fielding, Proust, Rolland, Dostoevsky and Tolstoy. I read feverishly, sometimes staying awake the whole night, listening to the never-tiring voice of the actor Alexander Scourby on record after record. This way of reading was so entrancing that I hated to turn sides or change records every fifteen minutes. The phonograph used to get hot and smell of burning rubber, but I read on into the night, certain that I could do my work at the ice-cream plant even if asleep.

TWENTY-TWO

The Steampipes

SUMMER was over, and I could not go to the Boys' Club for swimming any more. I did not know much about baseball, but I nevertheless enjoyed very much standing outside below the locker-room window and, with Joe as our pitcher, taking turns with Arlie, Kenneth and Other, trying to hit the ball. Joe was a baseball fiend, and he said that if he could see, he would join the St Louis Cardinals. Even as it was, he spent hours by the radio, listening to the baseball games, and when a team he liked got defeated, he used to cry like a child. The boys used to tease him about it. 'Get over it, Joe,' they said. 'You are twenty now, and your mother gave up feeding you a long time ago.' Pat sometimes said, 'What the hell do you expect from a boy who, although twenty, has not even gone beyond fifth grade?' He once called Joe a 'soft-bellied bastard', and then Joe wept for a long while, and Other and I had to work very hard to get him outside and pitch. We knew that would stop him from crying faster than anything else.

Joe used to stand a few feet away from us and try to aim at the bat, which he barely had sight enough to see, and we took turns in trying to hit the ball. Arlie, Kenneth, Other and I were totally blind, but nevertheless, by listening for the sound of the ball and calculating its speed, we would try to score a hit. And if we missed the ball, Joe would have his laugh, and Other would curse him roundly, but always in good humour, for not aiming well at the bat. And sometimes when we got tired of the monotony of just batting the ball, we would keep on with it simply because Joe liked to pitch.

When we were not batting balls, we went down to the woods behind the gymnasium, where I now spent most of my idle hours. There was always the sound of Kenneth stumbling down there, scrounging for skewers to roast wieners, and of Other loudly chewing tobacco and spitting intermittently as he hammered a piece of tin into shape to be used as a fireplace, and of Arlie exclaiming loudly as he found a good piece of wood for fuel. We ate the wieners, and while the summer was still fresh in the memories of the boys, they told about their experiences.

Kenneth told about a woman he had met who thought the blind never needed sleep because they had their eyes closed all the time. Other never stopped telling about the credulous people who readily believed that the blind had to have strings running from the blade of the knife and the prongs of the fork to their teeth, in order to find their mouth with the silverware. And Arlie always had a humorous incident to tell us about the kind of people he met that summer while he was tuning pianos. When our stories of the summer were exhausted, there were always the ever-present topics of religion, women, and sometimes even politics to while away the time.

Miss Doves had come to our school at the beginning of that year. She had a glorious voice, and Mr Chiles used to say that if it were not for her devotion to her religious work, her voice might take her to the Metropolitan. When she practised, some of us used to crouch by the door of her music room and listen. Once she caught me and scolded me for eavesdropping. The boys said that at heart she was a perfectionist and did not want to be overheard fumbling her way through a song.

I used to take piano lessons from her. I was still at the stage of playing scales, and as I ran my hand up and down the keyboard in time to the metronome, I used to wonder why she ever wasted time with beginners: she always got impatient if I wiggled on the bench because it was too hot, sat with bad posture, or did not curve my fingers just the way she had taught me.

About the third week of school, she stopped me in the middle of one of my lessons. 'Are you ever unhappy?' she asked.

'Occasionally,' I said.

'Sometimes you look so glum,' she went on.

'I certainly don't mean to,' I said, and then there was an awkward pause.

I went back to playing, but she stopped me again and asked abruptly, 'What is your religion?'

'I am a Hindu, I suppose,' I answered, not a little taken aback by the unexpectedness of the question.

'What does that mean?' she persisted.

'It is hard to say,' I said. 'More than anything it is a way of life.'

And while I groped for words she went on, 'Have you ever known Christianity?'

'I have known Christians,' I began eagerly. 'I went to an American missionary school for the blind in India.' And then, hesitantly, 'I met Deoji and the nurse there.'

'Who are they?' she interrupted.

'Christians, Indian Christians,' I said, somewhat abashed. 'I knew them well.' I thought I heard a sniff, so I checked myself.

'I am sorry,' she began compassionately, 'that you have never been shown the light – you who should be so sensitive because of your blindness and sufferings.' I started drumming my fingers idly on the bench. 'You must be baptized or you are damned for ever to hell and fire. It is still not too late for you to be saved, and I want to help you, Ved. Will you let me?' she pleaded.

My fingers tapped on the bench more nervously.

'You have to be saved,' she went on, 'so that you can go home and save others.' When I asked what saving was, she explained rapturously, her speech gaining in tempo, how I had to accept Christ and be prevented from sinning. If you were not saved, you were damned, for ever damned. Yes, all Hindus and Muslims were damned, even if no one had tried to show them the light. God always showed light to those whom he chose to save. Did I not understand that he was working through her to save me?

My fingers were making a regular noise now. 'Stop it,' she said emphatically. 'That noise gets on my nerves.' My hand froze in mid-air.

Jumbled sounds of numerous instruments drifted in from the

other practice rooms of the small music conservatory. Someone was playing the 'Twelfth Street Rag' on the clarinet. Pat was playing 'I Almost Lost my Mind' on the trumpet, and now and then I could catch a few disconnected piano notes.

Miss Doves took my hand. 'Will you let me pray for you?' I wished that had not been a question. Why wasn't the conservatory soundproof? 'Well, say something,' she said angrily. 'Why don't you say something?' Then, in a calmer tone, 'I can pray for you now, if you like; time is running out. Come, kneel beside me.'

She tugged at my hand, but I remained immobile. Pat was on the second phrase of the recapitulation of 'When I lost my baby, I almost lost my mind.' The medley of noise was getting louder and louder. Someone was thumping his feet, almost shaking the floor. The high notes of Pat's trumpet made the window in Miss Doves's room buzz and tremble.

'I can't,' I brought out, and she let my hand fall. 'It's too much for me. I have to think.'

'Think,' she blurted out. 'What is there to think?'

I was hot, and the small room was unbearably uncomfortable. Outside, the shrill bell rang lunch hour. Pat stopped playing.

'I'll pray for you,' Miss Doves said, and I heard her swallow hard. 'And I know that God will show you the light. You must pray too.' A thick drop of perspiration dripped on the back of my hand from my forehead. 'You have to seek, Ved, in order to find.'

There was a knock at the door, and Sue banged in to arrange for her next piano lesson. Awkwardly I backed out of the practice room and ran down the steps three at a time, knocking Billy over and sending his clarinet case rolling down the steps.

For some time after that day with Miss Doves, I stayed in a seething mental state. Every time I went for my lesson, she asked whether she might take me to her church to be baptized, and all through my faltering playing, I could feel her steady gaze upon me. Try as I might to avoid Miss Doves, she would always accost me in the halls, and even appear repeatedly in my dreams. I spent many wakeful hours thinking about religion –

the religion which sent *pandits* to my mother to make her atone for my blindness as though she had brought it upon me herself; which made men like Qasim Ali and Ram Saran cut each other's throats; and which now enlisted Miss Doves as its agent for my conversion. Conversion from what to what? I wondered. The most appalling thing, it seemed to me at that time, was that each individual was convinced that he was unerringly right.

Mr Chiles in his class had used the analogy of a circle, trying to explain to Ray how he should regard the various Protestant denominations. 'It is as though we were all standing in a circle and trying to reach the same centre, but taking different paths.' Did that analogy hold for various religions?

Ray had not accepted Mr Chiles's analysis. 'All paths can't be right. Some must be dead wrong,' he had said, and yet he was already a preacher in a church.

One afternoon, not too long after that piano lesson, a number of us were gathered around the vending stand, drinking cold drinks. Fat Charlie was helping Other carry in some cases of Coke.

'God damn it,' Charlie said, putting down the case, 'it snagged my pants.'

'Sssh,' Other shushed. 'Watch yourself, Bull. Remember, you are among girls.'

Charlie cursed some more, defiantly but in guarded tones. I doubt if many people heard him. All of a sudden the loud but shaking voice of Miss Doves exclaimed, 'Charles!' and the hubbub subsided as though the boys had been fighting and the commanding voice of Mr Woolly had appeared on the scene.

'Charles, you . . . you promised, and just a day ago, too,' the voice went on despairingly. 'What am I going to do in this school?'

Then I heard the clicking heels of Miss Doves's shoes rapidly shuffling down the hall towards the music conservatory. Everyone remained quiet, even after the sound of the echoing steps ceased. Then, all of a sudden, 'What happened?' 'What got into her?' 'What did you do, Bull?' and other voices

clamoured for answers. In spite of the pressing questions, Charlie
would say nothing, and, slamming the door, he left

'I wonder what made the old witch get on her high horse?'
Big Jim asked.

'God knows,' Ernest said, and Other said, 'She's new at the
school, and maybe blind people are too much for her.'

That night there was no sleep for Charlie.

'It's not like you to be so quiet, Charlie,' Jim persisted.

'What did you promise? Ernest asked.

With all the sleeping-hall boys for his audience, Charlie was
forced into explaining the enigmatic incident of the afternoon.

'You see,' Charlie began, 'at my music lesson yesterday, Miss
Doves questioned me about my beliefs. She asked me if I led a
good Christian life. What could I say?'

Some boys laughed, and others chided Charlie about being
the worst Christian in the whole school, because he didn't answer every call of the blind fellows to see if the colours of their
clothes matched. It was some time before the boys could get
Charlie to go on.

'I told her no. She lectured me about being damned to hell-
fire, and then she made me get down on my knees, and, kneel-
ing beside me, she prayed for my soul.' There was a pause.
'What could I do?' Charlie pleaded. 'I wish you boys could
have seen her there, her face calm and earnest, and even beautiful. She was praying, praying over me,' he repeated. 'I promised
to give up cursing and taking God's name in vain and all that.
I didn't mean to curse at the stand, but the words just came out
that way.'

The incongruous image of huge Charlie on his knees with
young and slender Miss Doves, who was almost his age, floated
across my mind. It did not take too much imagination for me to
picture myself in his place. Beginning with Other's howl, the
boys rocked with laughter. It was hard for me to laugh. I wondered how many other boys there were in the hall who had
gone through a similar experience with Miss Doves and whether they were laughing now.

'Boys,' Big Jim began, the laughter ceasing, 'Miss Doves's

religious work in our school will come to a close now, because word about her activities is finally going to reach Mr Woolly.'

'That it certainly will,' said Ernest.

'But even Mr Woolly,' Other remarked, 'can't stop secret prayer meetings behind the piano.'

It was spring now. There was the cool smell of sprouting grass and a fragrance of blossoming flowers, and the distracting sound of the lawn mower, which streamed into the open windows of the classrooms. Except, perhaps, the classes of Mr Chiles, all the other junior high and high school classes came to a halt, as though the temperature outside were touching one hundred and twenty degrees, as in Lahore, and it was too hot to study. Actually that spring was one of the mildest, and what heat there was was generated by politics – school politics.

Whether it was because our constitution was new, or because politics injected a new issue into the old and worn-threadbare topics of conversation at our school, students and teachers alike talked and campaigned as though it were a presidential election for the country, rather than the measly prospect for a few people of winning honour and perhaps some glory, but certainly not much power. Whether I went to the locker-room, lounge, or the sleeping-hall, there were always boys whispering and I always had to clear my throat loudly before entering so that I might not overhear. Blind people hate more than anything else being overheard, and I knew that well. Sometimes I would not clear my throat fast enough, and embarrassing phrases would fall on my ears. Although Kenneth had said, 'You shouldn't go into politics if you don't want your toes stepped on,' it was as though people were purposely aiming dumbells at my toes.

'Aw, don't you know that Jane is old enough to be his mother and the only reason he's going with her is so he can get all the girls' votes?' I overheard Billy telling Joe when I walked into the lounge. 'You don't want to vote for him.'

And mild-mannered Joe was saying perplexedly, 'God, I don't know what to do. Other and Ved are both nice guys.'

And I, because I was in the race and not supposed to overhear, could only keep on biting my tongue and rapidly walking through helplessly.

It was not until I overheard the accusation about Jane twice over from other sources that I really started losing sleep, and I wished I had never got into the race.

'What's troubling you?' Kenneth asked when we were in the shower cubicle.

'It's about Jane,' I said. 'I wish they wouldn't keep dragging her in.'

'How old is she?' he asked.

'Not you, too, Kenneth. If you believe . . .'

'But I am your campaign manager. You can confide secrets to me,' he said knowingly.

I bit my tongue so hard that it ached. 'Kenneth,' I said, 'I started going with Jane even before the idea of my running ever came up, and it's unfair.'

'But how old is she?' he persisted.

'She's never said and I've never asked her,' I answered, getting more and more disheartened. That day I knew for sure I would have to ask Jane how old she was, and I wondered how to go about it.

Jane was in my class and had just come to our school at the beginning of that year. She was shy and quiet, read all her assignments, and answered every question in class. Boys said the reason she was so good was that she could read large sight-saving print, and naturally, reading the Braille was much slower than that. Other had taken her out one time, but then stopped, probably because she never said very much.

Once I got to my English class early, and I heard someone turn a page stealthily.

'Who is it?' I blurted out.

'It's me,' she said, and then there was a moment or two of awkward silence. 'You have a letter from India,' she said. 'May I read it for you?'

And I could not help turning crimson. It was always an embarrassing business having people read letters from home. Every time I got a letter, I used to carry it for days. I did not like the housemaster to read it aloud in the lounge, as he did with many of the boys' letters.

'If you want,' I said, handing over the letter to her hesitantly. It was a note from my younger brother Ashok. He had decided not to buy a new pair of shoes for a while, because he wanted me to get my education.

'I have never heard you talk about home or your family,' Jane said.

Just then Lois came in, so our conversation was cut short. From that day we started going to the Saturday-night dances together. It was good also to have someone to take to the square dances which had just been organized a month before the election.

'You all jump up and you all come down. Swing your partner right around, Miss Harper was calling over the speaker. Around me there were continuous shuffles of feet, the shouts of some totally blind student who hadn't quite made the connexion with his partner, and the loud huffing sounds of fast breathing. Miss Harper was calling faster and faster.

'Come on, Miss Harper,' Kenneth shouted. 'We can do it faster.'

And Miss Harper asked under her breath, not interrupting the rhythm of the call, 'Can you do it, boys and girls?'

'We can,' the whole floor responded, and the pace of Miss Harper's calling picked up even more, until the words were hardly distinguishable from each other. I wasn't listening to her any more, but just going through the motions, which came naturally. I wished the square dance would never come to a halt, and that all that night, the next day and the day after, I would stay in motion. I did not want to know Jane's age. I couldn't tell why, but I just did not. I was not dizzy. It was the floor beneath me that was going round and round.

'Texas Star,' a shout went out, and no sooner had we switched the dance than Kenneth collided with Lois head on, and the whole movement came to a stop. It was as though the belt which had whirled the whole gymnasium floor about had snapped. The floor, however, was still going in circles, as though the momentum of the motion was too much to stop immediately.

'Oh, I am so dizzy,' Pat said

'Let's have intermission,' Miss Harper called.

There was a rush for the only water fountain. 'Come, Jane,' I said, and we walked towards the punching-bag at the back of the room. 'How old are you?' I said suddenly, and her hand pulled out of mine as though she had just received an electric shock.

'Why?' she asked.

'I have to know, I said.

'You see, for a long time –' she began, evasively, I thought.

'Age, Jane, please,' I pleaded.

'Twenty-seven,' she brought out with a great effort of will. It seemed as if all of a sudden the floor had been set in motion again.

We were right next to the punching-bag now. 'No one knows,' she went on. 'I thought it best to keep it to myself.' I wanted to hit the punching-bag hard, but I bit my tongue. 'I knew all the time, she went on 'that our relationship wouldn't last very long, but you look so lonely sometimes that I just wanted to be a sister to you.

I pressed her hand warmly and then walked her to the girls' side.

It was election day. I buried my head in my pillow and tried to shut out the voices which were calling me from both sides. I wanted to continue in the forgetful sleep, and I clung to it as though it alone were a land mass amidst the tempest of voices and the welter of wake-up bells. My bed was being tilted and octopus-like arms were tugging at my doubled-up and ever-shrinking body.

'Wake up,' voices heralded. 'You have the election in the bag.'

As though that mattered. Now the bed was solidly back on the floor and Mac was telling me eagerly what had happened.

'Other and a couple of other boys, we don't know who,' he was saying rapidly, 'went down to the basement this morning and started rattling steampipes. They shook those steampipes so hard, down in the basement, that they woke the whole bedroom up, and Arlie and Jack lectured the boys, with steampipes rattling, about your candidacy. They told them that Other wasn't fit to represent them if he had guts enough to disturb the whole dormitory, and I tell you, you've got it in the bag. Every boy who was awake then is with you one hundred per cent.'

'I hate politics,' I blurted out, 'the steampipes and all.'

'This is America, and you live in a democracy,' Kenneth said. 'Besides, I thought you wanted to go into politics as a career. You'll need a harder stomach than you've got.'

'I'm through with it for ever,' I said.

By nightfall, when the Braille election ballots had been counted, I had received two-thirds of the votes, and was the new president of the student body. Other was the first to come up to me. Flinging his hairy masculine arms about me and spitting tobacco above my shoulder, he congratulated me warmly, as though I were a long-lost brother. 'A real Arkansan,' the boys used to call him, 'solid as the Ozarks themselves, good-humoured as the best of the mountaineers.'

'You should have got the election,' I said. 'That was my sincerest wish.'

'To win and to feel remorse for your defeated opponent,' he said, 'is a privilege of democracy.'

'But the steampipes, Other,' I said.

'Hells bells, I did that knowing what I was doing. I wanted you to win.'

We had been fast friends before, but we were inseparable from that day on.

TWENTY-THREE

Between the Lines

WITH the passing of each day and with the learning of each new slang word or expression peculiar to America, the gulf between what was home to me and what I was fast becoming grew wider and wider, and sometimes in my gloomy moments it seemed for ever unbridgeable. There were always letters from home, but it was as though all of them came in semi-transparent envelopes. Everyone at home hoped that I was making the best of every opportunity. All of them longed to see me. I was in their constant thoughts. Would I please look after my health. Now and then a birth was reported in the home of one of our relatives, or the marriage of a distant cousin. Sometimes the news concerned my immediate family, like the marriage of sister Umi to Lieutenant Gautam. India was changing, she reminded me, because she had met Gautam in Bombay all by herself, without, as she put it, the help of the relaying stations of our relatives. Mother never wrote, because she could not use English, and there was no one in Arkansas who could read Hindi. Whenever I thought of this, I felt very depressed that I had come to Arkansas, where during my whole stay, I had not met another Indian or had a chance to speak Panjabi or Hindi.

Beneath the surface of the simple news from home of daily occurrences, now and then there was a line, or more likely a tone, which made me stop and think what sacrifices my family was going through to keep me in America. Ashok had decided not to buy shoes as yet, because I was in school, and the dowry of sister Umi did not begin to compare with that of sister Pom. The devaluation of Indian money right after my leaving home had really played havoc with family finances. Father wrote that he was working very hard to get some compensation for our lost home. Retirement from the Indian Government at the age of fifty-five was compulsory, although if you were 'absolutely indispensable,' there was an extension of one year. His extension would soon be up, and then he would be jobless, although brother Om, Usha, Ashok and myself were still in school.

Everyone at home wanted to know what I was learning. I could not write home that sometimes we played cards in class, using French words to denote the suits, pretending thus to learn a foreign language; that sometimes days would pass in a classroom without our ever reading a page. I wrote only about the classes of Mr Chiles, where alone we had daily homework, and where the class period was spent discussing these assignments.

They always received numerous clippings which appeared in the Arkansas papers, telling about my every activity as though I were a precious specimen whose growth and development had special bearing on all Arkansans. These clippings, along with the various letters written by groups who invited me to speak on India, were read by my family and many of our relatives with great satisfaction. Although often I felt discouraged that the papers exaggerated my achievements, and although there were times when I was quite frightened of speaking on India to groups who considered me the last authority on my country, my family took the paper cuttings and the letters at face value and as testimonials of my success. Whatever my fear, I could not communicate it across ten thousand miles.

Even with my next-door schoolmates, I had a similar difficulty in communication. To them, I was just another boy in his early teens who might well have spent all his childhood in those sheltered surroundings. I had wanted to become 'one of them,' and within the first few weeks I was 'one of them,' but with it I had flung away the chance of having anyone to talk to about sisters Pom, Nimi, Umi, Usha, or brothers Om and Ashok, or about the daily incidents on the frontiers of Pakistan and India. Even though there was no outlet for my gamut of feelings about home, my memory was fanned more and more as, with the marriage of sister Umi, the departure of brother Om for a school a thousand miles away, sister Nimi's leaving home to take a job,

I realized the family life of 'Pindi and Lahore was collapsing. Even Ashok was in a boarding school. 'There are no more dinner-table schools,' Father wrote, 'and no more trips to hill stations for us.'

If it had not been for the withdrawn hours in the night when my imagination could roam unhindered over the panoramic canvas of the past, the loss of the tonal texture in letters from home and the corresponding change in the fortunes of our family life might, indeed, have been too much to bear in that dormitory life of ours, a life where there was no privacy, even in the shower room.

The obscure hours in the night were not enough, however. I still sought communion with at least one person. It was with Mr Chiles, whom the boys called a 'father confessor' and the faculty called a 'walking encyclopedia', that I rested my hopes.

One day in civics class, a few weeks after I had been in school, I heard Mr Chiles's voice pitched unusually high. 'Are you deaf, Ved? Why don't you answer me?' It was as though Father had slapped me hard without reason.

'Ray, is he asleep?' Mr Chiles snapped.

'No, sir,' Ray said.

Then I heard in a tone more controlled, although still show-ing signs of exasperation, 'I think, Ved, you'd better go to the infirmary and have your ears checked.' At that moment, a mo-ment of complete humiliation in front of my class, I disliked Mr Chiles like a rebellious child who thinks he has been unjustly treated. Mr Chiles passed a question to Ray and ignored me for the whole period. All the time I tried to think back. What had happened? 'Why don't you answer me?' implied a question, but I had not heard the question. What had I been thinking about so hard? Had I been in a reverie about home? I certainly had not been asleep. When the class was dismissed, I waited for Mr Chiles to ask me to stay so that he could explain, maybe even apologize, but he did not, and I resented it bitterly. I decided I would never speak to him again, and in a rush of emotion, I was back in the Mehta *Gullie* fighting with Yog, defiantly telling him, 'Kuti' – 'I will never speak to you again.'

I felt then even more humiliated, like a child who thinks he is grown up, but discovers he is really a baby.

Later Ray told me that Mr Chiles had asked me a question, not once, but three times, and each time he had called my name. 'Where were you, old man?' Ray asked incredulously, and I could not convince him that I had heard neither the question nor my name being called. I immediately went in search of Mr Chiles. I found him playing the piano in the small reception room, but I could not see him because of the cluster of teachers who were gathered around the piano, singing. While waiting for him to finish, I was struck by the thought, What will I say to him, how will I explain my mental absence from the class-room? But I stayed nevertheless, and when he finished playing, I stumbled through an apology, telling him that I could not find a way to explain my mental blackout. I had just not heard his question. The simplicity with which he accepted my apology and his own expression of regret started a lasting friendship. From that day he became my confidant and interpreter of either the intricacies of American politics that I did not understand, or of what he called the 'American mind'.

Once I confided to him that the students I was meeting in the States seemed younger somehow than those in India.

'Ours is a young and luxurious country,' he said, 'where people can afford to be children longer, but once responsibility is forced upon them, they mature very quickly. One has only to see the difference in an American girl before and after marriage to understand what I mean. Americans play hard, but they work hard too.'

It was a favourite occupation among the boys to match Mr Chiles up with one single teacher after another. It was invariable that whichever teacher was revered second to Mr Chiles always became his bride in the imagination of the students. First it was Miss Harper, then Miss Wilson, and for a while, even Miss Greenway. As each of these teachers got married and left the school, the next attractive and most popular teacher took her place. The make-believe matchmaking had, I suppose, much to do with the wish of the students to see Mr Chiles happy, and the highest happiness, as Arlie used to say, was to wish a blind person married, because it is more necessary for him to be married in order to exist fully than it is for a sighted person.

Then, too, I suppose, the students felt a sense of community with Mr Chiles, because he was one of the few blind members of the faculty, and the only one who was a graduate of the school. He was a model for all the students and was good, extremely good, in mobility, which automatically rated him high in the minds of the blind students. Furthermore, he was one of the few graduates since the founding of the school to go through college, and even get his M.A.

Not satisfied with conjuring up brides for Mr Chiles, however, the speculative minds of the students had him teaching in the small private college from which he had been graduated. To be sure, a man of means, like Mr Chiles, did not have to teach at all. He taught because he enjoyed the activity of the mind.

I suppose he would have approved of the air castles the students built for him, because he always used to talk in civics class about the 'America behind the headlines' which he wanted to find, an America not shrouded by morbid radio programmes and scandalous tabloids. Students who knew him best knew also that his ideal was to be married and to settle in a small town and raise his family in its carefree atmosphere, away from the big and bustling city where each good action seemed lost to him. 'I'm not a big-time man,' he used to say. 'I just want to be happy.'

Miss Harper said once in her class, when we were teasing her about Mr Chiles, 'To hear you boys and girls talk, it is as though you were daydreaming for yourselves and not for him. Walking encyclopedias have a hard time of it.' And then she added, 'I would like some of you to wish away his nervousness, and maybe then he will be marriageable.'

'All sensitive and intelligent blind people are slightly nervous,' Other said. 'It's like asking one to wish away blindness.'

'It is so easy to daydream in these protective surroundings,' Miss Harper went on. 'It's like getting into a groove and not being able to snap out of it.'

But the students never stopped hoping that Mr Chiles would teach in the quiet of his small college, and that some day the imagined bride would appear in real flesh and blood.

Everyone on the stage was talking in hushed voices, because it seemed that people had started coming into the auditorium. It must not be very full, I thought, because I could hear the distinctive laugh of Big Jim. Ernest was calling the name of a girl which I could not make out. He probably wants to sit by her, I thought.

'I can hear Peggy,' Kenneth said, but Mac sniffed.

'She doesn't have a tongue.'

'Wonder if I'll ever see her again,' Kenneth said pensively. 'I wish I weren't graduating.'

'You can't live on here for ever,' Mac said.

Beyond the stage in the auditorium, the individual voices were no longer distinguishable. It was like the sleeping-hall now, multiplied manyfold.

'Why is everyone so sombre?' Other asked abruptly.

'You can afford to be cheerful,' Mac said, 'because at least you know a trade that you can practise.'

'Yes, Other,' Annabelle said. 'You can make enough money with piano tuning.'

'Maybe I'll never see Peggy again,' Kenneth said, 'and next year Pat will be dancing with her.'

'Sssh,' Mac shushed. 'Mr Woolly might hear you.'

'To hear you all talk,' Other continued, 'you would turn this place into an asylum.'

'Be quiet,' Kenneth said irritatedly. 'All of us won't be able to get jobs as you will with your piano tuning.'

I was getting uncomfortable. Mr Woolly, however, came up from the other side of the podium and told us that the school had never graduated seven before. Ours was the largest and the best class that he remembered. Then he walked Norman over a few steps to the podium so that he might not stumble when the time came to get his diploma. Norman had lost his sight late in life and was very clumsy in mobility.

After Mr Woolly left, Kenneth, Mac, Carol and Annabelle still talked despairingly about leaving school. Other was quiet now and I wondered if he was rehearsing his valedictory address. In my mind I ran rapidly through my speech: 'Board of Trustees, Mr Woolly, members of the faculty, and friends. Words cannot express the pleasure and honour that we, the class of 1952, have in welcoming you to this, our commencement programme.'

I wished they hadn't made me memorize my salutatory address. I felt nervous that Mr Davis was going to be our commencement speaker. I remembered how adamantly he had opposed my coming to the States for education. And since he was the head of the American Printing House for the Blind, his high position in educational work for the visually handicapped had given him power to block my coming to America. All the correspondence was in the backdrop of my memory, and I did not want to exhume the buried grievances. Maybe I could have gone to Perkins; maybe there they would not have played cards in the classrooms, and maybe its graduating class would not have minded leaving the security of school. But I did not want to think of any of that now, when all was in the past. I was just happy that I had been able to squeeze my eleventh and twelfth grades into one year and was graduating a year ahead of my class.

Other said, 'I'm not afraid of leaving the school and finding my own living outside. I feel unhappy only because I may never see many of my friends and teachers again.'

The rattle of the curtain rings cut him short. The ceremony from beginning to end was a blur, except when Mr Davis referred to our correspondence. Large beads of perspiration trickled down my back when he turned to me and publicly acknowledged that he, Farrell and others had been 'dead wrong' in advising me to stay home. I did not flush with triumph at this apology. I simply felt moved by the American candour and sincerity in his words.

When the exercises were over, all the parents of the graduates came up on the small stage. I tried to slip away, but Other had his arm around my shoulder. The auditorium started emptying, and so did the stage now. Ducking under Other's arm, I said, 'Excuse me,' as though I were a child and were excusing myself from the classroom, hoping that no one would ask why. 'You really swung it, old man,' Ray said as I came out into the hallway. 'Three years ago I would have bet my life that you wouldn't be graduating with us, let alone a year ahead of us.'

I did not blame Ray, because I recalled going into the fifth-grade arithmetic class. 'I myself expected to be a few years behind you,' I said. He laughed wryly. Lois came up and congratulated me for getting the Stanley award, which Ray had won my first year.

Mr Davis was there now. 'It is quite an honour to have the highest scholastic average in the whole school,' he said.

'Among the boys,' Ray corrected him.

I had heard of the gaiety, the dances and wild parties which accompanied graduation exercises, but all my class-mates seemed gloomy that night. There would be no parties, and I felt sad. All the class graduates had now joined us in the hallway.

'Other,' Annabelle said, 'your speech almost made me cry.'

'I thought it was the most cheerful valedictory I have heard in a long time,' Mr Charles said.

'It was just the idea of valedictory,' Annabelle said. 'I didn't even listen to him.' Everyone laughed, but somewhat nervously, I thought.

'What next?' Kenneth asked, discouraged.

The next day, the whole building was as empty as on the first day I had arrived there. There were still some teachers left, but the dormitories seemed ghostly. Having completed my packing the day before, I wandered around the school compound idly. Tomorrow I would go to see my father, who had retired from the government and was a visiting Fulbright professor at the University of California in Los Angeles. There would be a chance to catch up on all the home news and talk Panjabi. I just wished that I had got into Columbia, the only university I had applied to.

I passed the window of the auditorium and heard Mr Chiles

playing the small organ. I went in and sat down to listen to the
familiar melodies. When he stopped, we sat down on the stage
steps facing the empty auditorium and talked. He told me he
wanted me to go to his small college and that if I were there he
would look after me like an older brother. He said he had been
hurt by the treatment I had got with my application at Columbia.
'In big universities,' he went on, 'things like that happen.'
Perhaps they did happen, but what would I say to my father?

Mr Chiles said I should not feel bad, because some universities
just balked at accepting blind people, that the school had never
sent students East. In fact, most of its students didn't go to
college at all, and what connexions the school did have were in
Arkansas. He advised me to go to his college, major in history as
he had done, and then . . .

There was no answer to the question of what to do after that.
An image of Mr Chiles, his handshake, his voice, his particular
speech mannerisms, his shadow sitting next to me, which I
could perceive with my facial vision, passed across my mind. It
was hard to tell, of course, how nearly my image of him corres-
ponded to the real Mr Chiles, but somehow, sitting there, it was
not hard for me to picture myself in his shoes, even to the slight
nervous quality to which Miss Harper had referred. He was right
when he reminded me that the orbit of influence of any one
person is limited, but living in that school seemed even more
limited. It seemed like a self-imposed limitation. 'It isn't for me,'
I said. 'If Columbia thinks I am not for them, then I have to
look elsewhere.'

We talked some more about school and my years there, but
it was like the last few paragraphs of a novel whose action has
already been resolved. Only a few loose threads remain to be
tied up, such as what to do with the governess who brought up
the hero.

That night I had dinner with Mr Woolly. He gave me a tie
clasp with A.S.B. engraved on it.

'Son, I want you to have this, so that whenever you wear it,
people will know that you went to the Arkansas School for the

Blind. You and Mr Chiles are the best graduates we have ever had.'

I took the tie clasp, felt the long, smooth bar, the two suspended snake chains, and the pendant in the middle. Mr Woolly ran my forefinger over the raised design with the A.S.B. seal on it.

'You'll never forget us, will you?' he said, putting it on my tie.

'How could he?' Mrs Woolly said. 'We have put our seal on him.'

'I am deeply indebted to you,' I said. 'If it had not been for you, I wouldn't have got to the States at all.'

Mrs Woolly and the boys walked us out to the car, where there were a number of faculty members gathered. I said goodbye to some of them there. Others insisted they wanted to go all the way out to the airport. I rode through those streets for the last time. When I first arrived in Little Rock, I had not been able to keep track of the direction from inside a car, but now I could. I could not help feeling that the most precious thing I had acquired from the Arkansas School was mobility. I may not have my eyes, I thought, but I have the freedom of movement, a freedom of movement almost equal to that of sighted people.

At the airport Mr Chiles said, 'Who knows, you might come back after the summer and go to our college after all.'

And Mr Woolly, who had gone to the same college, argued warmly for my return.

I did not know then what was next for me, though I knew I was outward bound. I never again rode in those once familiar streets, but the warm friendships I made there still persist.

TWENTY-FOUR

College At Last

THE air hostess asked us to fasten our belts. From the bumpy jerks, popping ears, and a kind of falling motion, as when I stepped into a manhole unexpectedly, I knew that in a few minutes we would land at the Los Angeles airport, and I would see my father at last.

I was eager to know what had happened to India in the three years I had been away. When I left, free India was only two years old. By now probably she had learned to walk well, and, I thought, could not only ask for bread, but knew how and where to get it. I had lived through the birth pains of a nation and shared in the glory of the independence and the shame of the partition, only to spend three years in Arkansas, bottled up in a preserve jar. By coming to America I had exchanged a position at the nerve centre of a nation for an isolated valley of the blind, without even newspapers to read. In many residential schools for the blind they didn't have readers, and there were few, if any, Braille or talking books on India.

We were on the ground now, and my father was there, but it was not until we reached the privacy of his small and crowded apartment and the friend who had brought us home left, that I felt at one with him. In the flow of the familiar musical Panjabi all the nuances of awkwardness and estrangement vanished.

I never was a very good violin player, but I always liked the sound of it. When I did not hear a violin for some time, I used to get lonely for it, but it was hard to realize how lonely, until I heard the long drawn-out vibrato notes once more. In the same way, only when I started conversing in Panjabi did I long to go back to India and fill my soul with the melodic language.

My father placed his hands on my shoulders and quietly looked at me for what seemed a long while. 'You've grown, son, in the last three years,' he said, running his hands up and down my more developed arms. 'Let's see, you were ninety pounds when you left home.'

'I have put on twenty-five more,' I said.

'You look much fuller,' he said warmly, 'and certainly an inch taller. I wish your mother were here to see the change.'

But what surprised him more than my physical growth was something else. 'It is the confident way you walked down that ramp and followed those two ladies ahead of you to the terminal.' He added thoughtfully, 'It is also the way you hold your head, so high.'

But soon, in the press of my questions about the family, all else for a moment was pushed aside.

While I listened to my father talk about home, I paced up and down the apartment, and within a few minutes, I had surveyed my narrow surroundings. Father had disassembled the couch and had made two beds on the floor, one on the mattress and one on the springs. Books and papers were piled around, and save for the narrow passageway where I paced, there was hardly any room to move about. I thought of the large three-storey house with its abundance of rooms, and I felt a pang of pain for my father. This is what it had all come to, this small upstairs apartment in West Los Angeles, with no servants or butler to make the beds or stack the papers. But memories of the old splendour were soon deposited deep in the well of the subconscious as my father read to me, day in, day out, one old newspaper after another and passages from books which told about the surge of political and economic activity at home. I felt once more, as I had in the days of partition, the stimulation of the present.

The present which concerned Columbia, however, was quite another matter. My father had hoped not only for my admission to Columbia, but for a scholarship, and so it was with a discouraged heart that I told him about my failure. I had no illusions about the seriousness of the situation, and however happy I might be at what Mr Davis had said, or at how well I had done at the Arkansas School, I had to entertain the prospect of now going home.

Counting transportation, five thousand dollars had been spent already, twenty-five thousand *rupees,* enough probably for the full education of at least two or three people in India, and more than my father's annual salary, even though he was one of the highest paid officials in the Indian Government. The question was whether, after such an expense, I was any better prepared to live an independent life in India than I had been before leaving home. The answer, I knew, was an unqualified no.

My father reminded me that the training of Arkansas would count for nothing in India. Furthermore, the cherished freedom of movement which I had acquired would also have to be surrendered, because in India there were no red and green lights, no regulated traffic laws comparable to America, and the erratic *tonga* men, bicycles and ox carts could not be expected to look after the interests of a pedestrian, especially a blind one. Neither was there a comparable organization of streets or blocks. I could try, of course, to buck all this, if I were stubborn enough, but it would be tough.

I could not get a job in the States, because I was on a student's visa. To continue to live here, I had therefore to be a student, but when we asked someone at the University of California to estimate the cost of a school year, he gave the flat figure of three thousand dollars. There would be the expenses for board and room, for tuition, and then I had to allow about one thousand dollars to pay readers, to have the class assignments read to me. The B.A. degree, therefore, seemed not only four years, but twelve thousand dollars away. And my father told me that when he got his pension, it would be one hundred dollars, or five hundred *rupees,* a month, which was enough for three or four people to live on in India, leaving nothing to spare.

'Five hundred *rupees* in India are like five hundred dollars, but when exchanged for American dollars, it is like forfeiting four-fifths of their value,' he told me.

As for obtaining any assistance from the Indian Government or an Indian foundation, there was not even an iota of a chance, because the Indian Government had much more pressing problems than to look after the interests of any special group like the blind. My Arkansas diploma would not be of much weight in the scales of any foundation.

But for all this, my father said he would not think of my going home. He would borrow money.

'But how will you pay it back?' I asked.

'I will open a practice in India.'

'But that will take lots of money,' I said.

'I will get a job here in the States, then,' he said.

But I knew that was impossible, because it took Asians ten years, sometimes, to get into the States to become citizens. And then, too, they had to bring some money with them to prove that they would not be public charges.

'Don't you worry,' he told me. 'I'll manage it somehow.'

At night, however, we both pretended to sleep. I always knew when he was up, and he was up a good deal of the time. One time we said good night to each other at ten. I did not stir at all and tried to breathe heavily, pretending to be asleep. At two my father, without any warning, broke the silence with, 'You've got to look at it another way. I have managed to be here in the States with you. Three years ago, I could never have foreseen this day. I mean, what with Pakistan, I never thought I could afford to leave the country.'

'Yes,' I said. I knew the Fulbright people had paid just his passage, and the only reason he had come was so that he would be able to see me. He was forbidden to earn anything in the country.

'I have some savings,' he said, 'from the brief job with the World Health Organization I had after my retirement. They're all yours.'

'Yes,' I said, and thought of all the education of Ashok which was ahead, and of Usha, who hadn't even finished high school, and of sister Nimi, who had to be married and whose dowry had yet to be bought, and of brother Om, who still had two years to go before finishing engineering school. I could have wept for my father then.

If the nights were sleepless, during the day my father and I went from foundation office to foundation office, from one philanthropic person to the next. There was no scarcity of these philanthropists. They were as numerous as the cash registers in the stores, and it was not hard to get close to the cash registers, either. To punch the button, however, and draw some money was quite another matter. Every day we would get notes and telephone calls from our well-meaning friends, who would point out one person after another to be approached. We saw them and they were all generous people, but they either did not believe that a blind person could be educated, or had undertaken some more worthy project than my education. Established organizations like the International Rotary either were not interested in foreign students already in the States, or did not subsidize undergraduate education.

But along with the fatigue and disappointment, there were always humorous incidents, like a millionaire's quietly slipping a dollar into my pocket, with a note explaining it was for taxi money, or the old lady who kept us for a whole two hours, explaining her genealogical connexion with a Hindu *pandit* who lived in the fifteenth century. If I had been closeted in an Arkansas prison before, I was now moving in high society, coming into contact with a gallery of rich and adorned persons who were all kind and accommodating, but who nevertheless, for one reason or another, could not be of help to us.

One day, when the rank poison of failure after failure to get money had settled in my stomach and was beginning to turn sour, the scent of strong wine came from a wealthy family. 'They seemed not only to be interested in your promise,' my father told me, 'but I think are genuinely impressed by your independence and the way you have overcome your blindness.' Of course, their foundation had given scholarships only for graduate study, but my father felt they were ready to make an exception.

After that, I could never be in the presence of these patrons without being self-conscious, and I remember vividly, although with great mortification, the time when, while my grant still hung fire, at one of their dinners they served me squab. The clean tablecloth, starched white napkins, full dishes of the most expensive wild rice, and the eyes of their most intimate friends all surrounded me. All of them seemed to speak out: 'If you can't eat your squab with a knife and fork, you'll never get to college. You'll never get any scholarship – no grant.'

As I sat next to my hosts, slowly, deliberately drinking a glass of water before touching my silverware, the tiny bones covered with skinlike meat seemed to be the only things between college and me. Self-sufficient I was, but not self-sufficient enough to manage the squab. The old, the almost forgotten, interview with Baldwin rose to my mind. I could not fail my father again. I picked up my fork, started nibbling gradually at the wild rice and the water-melon rind, but carefully avoided the side of the plate with the squab. One of the guests on my right offered to help me with the squab. I yielded. For ten minutes she worked on the squab, while I sat idle, hot with shame. It seemed my very presence created a scene. When the plate was finally returned to me, there was nothing more to the squab than a few morsels of skinny meat, and I gulped them down as though I were eating a vegetable I did not like, rather than a very rare delicacy which should be held in the mouth to taste all its rich flavour.

Dinner done, I was again an exhibition piece, because in the living-room I had to tell the guests about my Arkansas experience. For all my speaking practice, my sentences were faltered and mangled, and the talk was disconnected, because I could not put the squab out of my mind.

'You are too sensitive about these things,' Father said as we went home. 'You overdramatize them.'

Perhaps I did, but I wondered how a surgeon would feel who had performed many operations successfully, but botched one right in full view of the operating theatre. If the gallery of watchers had no knowledge of his past successes, would he not be judged by that operation alone?

A few days later, however, a grant for two years, fifteen hundred dollars a year, was confirmed, and at last I could begin my college career. Although I was not a citizen of the United States, by special arrangement the state of California made available seven hundred and fifty dollars to pay my readers, provided

I went to school there. Even at that late date, after my personal appearance, admission was the least of my problems. I had a choice between the universities of California and Stanford, and Pomona College. I chose the last because it was small, because somehow it offered more prospect of a real interlocking of mind between professors and students than did the two bigger universities.

When my father left for India, I entered my college full of trepidation. Upon my admission, the deans at both Stanford and Pomona had said exactly the same thing to my father: 'Competition in our private school is keen, and if he comes out with a C average, you ought to be grateful.' Whether or not I could be grateful for that comment, the prospect of living on what had once been the frontier, and somehow still breathed the informal, carefree atmosphere of old, excited me, and I was happy to have a chance at both college and competition.

Although Claremont was placed among secluded surroundings close to the hills, and sometimes at night for a stretch of an hour one could walk down the middle of the street without meeting a car, still, in some ways it was reminiscent of Little Rock and the ice-cream plant. To be sure, Claremont was populated with students of four associated colleges, yet the awkwardness, the very misunderstanding I had experienced in Little Rock buses and in the ice-cream plant about what the blind could or could not do seemed, too, to grip my class-mates, a few professors, and even a dean.

I had for my English professor a man of consummate wisdom and skill in dealing with people. My second day in his class he asked me to stay for a moment after he had dismissed the other students.

'You shouldn't be crossing College Way without your cane,' he said. 'You'll get killed.'

'Yes, sir,' I said shyly, and went away.

Three or four class periods later he talked to me again. 'You're still not carrying the cane,' he said.

I knew I would never carry a cane, but I didn't know how

to tell him that or how to explain it. 'I will as soon as I get one, sir.' I guess within my soul I still hoped that people watching me cross the street would realize I could do it without a cane and would stop talking to me about it.

About a week later he stopped me again. 'The dean called me,' he said, 'and he's afraid you will get killed. I hate to keep on bringing up this subject, but your cane . . .'

In those two weeks since I had been at Pomona, I had crossed College Way at least four times a day, but still the question of a cane seemed to persist.

'I will not carry it, sir,' I said.

'If you are shy about it,' he went on kindly, 'just use it while you are crossing streets and then hide it under bushes before coming to class.'

'I am not ashamed of being blind,' I said, moved deeply by his sensitivity. 'That's written over me in larger letters than any cane could ever write. It's just that I don't need the cane.'

Whether it was my facial expression or his own sensitivity, he never mentioned the subject again, but the dean once accosted me in the middle of the quadrangle.

'Why won't you carry that cane?' he asked. 'You'll get killed.'

Trying to dismiss the subject with humour, I said, 'Death only comes once, and I am not afraid of dying.'

'It might come once, but once is enough to kill me. How about you?' he asked wryly.

In cafeteria lines it was like meeting so many hundreds of deans. No sooner would I enter the door than, although I was quite capable of finding the end of the line myself, all the men standing would start directing me, and once at the counter, would get the tray, silverware and even the food. Sometimes, when they put my milk on their own tray, they would drink it for me also. And if I did manage to ignore or slip through these scrutinizing eyes, find a tray, get my food, and at random sit down at a table, all of a sudden the conversation would cease, and after a while, when I was no longer an object of curiosity to be stared at – not for being an Indian, but for being blind –

people would ignore my existence at the table altogether, and would carry on talk unaware of my very presence. I liked pretending I was invisible. I sometimes wished I were Other. I could then have joked about it or entered the conversation on my own initiative. As it was, I also started ignoring their existence, and sometimes was rude outright.

Girls in class, too, shied from talking to me, not because I had a communicable disease, but, as one of them told me later on, because I seemed to her then 'detached from reality'. I never asked her whether it was my facial expression that seemed detached from reality or whether I was outside the pale of her reality. Wherever I was in relation to the skirts of reality, I knew well that these students had to be educated about the blind if I was to get my education.

As I learned on the first day of college, each and every assignment would have to be read aloud to me. There were few if any textbooks – indeed, not much non-fiction – in Braille or on talking books. I had never used readers before, except for what little my father had read to me that summer, but I knew that reading aloud, whether heavy or light books, Hegel or comic strips, all went at the same speed. My fastest reader would not be able to read more than twenty full-size pages an hour. These limitations I knew and accepted, and then started scouting around for readers among the more serious students, although as a freshman it was hard to know who they were.

I got some bad readers, who would call off an appointment without notice, and prefer to talk most of the time rather than read, or waste a lot of time finding sources. Just before my first half-term, when I needed help most of all, a few of them left me. By the end of the first three weeks of college, I was behind about four hundred pages, at least twenty hours of reading, and for the first month and a half the back-log of reading kept accumulating by geometric progression.

In class I found it difficult taking Braille notes, because the professor talked too fast, and besides, the clicking noise of the Braille stylus used to make me self-conscious. I could write Braille fast, very fast, but it still was three or four times slower than writing with pencil. Coming from the Arkansas School, where I had to write scarcely more than two pages of theme every two or three months, organizing and writing papers sometimes twice a month for a class was difficult. For all the accumulated handicaps, I could not afford to go to a professor and explain that I had no readers, or excuse my bad work because of my poor background. I could not afford to create the impression that any part of my problem was related to my blindness. Above all, I wanted to be treated as normal.

In my room I could not go to sleep. I used to turn my phonograph on at full blast and listen to the blurred music, wondering if I would get my grant for the next year or if I would have to go home. Sometimes in the middle of the night I would get out of bed, take the first bicycle standing without a lock, and ride up and down the empty familiar streets stealthily, because I wanted privacy. I would pedal hard and would come home tired, and even then I could not always fall asleep.

As the months progressed, however, I started losing less and less sleep over my work, because it started improving, and I got assurance that I would have enough money to see me through college. I banished worry for inner quietude and relaxation, and I perfected my technique of getting readers. Professors would point out to me their best students, and I would approach them either at the dinner-table or at the student union about reading our assignments together. I found that students working their way through college were more reliable. I also used as fill-ins some elderly readers that the dean, who had by now become a good and resourceful friend, referred me to. Even before the first semester was over, I had about a ten-hour-a-day reading schedule. After my rigorous reading schedule I still would not be tired, and would come home to read whatever literature I could find on talking books. Gradually I started cutting my sleep from the nine hours I had had in Arkansas to about six, or occasionally even five.

My acquaintance with the better students, students well nurtured and with solid training, pointed out my own deficiencies, but rather than fret about them as I had done earlier, I just accepted them and read as much as I could above and beyond the class assignments. My professor remarked once that I was a hothouse plant, but I knew there was nothing I could do about it.

Classes, too, became easier, because instead of taking notes, I simply concentrated on what the professor said, although for tests I occasionally used my readers' notes. For exams I learned to work accurately on a typewriter, or sometimes, when they were long, I dictated. Readers still would stop reading to me before exams, but if I had done my regular assignments throughout the semester, this did not seem a very great handicap. The most restful week of all was the week before final exams, when I had only two readers left out of nine.

I did not lose any sleep over my relations with other students, either. The earlier awkwardness and hesitation in the dining-room and classrooms passed into wonder, and students used to walk up to me and ask, 'How do you know when you get to that step?' or 'I saw you walk around that parked car as though you could see it.' To my amazement, I learned the most common misconception among my friends was that I counted steps, that I had had the whole town of Claremont measured by steps when I first arrived there, and therefore I knew where every sharp curve and gutter was. No matter how much I explained about facial vision, it seemed I could never explain enough for anyone to understand fully.

I suppose it was this failure which resulted in the story about a mutual friend, whom we called the Dauphin – a story circulated liberally among my friends. It was reported to me thus:

'The day I mailed your letter I ran into the Dauphin and we went up to his place to chat for a while.... Incidentally, he never believed that you were totally blind. We had a long argument about this, too. He felt that if you weren't, there would be something to be gained by keeping it a secret. I replied rather grossly to this, as I was a whit annoyed. I think the Dauphin keeps secrets just for the sake of keeping secrets.'

We had named our friend (now at Harvard) the Dauphin

because of his unique personality, after the memorable character in *Huckleberry Finn*. The Dauphin's opinion itself would not have carried much weight if it did not reflect the gamut of notorious misconceptions about my having some sight or being blessed with some supernatural power or perception which persists among the people who should know better.

TWENTY-FIVE

In Search of Sight

LEGEND has it that there are certain birds which, if kept in a cage too long, lose their faculty to fly, although I never tested this myth by letting my canary or parrot out of the cage. In the same way, it is said of blind people that if they become too entrenched in one environment, they become lethargic, too careful. Instead of becoming more skilled, they lose their powers of travel. In short, these blind people are 'shelved', or 'get glued to a rocking-chair'.

Having no love for either cupboards or rocking-chairs, during holidays I have travelled a good deal. I have not always travelled in style – it's impossible when you want to cover the distance from San Francisco to New York, from San Diego to Seattle, and from Miami to Cambridge. I have hitch-hiked in 1928-model jalopies, ridden in fuming buses and rattling milk trains. Sometimes I have also had rides in Cadillacs with buttons for rolling down the windows, smuggled myself into roomettes on Starlights, and flown in airplanes which had a bar and, because the plane was half-empty, a window seat for every passenger. All in all I have crossed the United States fourteen times and visited in or travelled through thirty-seven of the forty-eight states.

Of course, when you are blind, you miss the scenic part – that is to say, you miss the view of a snow-clad peak, the impression of skyscrapers lined up shoulder to shoulder, a vast stretch of countryside, or the way a city looks from a plane when draped in a thin veil of clouds. You become, however, more conscious of smells, the gamut of accents, or the unusual names streets have in some cities. But what you remember most of all, the thing which imprints itself permanently on your mind, are the people you encounter, even the ones you meet only for a moment on a street corner or sitting at a counter, or the kind driver whose motor you can hear coming faster and faster while you wonder whether he will pass you by like the one before him or stop. You remember vividly the moment when a car slows down, and a voice says, 'Hey, feller – want a ride?' or 'Where are you going?' or 'Can I give you a lift?' And when you come to the end of the journey, often the driver, who is now a friend, insists on getting out and helping you flag down the next relay.

Sometimes my hitch-hiking has turned into a circus. I remember, for instance, a kind elderly lady who was genuinely distressed with my parents' not taking better care of me and letting me out on the streets like a 'vagabond'. In a wayside place in Texas, under the pretence of taking me to a gas station to catch the next ride, she turned me over to a police deputy with a blistering harangue that I was probably a runaway state ward, and if the Democrats had been in power I would have received better care. I was irritated until, after she drove off, the deputy told me that she had left twenty dollars with him for a train ticket to take me back to Washington. We had a lively discussion about what to do with the money, and finally decided to send it to the Democratic campaign fund. The deputy then took me to a petrol station, where I caught my next ride.

Somewhere I also have tucked away the card of a cutlery salesman who thought my blindness would be a 'terrific asset' in salesmanship. 'So if you ever get in a jam,' he said in that thick Southern accent, 'come to me.' I kept the card as a souvenir. After all, he did take me two hundred miles. All these associations, sometimes embarrassing, sometimes touching, make the travelogue of those of us who are blind.

The summer after my freshman year at college I spent at the University of California, at Berkeley. It took me only two days to settle down in International House and to learn their campus. It was during that summer session that I met Simon. He was a South American, settled in the States, and I don't think he ever stood still. His body was always full of movement, as though he were doing a rhumba, a samba, or even a Charleston. Even in the shower when he sang – that was by no means the only place where he sang – the songs were marked by jumping, gay, motions.

Sam, who was bald, described him to me as having glossy hair and deep well-like eyes which were very effective when he sat on a sofa in the lounge – the International House abounded in lounges – and tried to catch or wink at the girls around him. Sam, who was an Iranian, nearing thirty, and wanted to marry an American girl very badly, used to call him the bouncing Romeo from South America.

It is not easy for me to meet bouncing Romeos or famed athletes, but because I helped Simon in one of his economics assignments, he became a friend of mine. One day, early in the summer session, I said to him, 'Simon, you go out so much. Why don't you get me a date?' I said it sort of bashfully, and feeling the necessity to explain, I went on rapidly, 'You see, at college I have such a rigid readers' schedule that every hour from eight in the morning to ten at night is taken up, and that way I haven't had time to develop friendships, especially with girls.' I was flushing more and more hotly, but I couldn't stop. 'Understand I don't live in a monastery. I have girl readers – brilliant and pretty, too – but I make a habit of not mixing business and pleasure. You know what I mean' – and I stuttered – 'when I go scouting for readers I don't want them to think there is anything else attached to it.' And then I tried to make a joke. 'I don't want them to think I am scouting for a wife. I have taken girls out, but it's been merely conversation, never anything more. I mean, that is, with the sighted girls.'

I would have gone on, but Simon was laughing, not unkindly, just gaily. 'Listen, listen,' I pleaded, 'I want to have some fun this summer, and it's always awkward meeting people until they get used to me. Would you help me?'

'But the expression on your face!' He kept on laughing.

I felt hurt, but I wasn't going to show it, because I knew that when you are blind, you have to make many compromises. 'Please, be serious,' I persisted, summoning all my wits.

'You mind if I tell you a joke?' he said.

I was disappointed, but what else was there to do?

'You see, there was a man, crippled – no, let's say lazy – and he was sitting with another man who was going to a john, and the lazy man told the other man to go for him, too. And being kind-hearted, as he was, he consented. When he came out, the lazy man asked this man if he had done what he had told him. "Well," the man who had gone to the toilet said, "you see, after I went, you didn't need to go any more." ' He laughed at his own joke. I felt crushed.

'You see how it is in this game? Each man for himself,' he said.

A wrong card, I thought to myself.

'You remind me of Sam,' he said, with an air of finality.

But Sam, who had listened too, didn't say anything. I could not let it go at that. I had hid my innermost feelings many times before. 'Iranians and Indians,' I said, 'are friends from old historic times.'

'Thank you,' Sam said, and only then was I glad that I had coupled myself with him.

'Simon, you're cruel,' Sam said reproachfully.

'I'll try,' Simon said, 'but one man's meat is another man's poison. Besides, the trouble with Ved is that he looks too much like a walking encyclopedia.'

I couldn't contain myself any more. 'Like hell I do,' I said.

Being new in a university where no one knew me at all, I found it hard to get readers. I asked the professor if he would make an announcement in my class, which was four or five times the size of any at Pomona, that there was a blind student who would like his assignments read and who would be willing to pay seventy-five cents an hour. But he did it in such an incredibly garbled way that, although after each class I waited for someone to come up to me, no one volunteered.

I started getting panicky and thought seriously about trying some other course, but on the fourth day I happened to sit next to Syl and tried to talk with her. She spoke softly and almost timidly, and at first it was not easy to carry on a sustained conversation. I gathered she was a junior at the University of

California and a sociology major, but had a keen love for literature and music.

'Have you found any readers yet?' she asked shyly.

'No,' I said.

'I'd like to do it,' she went on hesitantly, 'except that the braces on my teeth don't come off for another week. I thought they would bother you.'

'Heavens, no,' I responded, and from that day she began reading to me.

Before the week was up, I learned that she came from an exceptionally large family for America. They were seven, and she was the only girl. The father had named all his children after the great universities in the country. In their family they had Harvard, Yale, Princeton and Stanford.

Syl told me, 'My father wanted to name me Wellesley, but my mother called a halt when it came to me.'

Although her father only owned a small grocery store, every one of his children had gone through the state university, and even law and graduate schools. 'He has a mania for education,' Syl told me.

Her mother had died when Syl was young, and Syl had had to perform all the domestic duties until her father remarried. 'I worked hard,' she said, 'because I not only had to take care of the house, but help manage the grocery store. When you have a small business like ours, the whole family has to work.' But she admitted that, being the only girl in the family, she had been spoiled, too.

Now and then she would stop reading and say, 'Oh, I sound horrible. Honestly, it's because of these braces.' I used to protest, and then she would say, 'Oh, you are very kind. You see,' she explained, 'I should have had these braces a long time ago. It's hard to wear them at college age.'

'You take it too much to heart,' I kept telling her.

When she found out how far behind I was in my reading schedule in both my courses, she insisted on helping me catch up.

'I wouldn't think of it,' I told her. 'There are not many

people who can read aloud more than two hours a day. And besides, you still have to put in your hours at the grocery store on Sundays.'

She would not hear of it, and once or twice, when she read to me late at night, I walked her to her dormitory. And this was the beginning of our warm relationship.

She had thick hair, a slight and slender body, a round mouth, and a mellow alto voice which always sounded fresh and alive and which reflected the modulation of her emotions amazingly accurately. Her laugh was subdued but full, and she walked as though she had no weight at all. Whether we were at concerts, the theatre, movies, or restaurants, she always knew how to conduct me without an iota of embarrassment. There was, of course, nothing hard about directing a blind man, because it was I who escorted her, not vice versa. All she had to do was place her hand firmly in mine, and when walking through crowded aisles, not get nervous. She allowed me to order for her, open doors, help her off buses, and let me walk her home as anyone else would.

When we were on a day's outing together and went into a restaurant for lunch or dinner, she would say sweetly, 'Wash-up time,' and would explain to me from the table the twists and turns so well that I could walk directly towards the room without causing a scene.

'Isn't it strange and wonderful,' she exclaimed once, 'that I forget altogether that you can't see!'

When there were reminders, such as the girls at her dormitory marvelling at the way I found her bell and rang for her, or overhearing ladies conversing at a restaurant about how nice it was that a pretty girl went out with a blind man, she used to joke about it, as Other or Kenneth might have. If she had been self-conscious about the braces, she was proportionately relaxed when with me, and this gave our relationship an air of naturalness in which all the disagreeable reminders of awkwardness were effaced.

As at college, I still kept a rigorous reading schedule, but the difference was that every week night at ten I saw her, except for the days she read to me, when we studied scrupulously. I concentrated on my studies harder than ever, locked up in the library, always having the assurance that in the evening there would be the warm and fresh fragrance of Syl beside me, and her soft but firm hand in mine. The relationship was like discovering sight, getting in the bargain an unlimited open country to roam in, with all the problems of readers' schedules shoved into oblivion.

Try as he might, Sam had very bad luck in getting girls to go out with. He, like Simon, used to sit in lounges. In the dining-room he used to look for pretty girls to sit by, but as far as he was concerned, they were as cold as portraits. After a moment's acquaintance, he would call them up, ask them for dates, but invariably they would turn him down.

'I can't understand these American girls,' he told me once. 'Here I am, working for a doctoral degree in electrical engineering, getting paid the salary of an instructor, have a car of my own and plenty of money to take these girls anywhere they want to go, and still . . . Is it because I am a foreigner?'

He paused for confirmation, but I just listened. 'I want madly,' he continued, 'to marry an American girl and live here. And what am I forced to do? Every Saturday night I stay home and listen to the radio, or go out and get drunk.'

'I wish I could do something for you, Sam,' I said. 'I'll ask Syl, but she is shy, and besides, she doesn't know many people at the summer session. Maybe she can do something about it, though.'

I asked Syl that night if she could do anything for Sam. 'Maybe,' she began, 'I can arrange it with my room mate.' (She had just moved in with a girl.) 'But she is very particular,' Syl went on, 'and I don't even know what Sam looks like.'

'Hang it,' I said. 'You don't have to know. Just get him a date.'

Her room mate consented, and Sam insisted on Syl and me doubling with him. We would go to a play first, at the university and then go for pizza in Sam's car.

All the remainder of the week, Sam kept accosting me and asking if he could at least have a glimpse of the girl he was taking out. He was terribly agitated, a state unsuited for a first meeting, although quite in order for a bridegroom. He stopped scouting around for girls in the dining-room and sat next to me, as though to show his gratitude. I started wondering if I should have meddled in it at all, since Sam wouldn't give me any peace. Simon repeatedly insisted that he wanted to see Sam's date. 'Just to size her up,' he said, because Sam wasn't a connoisseur as he was. He decided he would take his girl to the play also, just to appraise the object of Sam's agitation.

When the night finally arrived, everything went off all right. Sam and I picked up the girls and it seemed to me that Sam liked his date, because they talked easily. After the play, however, when Simon came to 'size her up', he whispered something, possibly his judgement, to Sam. After that, everything was miserable. There were awkward pauses and dead silences in the car. Syl and I could do nothing to make the wheels turn smoothly. I dreaded a moment alone with Sam, so when the evening was over, I stayed a while longer with Syl.

The next morning at breakfast, however, poor Sam was the butt of it all. 'She looks exactly like a sheep,' Simon said, and Simon's girl-friend was laughing at his description of Syl's room mate.

'He doesn't look too much better than a goat himself, you know,' she whispered to me. 'You really matched them well.'

'One man's meat is another man's poison, Ved,' Simon said, and then to Sam, 'You should know better than to ask a blind man to get you a blind date.'

Although I think Sam really wanted to take Syl's room mate out again, because of Simon he did not. In those six weeks of summer school, however, I went to more concerts and more theatres than I had been to since my arrival in the States. Syl and I kept on going together, growing closer and closer to each other – that is, until the last night of the session, when Syl's friends arrived from Oregon.

There were two chattering girls and one boy just beginning college there. All of us started out towards the movies. Since the sidewalk was narrow, the girls were walking ahead, and

John and I were following. It worried me that I could not get a conversation going with John. He still felt awkward about my blindness; I therefore felt nervous. I should have perhaps taken his arm, because that is what I usually do if I feel nervous. That way the other person feels easier, too. But I felt slightly proud, perhaps, or maybe I was just too lazy to ask.

We were late for the movies, and we were walking faster now. I was on the street side and was making careful effort to dodge the lamp-posts. It seemed to me that the small streets abounded in oddly placed, slim lamp-posts.

'Come, the girls are leaving us behind,' he said, and we walked with rapid steps. Just as we were approaching a cross street, I heard the roar of a truck motor which drowned out all other sounds and dulled my facial vision. I ran smack into a lamp-post, and as my forehead hit it, it sent a vibration all the way down my spine.

I had run into iron posts many times before, but never with such gusto. I hoped hard that my forehead wasn't bleeding, but it was numb and I was too embarrassed to put my hand up. I didn't mind the internal pain, but an external blemish was another matter. I stood there stupefied, hating the truck, the driver, and the mechanics for making such a motor. I felt then in my side a nudge which sent me tottering half a step. The nudge wasn't severe, but it was like the push a mother might give, half-mad, half-embarrassed, to a child for breaking her favourite vase in front of a roomful of guests. I couldn't be sure that it had been Syl, because all of them were around me now, although I was standing upright.

'It's nothing. Let's go on,' I said.

But Syl had her hand up with a handkerchief, fragrant with the mild smell of her hand lotion. The motor of the truck was still rumbling. With a sort of quick, jerky motion, I pushed her hand away and started crossing the street, alone.

'It's really bleeding,' Syl said.

'I don't care.' And with this pronouncement, all of us entered the theatre, estranged.

In the dark I finally held my handkerchief up to my forehead and pressed it, but it ached. Syl was flanked by the girls, and I sat on the aisle seat. I did not follow the movie at all. When it was over, I tried to get beside Syl and have a word with her, but her friends were talking to her about the movie. Again with the girls leading, we started walking back towards the dormitory. John was on the street side this time and held me fast.

The reason no one has asked about my forehead, I thought, is because one of the girls put her finger to her lips. I felt as isolated from the group as though they were talking, not with words, but with gestures, and to divine their meaning, one had to see the movements of their hands. No matter how well trained one was in mobility, how well adjusted to a seeing society, there were always some lamp-posts left out of one's calculations.

I wished they would change the topic of conversation from the movie to something else, so that I might stop appearing like a chided, sulking child. But nevertheless, I yielded to a trance of reverie, the way a man in a trench, overpowered by odds, surrenders himself to private reflections.

When I pulled myself together and entered into the conversation, it seemed John had persuaded the girls to go on an all-night hike with him. They were to sign in at Syl's dormitory and then slip out the window. It was all so unlike Syl.

'While you girls are doing that,' John said, 'I'll walk Ved to the International House.'

'He'll come with us,' Syl said, but not a single one of her friends picked up the suggestion.

'I don't feel very well,' I said, my mouth completely dry.

'Don't force him to hike, Syl,' the girl on her right said, and then my presence was lost as the discussion shifted to the arrangements for getting out of the dormitory.

The girls went into the dormitory, and I left John impatiently pacing in front of the door. As soon as I was out of his sight, I walked slowly and deliberately towards Telegraph Avenue. Tomorrow Syl would be going home to the other side of San Francisco; I would stay on in Berkeley for another summer session, but compared to the first, it would be dull and dreary. Sure, I would see Syl again, but it could never be the same.

I thought about Sam and his bald head. He felt lonely because he was going on thirty and away from home there was no one to love him or for him to love. Simon was away from home, too, and like Sam he never wanted to return. But I was different from them both, because I wanted to go home. I wondered how many Sams there were – blundering Sams, who had bald heads, or looked like goats, or could not walk straight because they tried to forget their loneliness by drinking.

As I approached Telegraph Avenue, I heard the long drawn-out muffled notes of a violin. They were distant and hard to place, but they persisted, like the mellifluous melodies played on a flute late at night which I had heard so often at Murree Hills. Those musical flights of simple mountaineers seemed innocent compared to the subtle and rich notes of the violin.

I was abreast of the café; a few people were gathered around its door. It was clear that the violinist was inside.

'What is it?' I asked, stirred by the music.

'A beautiful girl is playing a violin,' someone answered, after a pause.

Another commented, 'She practises every night, after the café closes.'

'No one can go in?' I asked.

'The door is shut,' I heard.

I stood apart from the group clustered around the door. By and by they left, but the violin was still being played. Maybe they'll let me in, I thought, since I am alone now, and I knocked at the pane, first gently and then hard and frantically, but it did no more than just disturb the music for my ears. At that moment, Syl seemed as unattainable as the violinist. I could come and listen to her play tomorrow and the day after, but the yesterday of Syl and me was gone. There was no reasonable explanation for it, but I knew her friends had brought with them an imperceptible change, a change as looming and solid as the lamp-post.

I stood at the door for at least an hour longer, until the violin was put away. And then with my head hung low and the hands of my watch pointing to the early hours of the morning, I started walking towards International House, unconscious of all my surroundings.

'Hey, there,' I heard from behind me, but I kept on moving at the same pace.

'You, there, stop!' the man shouted again. I did not turn around, but simply waited for the intruder to come abreast.

'You are drunk,' the voice said militarily.

'What is it to you?' I said, starting to move away.

The intruder gripped my arm hard, and I felt too low-spirited to either struggle or be angry. In a moment the policeman was apologizing profusely. 'I thought, sir, you were drunk. I didn't know. . . . We are not supposed to,' he continued, 'but I would like to give you a ride.'

I was too weak to decline. He drove me to International House in his secure police car.

TWENTY-SIX

K and Prometheus

SUMMER was over, and I returned to the familiar surroundings of my college. There were old acquaintances and friendships to be renewed, and not least the figure of Prometheus, who had made a singularly unforgettable impression on me the first day I entered college. I remembered well the freshman dinner.

During that meal the conversation was desultory until our upper classman sponsor pointed to the figure of Prometheus on the opposite wall. There was a moment of silence in which, I gathered, all eyes were scrutinizing the mural, and then he told the story of this painting.

'It seems,' he said, 'that when Orozco was painting this mural, many of the board of trustees were appalled, mainly, I suppose, at the naked figure of Prometheus. They damned the mural and wanted to have it plastered over. If it had not been for the strong protest from the students, Orozco would never have been able to finish this painting.'

But however great the students' interest, the ambitious plan of Orozco to cover all the huge walls of the dining-room with frescoes had to be abandoned. Orozco left Claremont moneyless, and it remained for Dartmouth to give him his big chance, so that his frescoes, which might have today been the pride of Pomona, were at Hanover.

'Although the mural is cleaned regularly now,' the student sponsor went on, 'because the college knows it is its most famous possession, still, I don't believe the administration is paying due homage to Orozco's Prometheus.'

All of us were silent. I wished I could see it. Someone asked about the legend of Prometheus and what he symbolized, and at that a lively discussion began.

A few months later, as I was going out through the door next to the mural, I nudged K's shoulder, and stopping to apologize, I fell into conversation with him. He had been viewing the mural intently, and standing there, he explained to me pensively the meaning to him of the portrayed figure and the torch. Although it was hard for me to visualize the image at all, I was impressed by K's thoughtfulness in taking the time to explain something which, all during the months I had been there, no one else had. At last Prometheus, who brought the torch of knowledge and made men out of clay, became alive for me. This was also my introduction to K, who as the time went on became my fast friend.

Although I never got a single connected story about K's background, in snatches, sometimes from him, sometimes filtered through his Japanese friend Kaz, I did come to have a good notion of his past. He was a Nisei, and many times he felt conflicting loyalties to the Japanese and American cultures. Through the rigorous training by his mother in Buddhism and in the rich tradition of his culture, he had come to know Japan well, although at second-hand. All his life he had lived in a community which was segregated from the Americans and in which, as he used to say, 'my people try to make a little model of Japan'. He never liked to talk about the years he had been forced to spend in a relocation camp after Pearl Harbour, except to explain the long gap in his education. 'Sure, we had classes,' he told me once, 'out in the open, but we never did very much. We couldn't. Child that I was, I used to think the Americans would kill me, but I prayed for their victory.'

He did not know anyone in the camp who condoned or was sympathetic in any way to the Japanese cause, 'although,' he said, 'as long as we had Japanese blood in us, we were all suspect.'

After the camp, he went to work as a houseboy for an American lady. 'Otherwise I would have starved,' he said. He talked about this lady as though she were another mother, one to whom he owed as much as to the one who had brought him into the world.

'Can you imagine,' he told me once with surprise mingled with enthusiasm, 'she was as much devoted to my education as my own mother, and even though I came to her as a houseboy, she wanted me to begin college, and finish it, too, and maybe teach afterwards. It's strange – when I dream about my mother, I dream about her, too. Then I get it all mixed up.'

'Anyone would get mixed up with two mothers,' I said, and trying to make a joke of it, 'you can distinguish one as your Japanese mother, the other as your American.'

'It's true,' he said earnestly, 'that's exactly the way I feel about them, but. . . .' He did not go on.

With financial help from both his mothers he finished high school and entered a junior college. He had, of course, to work at odd jobs during the year. In the summer he picked tomatoes and earned enough for half his next year's expenses.

'I was fortunate,' he told me, 'that in junior college, the history professor got interested in me and helped me to get into Pomona.'

I came to Pomona as a freshman at eighteen, and K, who was twenty-two, entered the same year as a junior. Although he was two years ahead of me, he used to say, 'I am two years behind you really, all because of that camp. If only that hadn't come in between, I'd be graduating now.'

His age used to worry him a great deal, because ever since his father's death, his mother had had to work to keep their large family. 'She is such a weak and frail woman, I hate to see her work, but what can I do?' Saying this, K would start brooding. Then, after a while, 'I am not giving them a cent. My mother is helping me through college, and my sisters have to work too. It is I who should be helping them.'

K didn't know when he had started smoking, but now, in spite of his repeated attempts, he could not give it up, and because he could not give it up, he used to worry about it. He had to go often to his sister, who worked as a secretary in Los Angeles, to ask her for money 'to buy tobacco' in order to have a little something now and then to spend. 'She has got so used to my asking for money,' K said, 'that when I go in, she just slips it into my pocket so that I won't feel embarrassed. In Japan we would never accept money like that from a sister.'

Whether because of these conflicting allegiances, or because of the suffering he had seen around him in the camp, of which he never spoke, K was a very lonely man. Kaz and I were his only friends, and even to us he never revealed his inmost thoughts. When occasionally he asked a girl out and she did not go with him, one way or another we would find out.

I asked him once why he did not ask girls out more often. 'That way,' I said, ' the law of averages would be in your favour.'

'I don't know why,' he soberly replied, and then added, 'For some reason I would just as soon sit by my window and look at the girls below and listen to their laughter from the swimming-pool. They seem so distant from me.'

K liked America, and realized that, had he lived in Japan, he would probably never have gone as far as college with the means his family had. In this country he could work and go to college at the same time. 'Here people, instead of looking down at labour, value it,' he said, and although now and then he felt irked that he could not always get the jobs he wanted, or even a room to live in because he was a 'Jap' – that is, he looked Japanese – he didn't bear any grudge against America for that. 'Probably if the Japanese were in America's shoes,' he used to say, 'they would be much more cruel to non-Japanese.'

I remember coming home one time feeling especially good because I had been able to help a Pakistani. I had bought a type-writer at a special discount for my Pakistani friend, who was at that time attending college in this country, and had helped in its payment.

'You know,' I told K, 'for the first time I really feel that I am one with all of them, that I don't feel any grudge against any of them for our losing our house and all that.'

He got off my bed, shook my hand warmly, and I was glad we understood each other.

K majored in history, because 'that way,' he said, 'you can jump out of your time and even space.'

'Yes,' I said, 'you can cross all frontiers.'

He wanted to work for better Japanese-American relations, 'only if I have the capacity of mind,' he used to say modestly. He was never given to overconfidence in himself, probably because he was so uncertain as to who he really was. 'My background,' he reminded me, 'is Japanese, but my education American.' American because he never took courses in Japanese culture or Buddhism. He studied only Western civilization.

Of all his history teachers, he liked Dr Meyer best. Meyer's speciality was modern German and central European history and this made him unusually sensitive to the question of minorities.

'He knows,' K said once to me, 'when to raise and when not to raise the question – I mean about the Japanese-American problem – with me, and also how to do it.'

During his senior year, K fretted a lot about graduate school. There were only a few seniors in his department that year. Two of them got fellowships to go abroad or East, but K did not. The only feasible offer he got was from the Claremont Graduate School, which offered to pay his tuition, but board and room were still a problem. He applied to the dean for a resident assistantship. After the interview with the dean he said, 'I just couldn't communicate with him. Words came out, but feelings and responses did not. I just didn't seem to belong to his office.'

'All interviews go badly,' I told K. 'Don't worry, you'll get it.'

But it took Meyer's firm support to get him the job. He was all set for another year.

He went home and told his mother, 'One more year and I'll be on my feet. Then I'll be teaching school, and I'll take care of you, Ma.'

But when he started inquiring around about teaching jobs, some of the professors at graduate school discouraged him. They said it would be hard to place a Japanese-American in a high school, even with his good record and his teaching credentials. K started worrying again.

'My mother,' he said, 'just can't work more than another year.'

Meyer gave him another boost. 'K, you have a good mind,' he said. 'Teach in college. There you won't meet with any prejudice, and I'll help you get fellowships to see you through.'

He came home and told me that Meyer was a wonderful guy. 'If he has that much faith in me,' he told me, 'I won't disappoint him.'

K graduated *cum laude* in 1954. He felt sad that Meyer was going to be away the following year on a leave of absence, and it troubled him that he was already twenty-four years old, and that a Ph.D. was such a big gamble. Although the fellowships might make him independent, the time required for the degree would prevent him from helping his mother. But all these fears were put aside temporarily amidst the enthusiasm of his family about his graduation. His mother was glad that her son had won a degree from an American college, and his sisters proud because they, too, had worked and helped put K through school. His American mother wrote to him that all her confidence in K was completely justified.

The next year, however, when he returned to school, the conflict between getting a Ph.D. or a teaching certificate continued. He had an obligation to Meyer and himself, but he also had an obligation to his mother. He told me that year before the Thanksgiving vacation, 'I have done something very wrong. I haven't told my mother that I might go on for the Ph.D. She's expecting me to be through next year. I don't know how to go about telling her.'

Some time later he did tell his sisters. One of them had planned to go to college right after K finished. She told him, 'K, I don't care if I never go to college, if you can get a Ph.D.' She added, 'No one in all our ancestry has ever got a Ph.D. You'll be the first.'

By the second semester, he still had not decided, so he took some education courses and continued his work for the Ph.D. at the same time. When at our second-semester college convocation it was announced that I had led the Pomona College men, K wanted me to buy him champagne and take him out to dinner. I did, and since it was my pocket-book and my day, we ate handsomely. But at the end K paid the bill. 'I knew you wouldn't feast as well if I told you I would pay,' he said. I struggled and I argued, but it was he who took the cheque.

K had already begun to write his M.A. thesis, because he wanted something in place of the certificate to show his mother. He wished he could work on the minority problem, but since Meyer was away, he chose the topic 'The Idea of Progress'. In the essay he wanted to show the change in the conception of progress between the eighteenth and nineteenth centuries. He was overwhelmed by the material he had to read. 'The library,' he told me, 'is like a forest. I don't know where to begin. I could read for the rest of my life and still not get it all in.'

As soon as he started writing, he started fretting. Many a time I found him sitting at his typewriter in a small cubicle in the old dormitory where he was forced to live because of his assistantship, hammering away at sheet after sheet. He would write a page, wouldn't like it, and would throw it away. One page he wrote at least twenty times, and still he wasn't happy with it.

'Leave it, K,' I told him. 'Go away for a couple of days to a beach or the mountains. Just go away from this room and from this typewriter.'

But he kept on with it doggedly. He started saying, 'I am a moron, not fit for anything.'

At last he had the first draft of his thesis completed. One professor told him that his style didn't run smoothly enough, probably because it had been worked over too much. Another vaguely intimated that perhaps K should think about high school teaching quite seriously. I heard the whole essay through and tried to help him with the structure here and there. The deadline was May 2.

'K,' I said, 'why don't you get an extension?'

He blew up. 'You don't think much of my intellect, either, do you?'

'That was the last thing on my mind,' I said. 'I just wanted you to have a little bit more time to think about it.'

He ran out of my room. But he called me a few minutes later to say he was sorry.

When the spring vacation came, I asked K bluntly about what I had hinted at so many times. 'I have come to know your mother and sisters so well through you. Why haven't you introduced me to them as yet?'

'Because' – and he stuttered – 'I am ashamed of the way we have to live. I couldn't let you see our house. Besides, we are so poor. My . . . my mother . . .'

I protested. I pleaded. 'Do you think that matters?' I asked. I told him about my own parents and how we had had to live after the partition, but there was nothing I could do to dissuade him, and I could not very well invite myself to his house.

I hoped he would come back from the vacation refreshed, but he returned even more troubled. 'The day I went home I saw my mother picking onions in the field. Just think, picking onions eight hours a day. And here I am, the only man in the family, doing nothing.'

'They probably love to sacrifice for you, K,' I said, but he could not take it that way.

'I am caught,' he said, 'in the choice between further education and my duty to my mother.'

And I knew already which of these two worlds had won.

The next day, K got an offer of one thousand dollars from Wisconsin University to do his Ph.D. work there, but he turned it down, as he did subsequent offers. He took his own decision hard. Not going for the degree was the first major setback in his unceasing search for knowledge.

The next time I saw K he still seemed bothered. 'I talked to the dean of the graduate school,' he told me. 'He said no matter what I do, I can't be on my feet by the end of the year. I'll have many more education courses to go, after this semester. You know what that means.'

'Why,' I said, 'you'll have to come back to Claremont Graduate School in the fall, but you'll be able to get your certificate in the first semester. You didn't expect anything else, did you?'

'I thought,' he said, 'I could get a temporary place for next year without having finished my education courses. After all, those courses are just a technicality, but even if there is a job open, they won't give it to a Nisei. My mother is counting on my being out by June. If I'm not, I'll never be able to look her in the eyes again. I've failed my mother. I'm licked.'

'You work too hard,' I said.

We talked some more, and I thought by the end of it he was genuinely relieved. We saw each other so often that we never shook hands, but that evening he made a point of it and said strangely, almost shyly, 'I want you to know that you are my best friend.'

When he went out the door, I wondered if all the other students at Pomona took education as seriously as he did. Whatever else was true about them, there weren't many as sensitive and conscientious as he. Furthermore, they weren't as lonely as he was, either.

My father had been invited to come from India to present a paper to a medical conference. I was excited at the prospect of seeing him again, and I wanted to get ahead in my reading so that I could take a few days off when he came. I missed breakfasts and lunches, and spent every spare moment reading. For several days, therefore, I did not see K. When my father did arrive, in the last week of April, I went into Los Angeles to meet him. I did not return to Claremont with him until May 1, after his association meeting. I remembered the deadline of K's thesis was May 2, so I called him immediately. When he said hallo, his voice sounded distant, as though he were talking to me from the top of a precipice.

'How's it going, K?' I asked.

'Badly, very badly,' he replied cryptically.

I waited for him to say something else. 'You're exaggerating.'

'I can't have it ready by tomorrow morning,' he said solemnly.

'Hang it,' I said. 'The commencement isn't for another five weeks. You have only to ask your adviser and he'll give you an extension on it.'

'He's counting on my having it in tomorrow,' he said.

'Gleason will understand,' I said assuredly. 'He's a very understanding man.' There was a pause. 'K,' I said, 'give me your word that you will call Gleason right after you hang up, and get the deadline extended.' He hesitated. 'Promise me,' I insisted.

'If you say so, I will,' he said. 'I want to see you very badly. May I come over now?'

Without thinking, I said, 'My father is here. I'd like very much to have you meet him. Let's arrange to have dinner together.' I waited for a response. 'K, are you there?'

'Yes,' he said shakily, and all of a sudden I felt guilty for putting him off. 'I guess that's all,' he said then, definitively.

'I will come by tomorrow,' I said, 'and then we can make arrangements for our dinner together.' I reminded him about his promise to get the deadline extended, and we hung up.

Twice the next day I went over to his room, but he wasn't there. His bed was littered with papers; the wastepaper basket was full of them also. I took a paper out of the wastepaper basket and started to type him a note to call me as soon as he got back. But there was a page in the machine already, so I let the note go.

That night I left my father at the inn and went to the college to pick up some clothes and to see K. This was the first time since I had known him, except for the summer and Christmas vacations, that we had not seen each other for such a long interval.

No sooner had I entered my room than my telephone jangled.

'Ved – Ved, K is dead,' said the voice of a close friend. 'He shot himself five minutes ago.'

'Shot?' I gasped, and I sat down heavily.

That night I went to bed beside my father at the inn. I was glad that my father was understanding enough to let me find my way through the labyrinth of circumstances that had led to K's death. I tried to construct the living image of K and could not. I knew only his soft-spoken voice, his short thin hands, and the small physical shadow that he threw against my facial vision.

In his stead I heard a much deeper and desperate voice, blaming me for not going over to his room the night before, for not writing that note, and for having neglected for the last fortnight a human relationship that I valued so much. I thought about going over to his room right away, but see him I could not, and feel him I would not, because what made him real and alive was the texture, the quality, the modulation of his voice, and nothing else.

The telephone jangled once more, this time in a room with my father beside me.

'As his closest friend,' the warm and fatherly voice of the dean said, 'I wanted you to know that his mother has been informed.' The dean went on, 'He sought perfection, in the Oriental manner. He was too conscientious, perhaps oversensitive.'

A world which could not accommodate these qualities, I thought, was shoddy indeed, and as I hung up the phone, I thought about tomorrow. There would be other post-mortem analyses – analyses of a man so freshly dead. Some, I could not help feeling, would pronounce the fatal word 'maladjustment', and this word echoed across the memory buffer of six years. I reflected how much these analyses would be conjecture which had begun the very day K entered school as a Nisei. I wondered, too, to what degree K had assimilated the values around him as his own, and whether what had really killed him was the bullet clean through his breast, or a striving for dignity – dignity to hold to his own values at the risk of being 'maladjusted' amidst the jangling small-change opinions about the predicament of a man with mixed heritages.

Had his death really indicted him or us? Sure, tomorrow, when all was done, people would call him cowardly and would say that this was hardly a way to help his mother or improve Japanese-American relations, that it was selfish to leave the weeds growing when he might have helped cut them. No one, however, would stop to consider himself responsible for making K lose his grip on the sickle, for leaving him to find his own way in the jungle of weeds growing faster and faster around him, making a morass from which there was no escape save one.

K had been a light to me. And even the light of this lamp, I learned now, had been shaded, obscured, only to be shrouded for ever. To live, one had to form meaningful human relationships, but how did one lift the shade and look into the glare? People did live, certainly, knowing friends as though they were just so many faces in ticketed theatre seats, but I wanted something more, something as elusive as light to blind eyes, but as warm and certain as the full glow of the sun.

'Ved,' my father called, 'if you ever feel completely licked' – and I listened – 'promise me one thing.'

He paused for answer, but I could not even bring out 'What?'

'Promise that you will write to me first to pour out your heart, and then wait for my answer before you finally act.'

For me this was a big thing to promise, but not to my father. 'I promise,' I said. Then from the heavy breathing I could tell my father was asleep, but I still wondered how long he would be there to receive my letter, and what after him.

The next morning, K's mother and sisters came to get him, and although I wanted to see them very much, I did not, because I respected his decision.

After a week my father left for Europe, and I was back in circulation. People came up to me and warmly expressed their sorrow, as though I were K's blood relation. One said he wanted to write a poem in K's memory. Another remarked, 'It could have been any one of us.' And another told me how the night before K shot himself, when everyone had left the dining-room, he had stood before the damned mural of Prometheus and had stared at it intently.

TWENTY-SEVEN

Mary

ALTHOUGH I understood that the loss of one spoke in the gigantic wheel of the universe would not prevent it from turning and grinding in its endless orbit, that year, 1955, the year K shot himself, I wanted to leave Pomona altogether. I did not like going to classes, especially since the main path went by the window of his empty room. Every time I passed the overhanging window I hesitated a moment, thinking that I might hear his voice calling out from the second floor.

Somehow, all the weekly papers, the exams after exams, just did not seem important any more. In the three years I had been in college, I had run my readers ragged. Starting by getting a mark of 75 on papers, I had scored first place in my class in my sophomore year, and had led the college men in the first junior term, and my adviser said I would be elected to Phi Beta Kappa in the junior-year election. All these honours, which a few months before had stimulated me, seemed thin and wanting, based on wrong values – prizes of success, not for men really reaching for genuine education, but for those committed to vicious competition.

It seemed to me that the theory of education in which I had been reared at college asked me to stock the storehouse of my mind with so many tins of facts. These tins, neatly labelled and arranged, were to be pulled out for the right examination or for an impressive conversation. This name- and fact-dropping theory, implying presumably a fund of knowledge and wide reference, seemed to me at best inadequate. It appeared to ignore sharpening the tools of the mind for a rigorous methodology, for critical thinking, for expression and communication with style.

My disillusionment with the prevailing educational system

was only the coating of the real problem of wanting time, time for reflection, for just ruminating – above all, for developing my sensibilities as a human being. By no means did I wish to stop reading or give up education. My predilections towards history, literature and philosophy were as strong as ever. I simply wanted to study these subjects in my own time and in my own way, without any deadlines.

By the end of May, however, the finals began, and I suffered through them with that last bit of energy which a child has when he is lost in the woods and is trying hard to find his way home. After I turned in my last exam to my contemporary-poetry professor, he wished me a good summer. 'You should have a lot of time to think this summer,' he said. 'Remember, there is a difference between being sensitive and weak and being sensitive and strong.'

I left Pomona without giving the registrar a stamped envelope for my transcript. I started on a leisurely trip to the East Coast to spend my summer at Harvard, to study literature and writing.

There I passed the summer reading and taking long, tiring walks. The summer gave me time to try my hand at some short stories, and to start listening all around me for human situations. But it appeared that people did a very good job of hiding their 'traumas,' and often my imagination read more into situations than really existed. Nevertheless, the few short stories were good for unleashing my imagination, and the literature for replenishing some of my lost vitality. When I got back on the road once more, and headed towards California, I was ready with my chisel and hammer to pry open the storehouse of wisdom again.

It was in my senior year that I met Mary. Although after graduating from a private university in Tennessee she had come straight to Claremont, it took Christmas vacation and a religious conference for us to meet. To hear Mary speak was like being transported back to Arkansas – no, actually Tennessee. She spoke with that Southern slow, deliberate drawl which made one think that all the notions about Southern belles were absolutely true. Her speech abounded in peculiarly Southern expressions with Southern meanings; she called a reverie a 'brown study' and a porch a 'gallery,' and talked as though she had never had to do anything but just exist. At her college she had been elected football queen. She always dressed well, with costume jewellery, perfume and hand lotion, and complained of the boys in California not being gentlemen 'in the Southern way,' as she used to say. Although she drank coffee and now and then even took a cigarette if she was nervous, she said she would have to give up smoking and tone down her coffee drinking as soon as she went home.

She was seldom given to doubting about why she was here, where she was going, or what the reason was for this world's ceaseless grinding. She had no millstone around her neck, and no worry except to make people around her as cheerful and happy as she was.

'I have faith,' she told me, 'which I don't have to question because I know it's true.'

When someone goaded her, she used to say simply, 'I believe in God as our Father and Christ coming to earth to save us.'

She attended church regularly, and when on a rare occasion she was unhappy, as after a discussion about theological subtleties, she regained her calm by praying.

Our friendship began when she found out I had spent some time in Arkansas. I asked her out for coffee one day, and to my surprise, she consented. Soon I found that she was very understanding. She would let me do things like helping her wash her car, assist her in the selection of her clothes, and when she cooked dinner for us, she would now and then put a bite in my mouth to see if I liked the taste. She never felt embarrassed or awkward in taking me everywhere she went. She even asked me to go to the grocery store with her. We used to walk down the crowded aisle, wheeling the cart as though it were a perambulator and we were out for a stroll in the park. I liked to do all these things because they made me feel useful, and helped me forget all the time I was with her that she probably would prefer someone who had eyes.

She was never on time for dates, so whenever we went to concerts or plays I used to arrive early at the house where she lived with three other girls. While she dressed upstairs, humming a folk tune as though she were in a timeless world, I would wait for her with a heavy heart, because I thought she was used to boys' telling her how well she looked. But when she ran down the steps and greeted me as though she had been thinking about me the whole day, in her full presence all my trepidations fled.

'You know,' she said once, coming down the stairs, 'I think you may not know how I look, but you know how I feel. That's much more important.' I felt glad. 'I bet you even know how I look on a particular day, don't you?' she said suspensefully.

She is human after all, I thought to myself. It would have taken so little effort for me to say yes, except where facts about blindness were concerned, I was scrupulously honest.

'No,' I said.

'Then we'll pretend you do know,' she said cheerfully, and it was like receiving a shot of adrenalin. She seemed to me at that moment life itself, life which I had wanted for a long, long while, but which until now I had never met.

'We'll pretend, then, if you like,' I said, and hand in hand, with a light step, we walked out.

One evening, after we had known each other a month, she said to me, 'I think we are going too fast. I mean, it's so hard to tell,' she went on. 'We do things together, but I don't know where you stand.'

'I honestly don't know where I stand either,' I said.

She waited for me to go on, but I did not. It was late at night and the whole house was quiet. Through the cracks in the window there was a mild breeze. Mary nestled closer beside me.

'Do you think anything will ever come of it?'

'I don't know,' I said, and ran my hand through her short, silky hair. Side by side, we sat there quietly.

She broke the silence. 'You are a Hindu and I am a Christian,' she said, with a sigh.

'Just say you are a Christian, Mary,' I responded, beginning to feel uncomfortable.

'I am one of those people,' she pursued, 'who has to have faith to be alive.'

It was true, for it was hard to conceive of Mary without religion.

'I can't understand how anyone can be without it,' she persisted.

I left her side and walked to the window. 'Mary, it does no good talking about it,' I said. 'I am, if you like, still searching. I have no answers, and I am not sure I am in a position to make any commitments as yet.'

'But I wonder,' she went on, 'if you ever will. You talk as though it is an act to believe in God. You just think too much.'

I flung the window wide open and let in a draught. It must be two or three in the morning, I thought.

'Come here and sit beside me,' she said, and I did. 'I could not be close to anyone,' she observed, 'who I thought was rejected by God, the Christian God.'

'Do you really think, Mary,' I asked, 'that there is no salvation outside Christianity?'

'Yes,' she said, 'as far as I know.'

It was the first time she had qualified her yes. 'You've changed,' I said, 'if you can admit that much.'

'I am willing to change for you,' she said, 'but only so far.'

'I wouldn't want you to change. You're good, very good,' I said, 'but you have to understand me too.'

'How can I understand? Do I ever argue about who my father is? Then how can I about God?'

What struck me was the simplicity of her faith, yet I was sure her mildness and quietude, even peace, the very qualities which had attracted me to her, were engendered by it. I could have argued then as I had before with her and pointed out the simplicity of her belief, but it seemed to me useless.

'Mary,' I said, 'let's decide never to talk about religion.'

'We have to,' she said, 'for my peace of mind. Otherwise we can't go on like this.'

It was like confronting a glass of wine filled to the brim. In order to drink it I had to lift it, and clumsy as I was, I knew in bringing it to my lips I would spill some of the precious contents, and I could not afford to lose a single drop.

'Mary, we are happy together,' I said, 'except when we talk about religion.' I took her hand in mine. It was perspiring. 'Don't deny me, Mary, something I've really had for the first time,' I pleaded. 'You don't know how much all this means to me.'

She came closer.

As I walked home that night, the air smelled of rain, and before I reached my room it had begun to drizzle mildly. I was happy that the night had not ended badly, as it usually did when we talked about religion. But I also knew that for all our closeness, we could not reach each other as long as we talked on different levels.

A change, gradual and subtle, almost imperceptible, had come over our relationship since the night we had talked about religion. It was hard to say when, where, or how it had come about. Maybe it was the day we had an argument about Dick's editorials in the college paper. Although I agreed with her that Dick was a cynic to his teeth, I liked what he wrote, and always found occasion to be amused by the little Mencken of our campus. She disliked him intensely, because he wasn't 'good' and wrote about 'bad things'.

'You are like all the snobs at this college,' she had said, 'who think there is nothing higher than the mind. You all take pleasure in anything that comes from a mind, even if it's ugly. Why, Dick would pick up a stone, look at it, and then write an editorial about how ugly it is.'

For my part, I had called her simple-minded. 'Mary,' I had said, 'the world isn't all that it appears in the suburbs of Nashville.'

She had called me morbid, and said that I purposely reminded her that she had passed most of her life in Tennessee, because I did not respect her.

We had patched up this quarrel, but the deep-seated issue flared up again and again. After each of these arguments, I had a bad taste in my mouth, because in a sense she seemed to represent to me all that was good and kind and affectionate in this world, and yet the very naïveté for which I criticized her was the underpinning of her character.

Based on whatever reason or sentiment, it was apparent to both of us that the relationship was losing its savour. She started going out with Bud, who sang in the glee club and was a member of a powerful social fraternity. The boys teased him about calling up girls he had not even met and telling them that he was the handsomest boy in the school, therefore they should go out with him. Bud was often at Mary's place, and I could no longer just walk in. 'All Southern gentlemen,' she said teasingly, 'call before they come.' And if he was there when I called, she would say simply, 'I have company now. Why don't you call back later?' Sometimes when I was there and Bud would telephone, she would call him Ved, and then she would double over with laughter and embarrassment.

Once she told me about corresponding with two boys who were in the Navy. 'Supposing you had a choice between those two, whom would you choose?' she asked.

'Describe them to me,' I said, and she did, colourfully. With a smile I asked, 'Choose for what?'

'For marriage.'

I considered with a serious air, and then, alighting upon one, marshalled all the facts to make him attractive.

'Oh,' she said, 'you are playing games with me.'

'No,' I said, 'I am in earnest.'

'You bore me. You talk as though I were buying a house, not picking a man to marry.'

'That's the way things are done in India,' I said gravely.

She blew up. 'What's the matter with you? Aren't you ever jealous? Don't you care about me at all?' To my utter amazement she wept, while I sat helpless, clumsily putting my handkerchief up to her face.

She muttered, 'You don't care, you don't care.'

'Oh, but I do,' I said consolingly, 'but I know my place.' I reflected that if it was a good time she wanted, she could have a much better time with Bud than she ever could with me. He could take her to parties, banquets, and dances of his fraternity, and whenever I was with Mary, I preferred her all to myself.

'What do you really think of me?' she asked, probing me.

I pondered the searching question. 'You are for me,' I said, 'the soul of America to the nth degree. You are friendly, you are kind, you are generous, and above all, you accept me as I am.'

'I don't want speeches,' she said, and drying her eyes with my handkerchief, she moved closer to me.

Mary put both her hands on my arm. I could literally feel her gaze.

'You are joking; you aren't serious,' she exclaimed.

'I am in earnest,' I said, with, I knew, a broad smile playing on my face.

'Why didn't you tell me? We would have had a party, and a birthday cake and, if you wanted, twenty-two candles.'

'Oh, come,' I said, 'that's much too many for a cake.'

'I would have made one myself, large as a tray. Let's call up Jean and Jack and Nicholas and David, and have a real party.'

'I don't want a party. I just want to be with you,' I said.

She ran into the kitchen, and I followed her. 'Oh, it's so empty,' she said. 'I don't have anything here at all.'

'Let's have cinnamon toast and coffee, like we always do,' I said.

She found a napkin with 'Happy Birthday' written on it, and a few candles from the Christmas season. She made cinnamon toast and insisted on my blowing out the candles on the toast.

'You know,' I said, 'how to do little things and do them well.'

She felt genuinely complimented. 'It is our little celebration,' she said sweetly. 'I'll remember it always. But if you had only let me plan a party for you.'

She sat beside me in that small kitchen and sipped her coffee. It was like rediscovering home. Ever since the callous times of Pakistan, birthdays had gone unnoticed, but with her in the room it was like being transported all the way back to Rawal-pindi.

'Do you ever feel homesick?' she asked.

'Sometimes very much,' I said, 'but I keep my sickness under the blanket. It's always better to think about home when I am by myself, late at night.'

'Soon it will be seven years, won't it?' she asked, and the smooth and polished guise I had carefully maintained since I had left home seemed to dissolve, and I fell to reminiscing.

'People say that the longer you are away from home, the less you miss it. It has worked in the opposite way with me. I haven't seen my mother for almost seven years, or, for that matter, any-one else, except my father.'

Mary listened attentively, and as she poured cup after cup of coffee, I told her about the figures once so vivid, now almost ghostly silhouettes. I remembered their voices over the distance of seven years only vaguely, and yet for me, not their pictures, but their voices were the reality.

She said, 'You ought to share yourself more. Maybe if you talked about them to someone, it would make them more alive for you and help you to get it out of your system.'

I felt like a man rejuvenated, or one who had saved for a long time a lock of hair, a batch of letters, and all of a sudden their lost owner appeared, not so much to claim an old forgotten relationship, but to establish another one, with a totally new being.

'I think you need me, or someone like me,' Mary added affectionately, almost modestly. Once more, the image of a full and rich life rose before my mind. Oh, I could live quite self-sufficiently, have all my independence, and always, in a stalwart posture, contend that the loss of eyes was no handicap at all, but still, for all that, it would not lessen Mary's claim that I needed her.

'I need you badly,' I said, but then, thinking about the two sailors and Bud, I added, 'or someone like you.'

She put her warm palm on the back of my hand, resting on the kitchen table. 'Will you believe me,' she said, 'if I tell you

I like you better than anyone, for all our differences?'

'I do,' I said.

Then in an almost excited tone, 'Let's love each other in a special way. We'll pretend we are completely alike. There is no difference between us. We agree on everything, everything.'

'A game?' I asked, swallowing hard.

'Not at all, but a way of really finding ourselves. Let's pretend everything is really all right.'

'Let's,' I said, and I took both her hands in mine, and tried to get used to her complete reality, to her beautiful Southern drawl and her gentle and soft voice.

'Let's never talk about Dick,' she begged.

'Let's not,' I said, under the complete spell of life itself. I got up and put my arms around her.

When I walked home that night, late, Mary seemed to me Rawalpindi, home, and yet much more. In my mind she was that violin player in the small café on Telegraph Avenue, but this time she had opened the door, and had not only greeted me warmly, but served me coffee and held my fumbling hand in her long fingers and warm palm.

I got my A.B. degree that June, but strangely, even ironically, it did not mean nearly as much to me as I had imagined it would four years ago. K's death had snapped something, and Mary's arrival had pointed to another scheme of values which seemed to promise a richer, less lonely, more gentle life than I had thought possible.

But with the receding of spring, Mary's job came to an end, and I saw her off on the plane for Nashville. She kissed me good-bye warmly.

'God be willing,' she said, 'we will see each other soon.'

'We will,' I said, and she added, 'We must hope so, anyway,' and then she was gone.

With her, passed away the embodiment of spring itself, a promise of life, real and complete. The spring would return again, and a new promise would be given. Perhaps the next season would have a more solid prop, because it would not be founded on the quicksand of pretence. Yet however solid the prop of tomorrow, and even though it might support a relation-ship more mature, it would be deficient in the sensation of a first full experience, a new discovery.

Epilogue

I WAS graduated in June with the class of 1956, and soon thereafter took to the broad highway to the East Coast on the first leg of my journey to England. I felt sad, because before the summer season was up, the huge American continent would be behind me. I had come to love America almost as deeply as home, and I owed more to her than I did to India, because she had given me education, freedom of movement, a complete sense of self-reliance, and a glimpse into what a full life could be in the persons of Syl and Mary. All these things my own country had not been able to do, because I was blind.

Among the very best people I had met in the country were professors who had fathered my mind with such care and labour. Chief among them were Crane Brinton, Paul Engle, Theodore M. Greene, W. T. Jones and Frederick Ludwig Mulhauser. It had also taken the deft hands of Harry J. Carrol, John Gleason, Henry Cord Meyer and Edward Weismiller to knead and mould fresh clay. If these nine professors, who had taught me subjects ranging from the history of ideas, to the philosophy of art, to contemporary poetry, represented an ivory tower, they also together formed a kiln from which I had emerged, if not a finished figure, at least sufficiently baked for an Oxford glaze.

I was going to Oxford because six out of these nine teachers had attended that university and they encouraged me to look across the Atlantic to that Pantheon of knowledge. When these professors and the president of Pomona, Wilson Lyon, one of the very good Americans I have met, approached the Indian authorities and the only English source, the Rhodes Trust, for financial help, both of them balked on what they called 'technical grounds', the former because I had an American training, the latter because of my hybrid background, Indian citizenship and American education, and both of them because I was blind. Once again it was an American source, a source similar to those that had seen me through four years of college, which, circumventing technical grounds, decided to support me at Balliol College.

As I said good-byes to my friends in California, Texas, Tennessee and Maryland, they all pleaded for my return to America. These friends, with generous sentiment, suggested that I settle in America, instead of returning home by way of England. They argued that here I could find a fuller and richer life, and if settled in a university community, I could forget altogether the prejudices about blindness, and even many of the day-to-day irksome reminders which no handicapped man is allowed to escape.

Living in America is an alluring prospect for me in so many practical ways: the freedom of movement, in contrast to India's streets, which are poorly, if at all, regulated by traffic laws and lights; the accessibility of readers, which will be a great problem for me in India (it is almost impossible to understand Hegel, Aristotle and Eliot if your reader does not comprehend as well). And I shall also miss the intellectual stimulation of discussing the great tradition of English and American philosophy and letters with others.

But how could I indulge myself to this extent when I have such vivid memories of boys passing their youthful years in an asylum, and men and women committed to the drudgery of begging because this is the only good use they can make of their blindness? How could I justify giving up a larger and more rewarding cause on such selfish grounds?

With the Pacific shore line receding and the Atlantic Coast looming ahead, I thought about England and my decision to spend two or three years at Oxford, reading history, before making my way to the Indian Ocean. I had plenty of misgivings during the time I was making this decision. However much I argued that the two years at Oxford would further fortify my education, allow me leisure to read and reflect at my own pace, and give me more time to mature, I could not help asking myself whether all this was not rationalization, whether I was

dreading returning to India because I had become too American-
ized, whether this postponement of two years might not ultimately result in my returning to America to live.

Yet against all of these practical arguments I can place my
strong love for and devotion to India. My return there constitutes both a challenge and a responsibility. It seems to me that I
have acquired a human debt to my professors, to the people who
have educated me in American ways, and this debt can at least
be partially repaid if I return home to help solidify the bonds of
friendship between these nations.

Aside from this debt, there is the memory of Sohan, daring
and brave, who offered his life for his burning convictions. I
owe it to his memory and to the memory of others like him,
sacrificed to an unwise division of a nation and the betrayal of
an ideal of peace and non-violence, to go home soon and to try,
not so much to undo history, but to help guide it, in however
small a way, on a more calm and peaceful course. Perhaps going
to England is rationalization, but, looked at in another way, it
seems a logical route for heading home. I really want to come to
know these Englishmen to whom Sohan, sister Nimi and I had
delegated the responsibility for so much evil. I have a different
perspective on them now from the one I had in India. At home
I had seen them as agents of division and bloodshed. In America
I studied their historic institutions and came to love their inspiring literature. I have a compelling desire to see them at home,
even if it means owing my loyalty, not to two countries, but to
three, and making my 'maladjustment' complete.

My desire to get to know Englishmen, to work for peace at
home, to try somehow to alleviate the cultural tragedies to which
K and Sohan and millions of others had been sacrificed, in the
twists and turns of twentieth-century reality, does not divert me
from the real test of ultimately returning home. The question is,
what shall I do once I do get home, to translate my ideals into
working tools? In India I will not only have to surrender my
freedom of movement, but may have to join the thousands of
students with liberal-arts degrees who sit day after day in a park
because there is no job to be had. 'A country,' one of my friends

reminded me, 'locked in a struggle for industrial revolution has use only for professional people, preferably with technical skills.'

The ambassador from India, who had been visiting in Los Angeles some months before my departure, pointed out to me that I would not be allowed to take either the civil or diplomatic service examinations, because the Indian Government felt that blind persons could not hold jobs with the same degree of competency as the sighted.

'Do you think there is any chance for a change in its attitude?' I asked him.

'I think not,' he said.

As for entering college teaching or a journalistic career, similar handicaps exist in India, because no blind person has been able to pull himself up from the mesh of notoriously bad educational facilities for the blind and hold a top-flight job. Those blind individuals who have suceceded have either taken up a law practice or gone into education for the blind. But then another good-natured Indian told me, 'Lawyers are starving in India, and unless you are absolutely sure you want to be nothing else in your life except a lawyer, I would not advise your going into it.'

As for educational work for the blind at home, I cannot help feeling that working through bureaucracy is not the only way to help the wretched lot of the two million so handicapped. What is needed is a living example that, if given the proper opportunities, the blind can succeed. Such an example, from the outside, can do much more in creating opportunities than bucking the red tape or being another selfless Mr Chiles in the Dadar School.

All these handicaps are negligible when placed against the tremendous obstacle of correcting the attitude which looks upon blindness as a punishment inflicted by the gods for a sin committed in the previous incarnation. In a country where many people hold that blindness is a curse, all the accomplishments, all the signs of a successful adjustment to a seeing society would count for little. Having enjoyed a more understanding, less superstitious, and certainly more educated attitude here in

America, I ask myself, can I conceivably return to such a deadening climate? Can I rely ultimately on my love and devotion for India to sustain me there in such an atmosphere until a signal change can be brought about, which, heaven knows, might not come in my lifetime at all?

As I prepare to leave for England, I am surrounded by cartons full of books and records, two vices to which I have given free play in the last seven years. Each familiar cover of a book encloses not only a fund of knowledge, but a fond memory of the readers whose tireless efforts made these books come alive for me. The great history of Thucydides conjures up Ann; Goethe and Joyce, Albert; Plato and T. S. Eliot, Eugene. The records have their similar associations. The album of *Don Giovanni* brings the image of Dick, beside me in the auditorium; and Bach's B minor Mass, JoAn.

As I stack these books and records in boxes with a musty smell, they seem like so many fond treasures given to me by America. I should feel sadder and lonelier without these gifts, and without a hope that I shall hear and feel American life again, for now America is as much my home as any place is in this foot-loose world. But my taking leave is made easier, because as I look towards the island across the Atlantic, even now there is a plane approaching, carrying my mother, who is coming to see me. For the first time, after seven long years, we shall meet, and I shall hear her voice, speaking with the unmistakable accents of home.

TAMAN

Glossary

ACHKAN: A long coat for men with a high buttoned collar.

AGNI: Fire.

ALU-CHHOLE: Potato and chick peas cooked in a pungent sauce.

BAHAN: Sister.

BANIA: Trader or shopkeeper: see Caste.

BARAT: Bridegroom's party.

BHABI: Mother or grandmother.

BHAIRON: A scale pattern in music.

BIBI: A lady; wife.

BIRI: Cigarette.

BOW-CATTA: A cry following victory in a kite battle.

BRAHMAN: See Caste.

CASTE: The caste system refers, for its origin at least, to the time of the Aryan invasions of India. Orthodox Hinduism ascribes to the invaders four castes: the Brahman, or priestly; the Kshatriya, warrior or kingly; the Vaisya (Bania), mercantile and agricultural; the Sudra, artisan and labouring. The first three of these are considered as the original Aryan castes, and they have religious rites and privileges denied to the Sudras, mainly composed of the indigenous conquered people. The Indian name for 'caste' (*varna*) signifies 'colour', and the system seems to have originated in the endeavour of the light-hued Aryans to preserve their racial purity. The system has been crumbling in the wake of reformers and social revolutions.

CHACHA: Uncle.

CHONKIDAR: Caretaker or watchman.

CHULA: A small charcoal burner.

DHARMA: Religious duty.

DHOBI: Laundryman.

DHOLKI: A small drum.

DHOTI: Loincloth.

DIWALI: A great Hindu festival, held in the fall, when houses and streets are illuminated at night; an illumination or row of lights.

DIYA: A lamp.

DOLI: The ceremony of the groom taking away the bride.

DOR: A strong thread for a kite.

GAYATRI MANTRA: A prayer for the illumination of the intellect.

GHAT: Steps leading to a river; a place for washing and bathing.

GHORI: Horse; hence also the marriage procession led by the bridegroom on horseback.

GHUNGHRU: A small bell; an ornament worn around the ankles, with bells fastened to it.

GULLIE: Literally, a street.

GURU: A spiritual guide; a teacher, a religious instructor.

GURUDWARA: Temple.

HAKIM: A physician who follows the Unani or Greek system of medicine; quite often a quack or charlatan.

HALWA: A sweetmeat made of flour, butter and sugar.

HALWAII: A confectioner.

HAVAN: Offering or oblation.

HINDI: See Languages.

ISTRI-DHAN: Women's property.

JAI-MALA: Rite in marriage ceremony when bride garlands groom, symbolizing her acceptance of him.

JANJ-GHAR: A community building.

-JI: Suffix of endearment or respect.

JIO: Dear one.

JUTI: A shoe.

KAFIR: Heretic to the Muslim faith.

KIRPAN: Blade carried by Sikhs as a symbol of their force and power.

KSHATRIYA: See Caste.

LAKH: One hundred thousand.

LALA: Banker; father; head of a family.

LANGUAGES: Altogether ten main languages form the vehicle of thought for India, based primarily on corrupted Sanskrit or Prakrit, a dialect of this parent language. These may be divided into three distinct families. The Northern Indian languages are Hindi, Bengali and Panjabi. Marathi, Gujarati and Oriya are the languages of central India. Telegu, Tamil, Kanarese and Malayalam are spoken in south India. Hindi (along with Hindustani or Urdu, which is Hindi with many adopted words of Persian and Arabic) is spoken throughout northern India and is understood by a population almost as large as that of the United States. Hindi has been selected by the Indian Government to become the national language.

LATHEE: Heavy stick bound with iron.
LUSSI: Buttermilk.

MALI: Gardener.
MARATHI: See Languages.
MELA: A fair held in connexion with a religious festival.
MILNI: Ceremony of introduction; at marriage, between families of bride and groom.
MISTREES: Skilled labourers.
MULLAH: Muslim preacher.

NAMASTE: Literally, 'I bow down to thee'; respectful bow or salutation.

OM, SHANTI, SHANTI: Invocation of peace, used after a prayer.

PAGAL: Idiot.
PAN: Nuts and condiments rolled in a betal leaf.
PANDIT: A learned man; teacher; scholar; especially, a Brahman versed in Hindu religion, science and laws.
PANJABI: See Languages.
PHAL: Fruit.
PURIS: Small wheat pancakes.

RAGAS: Scale patterns for tunes.
RAJ: Imperium or rule.
RAM: Legendary idol of manhood.
RASTRIYA SWAYAM SEWAK SANGH: (R.S.S.S.): Literally, Nationalistic Self-Rule League.
RAWAN: The famous King of Lanka (modern Ceylon) who carried away Sita and was killed in war by her husband, Ram; in legend, a villain.
REHRI: Small cart; wheelbarrow.
RIG-VEDA: The oldest and most important of the Vedas (most ancient and sacred literature of the Hindus), comprising more than a thousand hymns.
ROTI: Bread; especially, thick wheat pancakes.

SAHIB: Sir, master.

SARI: The principal outer garment of a Hindu woman, consisting of a long piece of cloth worn wrapped around the body, with one end over the head.

SATYAGRAHA: Civil disobedience.

SHEKH: A venerable old man, the first of the four classes into which Muslims are divided.

SIKHS: Followers of Guru Nanak (1469–1538), a leader of the reform movement in Hinduism, and his successors.

SITA: A legendary idol of womanhood.

SITAR: A stringed instrument.

SUDRA: See Caste.

SURMA: Medicated preparation for the eyes.

TABLAS: Small tambourines.

TAMBURA: A drone instrument with four strings, forming a chord for the accompaniment of singing.

THALI: Flat dish or platter.

TIKKA-SAHIB: The eldest son in the family.

TONGA: Horse carriage.

URDU: See Languages.

VEDI: Altar.

In general I have followed *The Student's Practical Dictionary Containing Hindi Words with Hindi and English Meanings,* published by Ram Narain Lal, Allahabad, India (8th ed.), 1949.